# IMAGERY ON FABRIC

## Jean Ray Laury

C&T PUBLISHING

Copyright © 1992 Jean Ray Laury

Edited by Harold Nadel
Trademark information researched by Elizabeth Aneloski

Design by Rose Sheifer – Graphic Productions
Walnut Creek, California

Published by C & T Publishing
P. O. Box 1456
Lafayette, California 94549

ISBN 0-914881-56-6

Library of Congress Catalog Card Number: 92-53802

Library of Congress Cataloging-in-Publication Data

Laury, Jean Ray.
      Imagery on fabric / Jean Ray Laury.
          p.   cm.
      Includes bibliographical references.
      ISBN O-914881-56-6 (pbk.)   $24.95
          1. Textile printing.   2. Dyes and dyeing—Textile fibers.
I. Title.
TT852.L38      1992
746.6—dc20                                                    92-53802
                                                             CIP

Printed in the United States of America

10 9 8 7 6 5 4 3 2 1

# Table of Contents

# *Introduction*

Printing fabric images makes magicians of us all. We can now transfer practically any visual image to cloth in one way or another. Slides of your travels, projected in a color copier, can be heat-transferred to fabric. Favorite old photographs can be photo silk-screened or cyanotyped. Quick screen is perfect for children's drawings; natural grasses, leaves, or flowers add delicate patterns for light-sensitive prints.

The addition of words and lettering opens a closetful of possibilities: invitations, quotations, traffic tickets (your spouse's, not yours, of course), old love letters, or the deed to your house may find their way onto panels or pillows, clothing or quilts. Newspaper headlines, birth announcements, and advice from your mother all help to make pieces uniquely personal.

Portraits have an appeal that is virtually universal. Most people are totally enamored of their own images staring back at them from pillows or T-shirts, and (though they may not admit it) few things give them greater pleasure. If a gift is to be especially well received, we need only add the recipient's face to it to assure a positive and enthusiastic reception. Perhaps the print offers a toe-hold on immortality, since pictures generally outlive their subjects. Or perhaps we want a glimpse of ourselves as others see us. Old junk-shop family photos exert a compelling power. It's hard for me to discard or burn a photo, even an unidentified one, as it seems I would destroy some magical energy and presence with it. Fabric works incorporating photographs seem permeated with some of this same energy and power.

There are many ways of accomplishing the transfer of images to cloth. A few methods are very simple and can be used with children. Other more complex approaches require greater skill and care. But even the simplest methods have great potential. A full range of methods, each with specific possibilities and limitations, is presented in this book, and at least one of them will be absolutely perfect for your needs. A few have been around for generations. Silk-screen printing is an old process, and cyanotype prints were made well over a century ago. Other processes, however, come directly from new technologies and didn't exist before copiers, computer printers or thermal imagers.

Whatever the form of your original images, they can be reproduced. Pencil or ink sketches, crayon drawings, photographs, negatives, or color prints — all can be transferred in one way or another, and you'll often have a choice of methods.

My intent in *Imagery on Fabric* is to offer as comprehensive an array of processes as is feasible in one volume. This book, therefore, makes it possible for you to compare methods and select the one which best suits your needs. I also want to offer my own experiences and experimentations, as well as those of other artists, and to invite you to share the fun and excitement.

Here are precise descriptions and all the basic instructions. Illustrations show the works of fiber artists and quilters across the continent. Their generosity and willingness to share their work has given spirit and clarity to this book. It is with their wonderful examples that the processes come to life. You'll invent your own variations, improvements, and changes as you work with the techniques. But here, in a large nutshell, is everything you need to know in order to begin.

## SYMBOLS USED IN THE TEXT

→ : There is an entry in the Additional Help appendix.

↘ : Additional discussion follows in the chapter.

✳ : There is an entry in the Sources and Supplies appendix.

☛ : Warning of potential health hazard

PFP fabric: fabric which has been prepared for printing, free of finishes

CLC: Canon Laser Copier

b/w: black-and-white (photograph)

## ABOUT COPYRIGHT

While transfer methods make it simple and easy to copy almost anything, it is neither legal nor ethical to use copyrighted material without permission. To obtain permission, write to the publication or person involved, explain your intended use, and simply ask. Enclose an SASE for the reply. If you write a return note that requires only a signature (not a letter), you will be more likely to get a response. I have never yet been refused permission to use copyrighted material. (But then, I've never asked Disney to let me print Mickey Mouse. It is unlikely that you'd be given permission to use any commercially successful and familiar image.) The purpose of the copyright is to protect the originator of a work, who should be the only one to have the right to use it or to profit by it. If copyrighted material is incorporated into any piece which will be exhibited or publicized, it will be important to have copyright permission. There are many copyright-free publications from which you can select and use any image you like. And it's also pretty simple to slip a roll of film into your camera and take your own pictures; then you are free to do whatever you'd like with them. To determine if a piece is copyrighted, look for the © symbol. In publications, the entire book or magazine is usually covered by copyright.

Copyrighting is here to protect you, too. If you have developed a design which you'd like to keep (whether or not you plan to make commercial use of it), you can copyright it. Place the copyright symbol, plus your name and the year, on the work itself. Then, to register it, write for form VA at the Register of Copyrights, Library of Congress, Washington, DC 20559. There is a small registration fee, a relatively simple form to fill out, and your design will be copyrighted.

## CARING FOR YOURSELF AND THE ENVIRONMENT

Know the art materials you are working with, and read all information regarding their safe use and disposal. Non-toxic water-based paints and safe materials are used and recommended throughout this book, with just two exceptions. The light-sensitive methods (cyanotype, for example) have unique and special characteristics which can be achieved only with the use of some toxic chemicals. A second exception is the occasional use of solvents. Read all the information and consider the risks before determining which methods you will use.

Material Safety Data Sheets are available with any hazardous material you purchase. These identify for you exactly which elements are harmful, what precautions you should follow, how to clean up and how to respond to a mis-use of the product. Always request this sheet when you make a purchase, so that you have on hand the information you need. Details on the disposal of leftovers will be included in the data sheet. Carefully estimate the amounts you need, so there will be no leftovers to dispose of. Further details are given in the appropriate chapters.

When the data sheets talk about "shoveling up" spilled materials, we know they are talking about quantities vastly larger than we are using in home studios! The agencies I talked with all regarded home studio amounts as "minute" and "negligible." If you are making occasional careful use of a product, it is unlikely that you will encounter a problem. If you are going to work with it extensively or if you plan to teach the process, then you must take greater precautions.

Never mix home and studio areas if you are working with any toxic materials. Allow no food, drink, or smoking in the work area. Keep measuring tools and mixing dishes for workroom use only and identify them so that they will not find their way to the kitchen. Be particularly attentive to the use and storage of toxic materials, especially if you have small children around. Specific precautions are given in any chapters where there is a need for concern. See the Additional Help section of this book for further information under Disposal of Hazardous Materials.

## REFERENCES

### BOOKS

Croner, Marjorie. *Fabric Photos*. Loveland, Colo.: Interweave Press, 1989.

Howell-Koehler, Nancy. *Photo Art Processes*. Worcester, Mass.: Davis Publications, Inc., 1980.

Laury, Jean Ray. *No Dragons on My Quilt*. Paducah, Ky.: American Quilter's Society, 1990.

McCann, Michael. *Artist Beware*. New York: Watson-Guptill, 1979.

McCann, Michael. *Health Hazards Manual for Artists*. New York: Nick Lyons Books, 3rd edition, 1985.

Nettles, Bea. *Breaking the Rules: A Photo Media Cookbook*. Urbana, Ill.: Inky Press Publications, 2nd edition, 1987.

Shaw, Susan D. and Monona Rossol. *OvereXposure: Health Hazards in Photography*. New York: Allworth Press, 2nd edition, 1991.

Swedlund, Charles and Elizabeth. *Kwik Print*. Rochester, N.Y.: Light Impressions Corp., 1989.

### PERIODICALS

*Art Hazards Newsletter*. Center for Occupational Hazards, 5 Beekman Street, New York, NY 20038 (212-227-6220).

*Rubberstampmadness*. RSM Enterprises, 408 S.W. Monroe #210, Corvallis, OR 97333 (503-752-0075).

*Surface Design Journal*. P. O. Box 20799, Oakland, CA 94620 (510-841-2008).

*Threads Magazine*. Taunton Press Inc., 63 South Main Street, Newtown, CT 06470 (203-426-8171).

| USE THIS METHOD (IF YOU HAVE →) | B/w photo | Color slide or print | Negative | B/w copy on transparency | B/w copy of original | Color copy of original | Map, diagram, magazine | Natural forms | Cut-outs, stencil | Child's art | Drawings | USE THIS FABRIC (all cottons are PFP) | PERMANENCE ON FABRIC |
|---|---|---|---|---|---|---|---|---|---|---|---|---|---|
| Color heat transfer | ● | ● | | | | ● | ● | | | | | cotton-polyester blends | hand washable |
| Contact paper transfer | | | | ● | | | | | | | | cotton, silk; no acetates | hand washable: may vary with copier |
| Mending tape transfer | | | | ● | | | | | | | | cotton, blends, silk | hand washable |
| Transfer medium: bottled | | | | ● | ● | ● | | | | | | cotton, silk | hand washable: do not dry clean or iron |
| Transfer medium: transparent base | | | | ● | ● | ● | | | | | | cotton, silk | hand washable: do not dry clean or iron |
| Transfer medium: acrylic | | | | ● | ● | ● | | | | | | cotton, silk | hand washable: do not dry clean or iron |
| Solvent transfer | | | | ● | ● | | | | | | | natural fibers (test others) | hand washable |
| Transfer crayon | | | | | | | | | | ● | ● | satin acetate, 65% to 100% synthetic; not permanent on cotton | hand washable |
| Dye sticks | | | | | | | ● | ● | ● | | | natural fibers, blends; not permanent on synthetics | hand washable |
| Transfer paper: Deka IronOn | | | | | | | ● | ● | | | | 100% synthetic (preferred), 65% blend; not permanent on cotton | hand washable |
| Transfer paper: Design Dye | | | | | | | ● | ● | | | | polyester; not permanent on natural fibers | hand washable |
| Fabric through b/w copy machine | ● | | ● | | | ● | ● | | ● | ● | | cotton, silk | hand washable: varies with copier |
| Fabric through typewriter | WORDS | | | | | | | | | | | cotton, silk | permanent indelible ribbon: some can be heat set, most wash out |
| Computer printer: heat transfer ribbon | ANYTHING ON SCREEN | | | | | | | | | | | 50% synthetic (preferred), 65% blends | hand washable |
| Fabric through printer | ANYTHING ON SCREEN | | | | | | | | | | | cotton, silk | hand washable: varies with printer ink |
| Quick screen: freezer paper | | | | | | | | ● | | | | fabric appropriate to paints or dyes | washable: follow paint directions |
| Silk screen: paper stencil | | | | | | | | ● | | | | fabric appropriate to paints or dyes | washable |
| Photo silk screen | | | ● | | | ● | ● | | | | | fabric appropriate to paints or dyes | washable |
| Thermal imager | | | | ● | ● | ● | | | ● | ● | | fabric appropriate to paints or dyes | washable |
| Cyanotype | | ● | ● | | | ● | ● | | | | | cotton, silk (test others) | hand washable: may fade; can be dry cleaned (test) |
| Van Dyke | | ● | ● | | | ● | ● | | | | | cotton, silk (test others) | hand washable: may fade; can be dry cleaned (test) |
| Kwik-print | | ● | ● | | | ● | ● | | | | | satin acetate and synthetics; cotton and silk retain some residue | washable, can be dry cleaned |
| Inko print | | ● | ● | | | ● | ● | | | | | cotton, linen, natural fibers | very permanent |
| Stamp print | | | | | | | | ● | | | | fabric appropriate to paints or dyes | washable with permanent inks |

| WASHING INSTRUCTIONS | CHANGE IN FABRIC | USE WITH CHILDREN | HEAT SET | COLOR OR B/W | HEALTH HAZARDS |
|---|---|---|---|---|---|
| cool wash (max. 90°); no iron; cool or air dry; no additives | slightly stiff | no | no | full color | |
| warm wash; air dry | no change | no | yes | b/w from copies; color if added | acetone |
| cool wash; air dry | slightly stiff | no | no | b/w | |
| cool wash; air dry | adds stiffness | no | no | full color or b/w | |
| cool wash; air dry | adds stiffness | no | no | full color or b/w | |
| cool wash; air dry | adds stiffness | no | no | full color or b/w | |
| cool wash; air dry | no change | no | yes | full color or b/w | solvents |
| warm wash; no bleach; line dry | no change | with supervision | yes | limited range of colors available | |
| cool wash; air dry | no change | with supervision | yes | limited range of colors available | |
| cool wash; no brighteners; line or cool dry | no change | with supervision | N/A | limited number of colors: can be mixed | |
| cool wash; no brighteners; line or cool dry | no change | with supervision | N/A | one color at a time | only with powders |
| cool wash; air dry | no change | with supervision | after curing | b/w | |
| cool wash; air dry | no change | with supervision | advised | b/w and indelible color | |
| cool wash; air dry; no bleach | no change | with supervision | N/A | by color of ribbon | |
| cool wash; air dry | no change | no | yes | color or b/w | |
| warm wash; cool dry | slight stiffening: softens with washing | with supervision | yes | one color at a time | |
| warm wash; cool dry | slight stiffening: softens with washing | with supervision | yes | one color at a time | |
| warm wash; cool dry | slight stiffening: softens with washing | no | yes | one color at a time | light-sensitive emulsion |
| warm wash; cool dry | slight stiffening: softens with washing | with supervision | yes | one color at a time | |
| no phosphates; no bleach | no change | no | no | blue-green to indigo | light-sensitive chemicals |
| no phosphates; no bleach | no change | no | no | brown | light-sensitive chemicals |
| cool wash; cool dry | no change | no | no | one color at a time | light-sensitive chemicals |
| cool wash | slightly stiff | no | no | one color at a time | light-sensitive chemicals |
| warm wash; cool dry | slightly stiff | yes | yes | by color of ink used | |

## Thank You!

I wish to express my warmest thanks to the artists who generously shared their information, knowledge, and finished pieces. They added both spirit and substance to this book. Betty and Bill Ferguson, in the midst of moving, took time to read and double-check the portions on blueprinting. Jackie Vermeer, Susan Smeltzer, and Nancy Clemmensen were helpful and high-spirited when it mattered most. I'm grateful to them all. I thank Diane Pedersen for her enthusiasm about this project from the beginning, and Harold Nadel for his patience in reading and re-reading.

And thanks to Frank, for always being there.

# l. Copy Transfer
## (Color and b/w)

If a textile artist had to choose, the copy machine would rank up there with a dishwasher or microwave oven as a non-expendable appliance. This time-saving machine stretches the possibilities for including drawings, photographs and other designs on fabric. The photocopier lets us select and work with one photo from the thousands which bombard us daily. In selecting any one image, we pluck that moment out of life and isolate it so that it can be re-examined. Our current push-button technology turns the photo image into source material — a beginning, not an end.

Since transferring black-and-white copies is relatively easy and inexpensive, the copy machine allows for play, invention, and imagination. Transferring color copies is also easy, somewhat more expensive, and very inviting. Even if you live in an area with no access to color copiers, there are companies that will do the color photo transfer for you.

Dependability, fickleness, or loyalty are traits we tend to attribute to machines as we become familiar with them. Like snowflakes, no two are exactly alike. Photo-copy inks and transfer technologies vary among brands and models. Copies which look identical may transfer differently because of the variables of toner, the heat required to transfer them, and the age and adjustment of the copier. Find a copy shop where attendants know their machines and will work with you. Experience and familiarity with the copier will be your greatest help. (Experience and familiarity with the attendant probably won't hurt, either!)

Photo technology changes constantly: an exciting innovation for fabric artists who like using computers involves the use of PARO transfer paper. With a special attachment (the EFI Fiery cLc Controller), a color copier is turned into a computer printer. Four-color photo realistic scans go directly from word processor to cloth!

All copy machines deposit toner (or ink) onto a sheet of paper. When freshly printed copies are stacked, ink may lift off or transfer from one sheet to another. This latent tendency to transfer can be enhanced in various ways:

## METHODS OF TRANSFER

I. TRANSFER SHEETS for color (thermal or heat transfers)

II. TRANSFER SHEETS for b/w (improvised)

III. TRANSFER MEDIUM for color

IV. SOLVENT TRANSFER for color, b/w

[V. DIRECT PRINTING by running cloth through the printer and by running cloth through the photo copier are both covered in detail in Chapter 4.]

Read all directions before beginning.

All one-step transfer processes are reversals. A copy, placed face down on fabric for transfer (with heat, solvent, transfer sheets or transfer medium), will produce a mirror image of the original. The Tower of Pisa, leaning to the left in your original, will simply lean to the right when transferred. A photo of your son in his #35 football uniform, however, will be noticeably affected by a reversal of the numbers. A mirror image results unless you take one of several steps. 1) For color, use a copier that can print in reverse so it will be "right" when it is transferred (the Canon Laser Copier 200 or 500, for example) or, 2) use a slide (color transparency) and project it backwards when you make the color copy. 3) Have a color transparency made of the photo. It is more expensive but will accomplish the reversal. 4) For b/w, copy onto a transparency, then flip it in the copy machine to produce a reverse copy which will be "right" when it is transferred. 5) For either color or b/w,

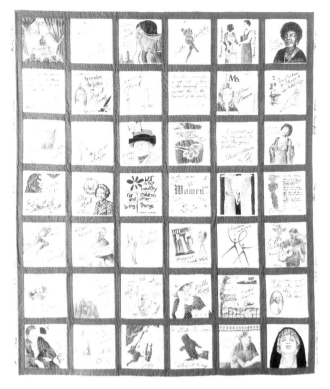

Plate 1-1: "A Tribute to American Women" by The Hamish Amish Quilters, 78" x 90".

*Anne Becker, Sylvia Edelstein, Esther Glusman, Beverly Katz, Eve Marsh, Ethel Rosenfeld, Mildred Kaplan, Ellie Sazer, and Ruth Silver, with Seymour Kaplan, art consultant, produced this piece using color heat transfer.*

Plate 1-2: *Detail of "Remember the Ladies" from "A Tribute to American Women" by the Hamish Amish Quilters. Blocks are about 10" square.*

produce the original in reverse. Or, simply select an original where reversal doesn't adversely affect the design and you can ignore it.

To make a transparency →, your illustration, design, or photograph ↘ is copied onto a sheet of clear acetate which can be flipped (placed face-side up instead of face-side down) in the copier. This will make a backwards or reverse copy. When this reversed copy is transferred to fabric, the Tower of Pisa will once again lean to the left and #35 will be recognized by his admirers.

The Hamish Amish Quilters of San Fernando Valley made their colorful and celebratory "A Tribute to American Women" using color thermal transfers. Original art work was made up in reverse so that, when transferred, the lettering read correctly. The large quilt is shown in Plate 1-1 and Color Plate 1. A detail is shown in Plate 1-2.

Copy transfer is direct, simple and inexpensive, allowing you to work with photographs without a darkroom. The transfers are diffused and invite the addition of hand coloring, embroidery or drawing over the surface. You can add your favorite aunt to a pillow top or your three-year-old to a quilt.

Gang several pictures on one sheet when making either color or b/w copies from a collection of photos. Good dark-light contrast will transfer best, but you will soon learn to predict which photos are suitable. Once you have a good copy, put your original in safekeeping, as all remaining work will be with copies. No need to panic about an old photo for which no negative exists.

It's now simple to adjust, retouch, or cut up the copy. Eliminate background clutter of cars or buildings by trimming them away. Select one face or person out of a group picture, eliminating all the rest. An arch-enemy can be annihilated with a clip of your scissors, or a spouse's "ex" can be removed from the scene!

Try altering images → and re-combining parts of copies. Snip out your own portrait (paper-doll fashion), and place yourself on a tropical beach or at the North Pole. Put your head on Jane Fonda's body or give yourself six arms and two heads. (Or keep the six arms and put the two heads on your sister-in-law.) Plant yourself on a surfboard, join the Bloomsbury group, or seat yourself in George Washington's boat as he crosses the Delaware. This cut-and-paste is the entertaining and exciting part of copy transfer.

# I. TRANSFER SHEETS for color copy transfer (thermal transfer sheets✳ or heat transfers sold as Magic Paper, Copy Trans Heat Transfer , Quick-Way Color Copies ✳, PARO ✳)

You will need:
- Transfer paper ➘ (the copy shop may carry it)
- Original (photo, drawing, map, document, slide)
- Access to CLC
- Iron and board →
- PFP fabric → to receive transfer

The process in brief:
a. Copy your art work, slide or print onto the special transfer paper in the CLC.
b. Cut away or alter the transfer copy of the image, if you wish.
c. Place the transfer copy face down on fabric.
d. Transfer to fabric by heat setting with pressure.

Have your selected images copied onto the special CLC transfer paper. Transfer sheets are color-copy papers coated with a polymer emulsion which can be permanently heat set to cloth. It is less expensive to provide your own paper, but be sure it is compatible with the specific machine you are using. PARO paper, for example, is for the Canon 300 or 500 only, though papers for other copiers will soon be available. Group several photos on one sheet or enlarge smaller ones to take full advantage of the transfer sheets. Cut out the photo or the area of the photo to be transferred. All scraps can be used, so save leftovers.

With the transfer face down on the cloth, heat set for 10 to 20 seconds with your iron at the highest temperature the fabric will tolerate (optimum temperature for transfer is 350° to 375°). Transfer sheets are designed for use in a hydraulic heat press, like those used to print T-shirts, and require both high heat and pressure. Use a dry mount press or become a human heat press by leaning very heavily on your iron. A hard surface under the iron works better than a heavily padded one. The amount of heat needed is dependant in part upon the temperature at which the copy transfer was made, which varies from one machine to the next. Use no steam.

Peel the paper away while it's still hot, starting at one corner to check the transfer. If your photo is not trans-ferring well, you are probably applying inadequate heat or pressure. Use the point of the iron on difficult spots. Practice is essential, but successful transfers with hand ironing are not difficult. Some T-shirt shops, copy shops, or specialty transfer companies ✳ will heat press a design for you. (You may, unfortunately, encounter copy shops which will not use transfer paper at all since, inserted wrong side up, it can play havoc with machines and service contracts.)

In addition to single-sheet transfer, PARO also has a two-step process, much like PAROdraw described in Chapter 3. The transfer reads like the original, with no reversal. It requires a heat press (hand ironing does not work well), but some copy shops are now equipped to transfer directly to your fabric. Graffoto, the manufacturer, can provide you with the name of a shop in your area.

Black-and-white photos can be printed on the CLC copier transfer paper in a single color (magenta, blue, etc.) or a mixed color (green, brown). The effect is especially nice on old photos. Color work can also be printed in a single color rather than the full range, if you prefer a monochromatic effect. Using a single color with black overlay gives more depth to the color. Copy shops have at least one employee specially trained to work with the color copier, who can help you in adjusting the colors.

Magic Paper transfers to cotton or 50/50 blends. Copy Trans, in addition to those, works on polyester. Read all directions that come with the products, as they vary slightly. Once transferred, the prints can be washed in cool to warm water (not over 90°), then air or line dried. Avoid touching the iron to the finished image, though this is less crucial with some brands. All fabrics printed with transfer sheets will be slightly stiff.

Most fabric artists combine transfers with various other processes in their work. Jacqueline Treloar makes extensive use of copy heat transfer in her rich and complex "Villa Torrigiani," Color Plate 2. Figures transferred to silk organza were used in overlapping layers with dyes, water colors, and Pilot permanent pens. Small statues on the rooftop and in various niches on the facade are also copy heat transfers.

Jennifer Argus's arresting combinations of images combine color heat transfers with stitching and beading. Using a commercial (hydraulic) heat press, available to her at a visual arts center in Toronto, her images are transferred to cotton or felt, then embellished. The issues and ramifications resulting from British Colonial rule animate

Plate 1-3: "Zebra Woman" pillow by Jennifer Robin Angus, 18" x 24".
Lavish beading and embroidery enhance the color heat transfer images in this pillow.

Plate 1-4: Detail of "Imprisoned" by Jennifer Robin Angus.
Photographic and architectural elements are combined in this fabric composition. The compelling images juxtapose the familiar with the bizarre in these visual expressions of her response to British Imperialism.

Plate 1-5: Detail of "Speckled Hound" by Gretchen B. Hill.

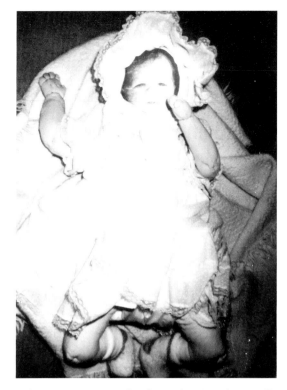

Plate 1-6: *"Speckled Hound" by Gretchen B. Hill, 30" x 48".*
*A dalmatian poses with color transfer pictures of his predecessors.*

Plate 1-7: *"Anna's Baby" by Linda M. Pool, 20" tall.*
*Linda transferred a baby's photograph to fabric for the face of this startlingly realistic doll.*

her strong and evocative pieces. See Plates 1-3 and 1-4. Other examples of her complex and ornamented works are shown in Color Plates 3, 4, 5, and 6.

If Gretchen B. Hill sees spots before her eyes, it's undoubtedly one of her dalmatians, Plate 1-5. Her wallhanging depicts the various dogs she has owned. Posing with the wall piece in Plate 1-6 is her current hound.

The face of the remarkably life-like doll in Plate 1-7 started from a 7" x 9" photograph of a friend's granddaughter. The realistic effects achieved by Linda M. Pool result from her use of soft sculpture, clothing, and color heat transfer. Cheryl Berman's daughters peer out from their playhouse, where they were deposited using color thermal transfer (Plate 1-8). Heather Urquhart's pieced "Don't Make War So Beautiful" panel combines a series of images in color thermal transfer with quilting and surface embellishment in Color Plates 7 and 8.

Wendy Lewington Coulter, in "A Piece of the Pie," shows lots of pie slices, each filled with collaged images taken from parts of our threatened environment. A detail in Color Plate 9 shows her combination of color heat transfer with piecing and quilting in a powerful and

Plate 1-8: *Detail of "Playhouse" by Cheryl Berman.*
*This appliquéd playhouse is inhabited by the quiltmaker's daughters.*

irresistible visual statement. For "Art Object," Color Plate 10, Wendy made up her originals by collaging photos and prints. The viewer, seeing the fragments, makes visual connections between the parts. Her originals were copied onto transfer paper by laser copier at a graphics shop which also heat set them on fabric using a press (similar to the T-shirt process). She painted final details with acrylic paints and metallics.

## TROUBLESHOOTING FOR COLOR THERMAL TRANSFER SHEETS

**Problem:**    Image has not adhered or is incomplete.
**Solution:**    Apply more heat or pressure, or use a fresher copy.
            Fabric may have finishes which resisted the transfer.

**Problem:**    There is only a partial print, or a line through the print.
**Solution:**    Re-heat and then pull the paper away. Image probably cooled before
            sheets were separated. Use a single steady pull, as uneven pulling may
            create lines.

## II. TRANSFER SHEETS IMPROVISED (for b/w copies)

Improvised transfer sheets are those which are adapted for transfer but were not designed for this purpose, such as a contact → adhesive paper or iron-on mending tape →.

### A. Contact Paper ✳

A really nifty and inexpensive way to transfer b/w copies to cloth is done with clear, self-adhesive shelf or contact paper (Con-tact, Magic Cover, Grid-Grip, etc. ) My sister, on a recent visit, was determined to find a way to utilize this self-adhesive paper for transfer to fabric. It seemed eager to stick to everything. Surely it would stick to copy ink, too. Like many other methods, it required effort and experimentation, and finally it worked! Remember that variations in toners and machines affect how the process works. The fabric is left soft and flexible.

You will need:
- A b/w copy
- PFP fabric → on which to print (not acetate)
- Brayer → (or rolling pin)
- Sheet of glass or masonite larger than the image
- Clear adhesive shelf paper
- Small piece of cloth or cotton flannel
- Acetone ☛

The Basic Process:
a. Select a small linear design and make a strong b/w.
b. Cut a piece of contact paper slightly larger than the printed area.
c. Remove the paper backing. Apply the sticky side of adhesive paper to the inked side of the copy, slipping a small paper tab between the edge of the copy and the film .
d. Run the brayer over front and back several times to get a firm contact.
e. Cut around the image (but not through the tab) if you wish to remove extraneous detail.
f. Peel paper from contact film, pulling the tab. The image will have transferred to the adhesive.
g. Place film, sticky side down, onto cotton fabric and run the brayer over both fabric and contact side.
h. Outdoors, on a piece of glass or masonite, place the laminated fabric with paper side down. Observing all precautions and wearing rubber gloves, moisten a small cloth pad with acetone. Replace cap. Dab or wipe pad over the fabric to moisten it. (Exposure is very brief.) The design will show through the fabric at this stage.

Plate 1-9: "River Trout" by
Jackie Vermeer, 12 ½" x 18".

*Fish were transferred to fabric
using contact paper. They swim
both upstream and downstream
through the use of a transparency which allows for image
reversal.*

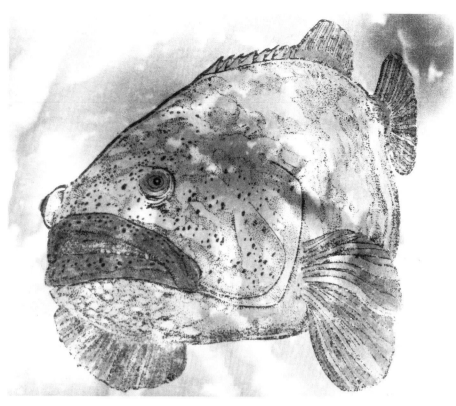

Plate 1-10: Detail of "Fish" by Nancy Clemmensen.

i. Quickly and firmly, roll the brayer over the surface and remove the film immediately.

j. Let dry several hours. Place printed side down on paper and heat set with a medium-hot iron. If the surface is slightly tacky, place it on clean white paper and iron. Repeat, changing papers, until the surface feels clean.

As with most transfers, these will be grayish rather than black. Copiers deposit different amounts of toner, and at different temperatures; therefore some copies, even a year old, will transfer while others just a week old won't budge. Differences in the adhesive on contact papers also affect transfer. Some papers require more acetone or more pressure than others. It is important to work through the process to find the compatible combinations.

To sharpen the transferred image, outline it with a fine-line permanent marker such as the Sanford Sharpie fine point or the Itoya Finepoint System. Look for permanent inks and test them on your fabric. Color can be added to the fabric images with pastel dye sticks →, fabric crayons →, dye transfer papers →, or by coloring prints → with textile paint. Or add color to the contact paper as described in Chapter 3 on dye transfer.

The fine-line b/w fish in Plate 1-9 were transferred to fabric, using contact paper, and then outlined with fine-point marker, also shown in Color Plate 11. The multi-hued fish in Color Plate 12 was first transferred from copy to contact paper, then colored with Caran d'Ache water crayons. After coloring, the transfer to cloth was completed. Plate 1-10 was copied and colored in exactly this same way.

# TROUBLESHOOTING FOR CONTACT PAPER

**Problem:** The image didn't transfer from copy to contact paper.

**Solution:** Use more pressure on the brayer when adhering contact to copy.

Try a fresher, darker copy.

**Problem:** The image didn't transfer from contact to cloth.

**Solution:** Use more solvent.

If the image on contact was good, burnish more vigorously; if the image on contact was pale, use a darker original.

Pull contact off fabric immediately after solvent is applied.

**Problem:** The contact paper sticks to the copy and can't be separated.

**Solution:** Try fresh contact.

Try a different brand of contact.

Burnish more lightly, so the bond isn't as firm.

Insert a tab for separation.

**Problem:** The fabric is sticky after transfer.

**Solution:** Trim excess contact from the image before pressing to fabric.

Place paper on the sticky fabric, iron to remove the adhesive, then keep ironing until all stickiness is gone.

**Problem:** There are stains on the fabric.

**Solution:** Change the acetone pad. It may have picked up toner.

**Problem:** The image on fabric is blurred or disappears.

**Solution:** Use less solvent.

## B. Iron-on Mending Tape ✳ → (for b/w copies)

A transfer medium similar to contact paper is iron-on mending tape. The polyester-cotton tape has a heat-transferrable coating of adhesive which can pick up toner (or ink) from a copy and transfer it to fabric. It is available in notions departments, fabric shops, or dime stores as Bondex from Wrights or mending patches by Coats and Clark.

The process is similar to the one used for contact transfer but uses no solvent. It is subject to the same variations in toners and copiers and will require experimentation. This version is detailed in Marjorie Croner's excellent book *Fabric Photos*.

You will need:
- A b/w copy
- PFP fabric → on which to print
- Ironing pad →
- Iron-on mending tape

The process in brief:
1. Place iron-on mending tape over a copy of your image.
2. Transfer image to mending tape by using an iron at wool setting for about 30 seconds. Do not use added pressure. Remove tape.
3. Place fabric on which you are going to print on a

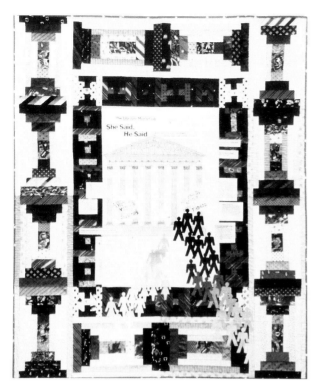

Plate 1-11: "The Oldest Men's Club At Work" by Ann Rhode, 48" x 60".

*Mending tape copy transfer, appliqué, piecing and machine drawing combine in this political statement.*

Dolls" in Color Plate 13. The images were transferred with the two-step mending tape method and then embellished with a profusion of French knots and embroidery. The dolls were added to a special quilt made for the newlyweds.

In "The Oldest Men's Club at Work," the artist added words and lettering to her visual commentary on the Clarence Thomas hearings, Plates 1-11 and 1-12. Drawn from magazines and newspapers, the words were arranged and photocopied in b/w, then transferred with mending tape to cloth. Transparent white figures and opaque black ones were fused to the backing; stitching created the architectural details and pieced blocks added pattern.

flat, smooth ironing surface. Place the mending tape (with the copy transferred to it) face down on the fabric.

4. Transfer image to fabric with a second, higher temperature, heat set process. Iron one minute, at cotton setting, with pressure.

The method requires lots of practice, but many designers work with it very successfully. Copiers vary and affect the amount of heat and pressure needed to transfer an image. The final transfer on fabric is permanent and washable. Any textile paint or permanent fabric marker can be used to add color. Both Bondex and mending patches are available in strips or small pieces (about 5" x 5").

Photographs of the bride and groom were used for the faces of Karen Page's "Wedding

Plate 1-12: *Detail of "The Oldest Men's Club At Work" by Ann Rhode.*

*Machine-stitched architectural details contrast with the fused-fabric men and women grouped on the steps, surrounded by Courthouse Step pieced blocks.*

# TROUBLESHOOTING FOR MENDING TAPE TRANSFER

Problem:    There is a poor transfer from copy to mending tape.
Solution:    Use more heat (try the cotton setting).
               Remove the paper before it cools.

Problem:    You can't separate the mending tape from the paper.
Solution:    Insert a tab as described for contact paper.

Problem:    There is poor transfer from mending tape to fabric.
Solution:    Use more pressure to aid in the transfer.
               Use more heat, increasing the temperature for a longer time.

Problem:    The mending tape sticks to the fabric.
Solution:    Reheat, then pull the mending tape off before it cools.

Problem:    Lines or streaks appear in the transferred image.
Solution:    Pull the mending tape in one long pull, not in steps.

## III. TRANSFER MEDIUM✳ for color copies (bottled transfer, transparent base, acrylic medium✳)

Any of several thick, non-toxic liquids can be painted onto plain color or b/w copies to facilitate their transfer to fabric. These include transfer mediums made for this purpose as well as the thicker transparent extender base used in silk-screen printing or with acrylics. CLC copiers have given the best color results, but other copiers work as well. Clay-coated pages from magazines or flyers can be transferred, since the ink can be lifted off the coating. Glossy or shiny pages supposedly work less well than matte or flat prints. So many different kinds of inks, coatings, varnishes, and finishes are now used on paper that it's difficult to predict which can be transferred. Some designers have even lifted inks from paper napkins. Do not apply medium directly to photographs. All transfer mediums add some stiffness to the cloth.

## A. Bottled Transfer ✳ (Stitchless Fabric Glue, Picture This, Transfer-It ) for color or b/w copies

Directions come with each medium and, while all are similar, there are variations you must be aware of. You will need:

- Clear copy of original
- Transfer medium
- Wax paper (or clear wrap →)
- Brayer → or rolling pin
- Foam applicator or brush
- PFP fabric → on which to print
- Paper towel
- Iron and pad→

The Basic Process:
1. Make a color or b/w copy of your art work or photograph.

2. Place any smooth PFP fabric over wax paper or clear wrap on a flat surface. It may be helpful to pin the fabric (for example, on an ironing board) to hold it smooth and taut.

3. Cut out the portion of the copy you wish to transfer, trimming to the edge and leaving a tab for handling. Place it face up on a second piece of waxed paper.

4. Paint the copy with an even, thick layer of transfer medium, up to ⅛", which almost hides the image. Some designers find that ⅟₁₆" is more than adequate. Apply with a 1" brush or foam applicator, a smooth plastic edge, or a credit card.

5. Carefully lift the wet print and place the coated side down on the fabric.

6. Cover with waxed paper or paper towel. Press with a brayer or rolling pin (very lightly) or by hand (very firmly) from the center out to the edges, to remove any air bubbles. When the paper backing of the color print begins to wet through, run the brayer over all layers again.

7. Let dry 24 hours. Curing time is critical and may take longer in high humidity.

8. Cover with a press cloth and heat set using a dry iron at medium setting. (Heat setting depends upon the specific transfer medium. Some, such as Picture This, do not require this step.)

9. Remove the backing paper by gently sponging with water and rubbing to reveal a mirror image of the original. Or, place a damp sponge on the paper for several minutes to loosen it. If it's stubborn, let it dry, re-wet and repeat.

10. When print is clean (when all backing paper has been rubbed off and the image is visible and clear), rub a few drops of the transfer medium into the image to seal it.

## Reversal

This transfer process reverses the image. In some instances, it will be important for your image to read correctly. In addition to the reversal methods listed in the beginning of this chapter, it is possible to make a decal of a copied image. This is important for lettering or maps but, as it requires two layers of medium, the finished piece will be slightly thicker, somewhat glossier. It will also be easier to remove the backing paper, and no heat is required for the transfer. The finished piece should not be put in a drier. To do the reversal:

1. Brush a light coat of the transfer medium onto the printed side of your untrimmed copy and let it dry for two hours.

2. Add a second coat and dry for 24 hours.

3. Soak the coated paper in water for several minutes, then place it face down on clear wrap over a hard surface.

4. To remove paper, moisten and rub gently, leaving a thin film with ink on it.

5. Blot, dry, and trim edges.

6. Place face down on wax paper, coat the back and, while wet, place it painted side down on the fabric for transfer. Cover with paper.

7. Press with brayer or rolling pin.

8. If transfer medium oozes out the edges, remove it with a damp cloth.

9. The transferred image will be directionally identical to the original.

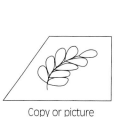
Copy or picture

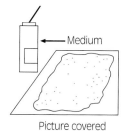
Medium

Picture covered with medium

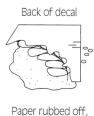
Back of decal

Paper rubbed off, leaving decal

Decal trimmed and applied to cloth right side up

When trimming or cutting the shapes to be transferred, some artists leave a tab to help lift the wet transfer. B.J. Weldon uses a brayer over waxed paper to press the wet transfer onto her cloth. Several designers use rolling pins (rolling in alternate directions), while others rely on finger pressure.

Bottled transfer is used by many designers with great success. Nancy Taylor has achieved beautifully clear and

Plate 1-13: Detail of "Peg's Quilt" by Nancy Taylor.

*A birthday celebration prompted the transfer of collected family photographs (all black and white) to this nostalgic and personal quilted piece.*

Plate 1-14: "Memories from the First Quarter" by B.J. Welden, 26" x 32".

*The desk top depicted on this quilted panel displays an assortment of family photos transferred to cloth, along with a resplendent appliquéd bouquet. (Collection of Marc Villa)*

crisp results with Stitchless Fabric Glue. She soaks the transfer, then rubs off the paper backing while it is still immersed in water. That allows paper fibers which may be caught in the emulsion to work their way out slowly. She starts at the center of a photo and works to the edges. Nancy's pieced "Peg's Quilt" (Plate 1-13 and Color Plate 14) is filled with the recollections evoked by family photographs; it was made especially for her mother's seventieth birthday.

B.J. Weldon's charming collection of b/w and color family photographs was transferred to cloth (Plate 1-14) using Stitchless Fabric Glue. Though it was not suggested in the directions, she achieved better results by covering the transferred photo with a press cloth and heat setting at medium hot with a dry iron for one to two minutes. Picture frames and the splendid bouquet on the fabric desk are appliquéd.

Plate 1-15: Detail of "A Cautionary Tale" by Joan Schulze.

Construction tape, cautions, and warnings surround the photo transfer images of The Big Shake-Up.

In Joan Schulze's "A Cautionary Tale" in Color Plate 15 and Plate 1-15, photos of earthquake-damaged buildings were transferred to cloth with bottled transfer medium. Some imperfections in the transfers enhance the feeling of rubble and disintegration. Construction-site plastic tapes were cut up and reassembled so that the letters themselves seem to have been jarred out of place.

In "Cloud Watching," Joan transferred both color and b/w photos to cloth. Unclear photo images (not actually of clouds) became clouds as she arranged their patterns of lights and darks. Magazine lifts are also incorporated into the composition as Joan overlaid one transfer of color and form with another. Magazine lifts, usually done with acrylic or polymer medium →, were worked successfully with the transfer medium. See Color Plate 16.

## B. Transparent Base✳ (Naz-Dar Clear Base, Hunt Speedball Extender, etc.) for b/w or color

Transparent base is a gel-like medium the consistency of sour cream or butterscotch pudding. But don't lick the spoon. It's really printing ink without any color — the Hamburger Helper of print-making! It must be applied in a thick layer in order to transfer a color copy. Use a brush or, even better, press your credit card into service to spread the medium. The extenders made for oil-base paints (Naz-Dar) work best, but some designers have had good results with the water-base (Speedball) as well.

You will need:
- Copy of original
- Transparent base → (buy the smallest container available)
- PFP fabric →
- Brush or card
- Iron and pad

The process:
1. For color: Make a copy of the original in color.
   For b/w: Copy the original on a machine that deposits powdered toner.
2. Coat the copy with a thin layer of the extender, using a soft brush and even, smooth strokes. Paint horizontally, then vertically, then diagonally, to be sure the coverage is even. Some brush strokes may show.
3. Immediately place the coated copy face down on fabric, cover with newsprint, transfer in a litho press or dry-mount press if possible. If not, use as much heat and pressure as possible and iron on both sides. If you have used too much medium, it will just squish out the sides. Wipe away excess.
4. Peel the paper while it is still hot, in a steady pull. If you hesitate or stop, the color impression will be uneven. Let dry for 24 hours.
5. Do not touch iron directly onto the finished surface.

Designers have had varying degrees of success with this method. It is inexpensive, and some swear by it. Others only swear. How well it transfers the image is again probably a function of the temperature at which the original copy was set.

## C. Acrylic Medium✳ (Liquitex, Hyplar, or any other matte or gloss polymer medium) for b/w or color

Acrylic and polymer mediums will work to lift color from smooth or clay-coated magazine pictures, or from newspapers. They pick up or lift the inks from the paper so that the image is contained in a thin, flexible film of medium. The film can then be applied to fabric with more of the same medium. It will be important to experiment with color pages to determine which will work best. There are mysterious variations that let the color section of one Sunday paper work while another will not.

The process:
1. Brush the image with acrylic medium and let it dry.

2. Repeat this process anywhere from 4 to 8 times, changing direction of brush strokes, and letting the medium dry each time.
3. Soak the paper in warm to hot water for several minutes.
4. Rub the paper backing to remove it. This will leave a thin sheet of acrylic film with the image printed on it. It turns whitish when wet, but will clear up when dry. Dry it again.
5. To apply to fabric, re-coat the back and, while wet, place on cloth. Roll it with a brayer to remove any air bubbles. Let dry.

The acrylic film is flexible and can be stretched or distorted, intentionally or otherwise. It can also be sewn to fabric, or it can be held in place by appliqué which overlaps its edges. Suitable for use in wallhangings and pieces that will not require washing, it will tolerate gentle washing by hand and air drying, but it turns milky when wet.

Because photo images have clear areas where the white paper background shows through, a transfer to dark fabric is not as satisfactory. To retain clarity, transfer the image to a white fabric first. Cut this image out and stitch or glue it to the dark cloth, using additional medium.

If any edges of your transfer were inadequately covered with medium, they will remain loose. Use a drop or two of additional medium, slip it under the loose edge to re-attach, and again let dry for 24 hours.

Another way to secure edges is with a bottled medium, such as Stitchless. Squeeze a line around the edge of the design to connect the loose edge to the cloth. When dry, it can be used that way, or colored or metallic foils (such as Foiling Around) can be adhered. Place foil over the lines, shiny side up. Set iron to medium setting and, using the point, set foil to glue. Let cool before removing excess foil.

Check your transfer medium label for washing instructions. Most can be hand washed in cool water but cannot be dry cleaned or touched with a hot iron. Do not place finished prints face to face, as they tend to adhere.

Another transfer medium, Decal-It, made primarily for use on wood, was used for the face of Elaine Brunn's juggler doll in Color Plate 17. The surface is not washable and adds thickness or body on the cloth. On the doll, brush marks add a painted look.

# TROUBLESHOOTING FOR TRANSFER MEDIUM

Problem:    The paper won't rub off the image.
Solution:    Not all color pages transfer equally well.
        Soak for a longer time, using more water.
        Rub more vigorously.

Problem:    The image rubbed off with the paper.
Solution:    Rub less vigorously.
        Soak longer before rubbing.
        Your print may be on unworkable paper (try clay-coated or other smooth-finish paper).

Problem:    The transfer is uneven.
Solution:    Use a heavier, even coat of medium.
        The fabric finish may resist transfer.
        Press or bray with even pressure.
        Be sure your work surface is smooth.
        If you are heat setting, apply the heat evenly.

## IV. SOLVENT TRANSFER → (for color or b/w)

All solvent transfers use liquids to help melt toner off a copy, and pressure helps transfer it to fabric. They always give reverse prints unless a transparency → is made first. Fresh copies will release their inks more readily than old ones, so transfer the same day if possible. It's worth trying an old copy, but success is less likely. It's easier to handle small prints than full pages. If several images are grouped on one page, cut them apart and transfer them individually. As both solvents and inks vary, only experimentation and a process of elimination help determine the most satisfactory combination.

### Solvent Transfer ✳ using turpenoid, mineral spirits, or acetone

☞ WARNING: All solvents are potentially hazardous. Protect yourself: read all labels on the products you buy and observe precautions. If ingested, solvents are highly toxic. Avoid breathing the fumes by working outdoors or in a hood-ventilated area and wash hands after contact. Protective gloves and masks are recommended. Keep away from children. Do not allow smoking or open flames anywhere near open containers. Purchase solvents in small amounts and use directly from the can to avoid leftover disposal.

Observing all precautions for solvents, you can work comfortably. It is not necessary to become paranoid, but you must protect yourself. Occasional use is unlikely to cause any problems, but for extensive use, extra care must be taken.

### General Directions for all solvent transfers

You will need:
- Clean, smooth cardboard about 10" x 12" (not corrugated)
- Clear or masking tape
- Solvent
- Cotton or flannel, about 6" square
- Burnisher (an old spoon or an iron)
- PFP fabric → on which to print (anything not melted by acetone)

The Basic Process:
1. Select the photograph or design you wish to transfer and make a fresh copy. Linear designs and patterns of alternating dark and light work best. Large areas of black or gray do not transfer clearly.
2. Cut a piece of fabric larger than your design, iron it smooth, and place it right side up on cardboard. Tape the edges so that the fabric is perfectly smooth.
3. Place your copy face down on the fabric and tape it at the top only, to form a hinge.
4. Select your solvent. Read all cautions and warnings. (You may prefer to base your selection on this information.)
5. Take copy, cardboard, solvent, cloths, and burnisher to an outdoor work table, or work with good ventilation such as a hooded fan. (Read cautions on container. No open flames or smoking!) Wearing rubber or neoprene gloves, saturate a small soft cloth with solvent by holding the folded cloth over the opened container spout and tipping the can to moisten the fabric. Immediately replace the cap.
6. Wipe the cloth over a small section of your copy (you will be moistening the reverse side). The paper will soak up the solvent and appear to be wet or translucent. Immediately burnish that area, using the bowl of an old spoon or any similar hard, smooth object. This helps press the ink from copy to fabric.
7. Peek under a corner to see how the copy is transferring, but do not lift the entire sheet. If the image has blurred, you used too much solvent. Start over with new materials. If it is too light, use more solvent on the paper and more elbow grease or pressure with the burnisher.
8. When transfer is complete, remove the paper from the fabric. Air dry for a day.
9. Heat set. Add colors, using permanent markers → , fabric crayons → , or any water-based textile paints → .

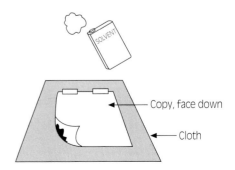
Copy, face down
Cloth

## A. TURPENOID (OR ODORLESS PAINT THINNER)

This synthetic turpentine can be used in the transfer process described above. It is less hazardous than gum turpentine. Use with good ventilation and wash your hands thoroughly when finished. Read and follow all directions and precautions on the container. Liquids and toners vary in their compatibilities.

Holley Junker has had great success working with solvent. Featured in her handmade book *Minnie Beyond Her Sphere* is an old family photo transferred with turpenoid (Plate 1-16).

## B. MINERAL SPIRITS

This solvent works well for copy transfer and should be used outdoors because of the fumes. Observe all precautions. In *OvereXposure* by Susan D. Shaw and Monona Rossol, mineral spirits is described as a moderately toxic solvent, whether by inhalation or skin contact, but highly toxic by ingestion. Never set your teacup on the work table!

In Plate 1-17 Gretchen Vander Plas made a color photocopy of her hand and transferred it to silk using mineral spirits as the solvent. The hand is overlaid with a pattern of threaded silk and paper images which fan out on delicate threads. A page from *The Button Book* includes another hand, solvent-transferred to transparent fabric and stitched. A copy of the button (the heroine of this book) was used to suggest a ring on fingers that fold up into a page-size fist (Plate 1-18).

For the title page of her book, Gretchen made single-color prints in the color copier. Instead of the full-color range, she had sheets printed in individual colors (blue, magenta, yellow, etc.); she used no image in the copier. She then cut one of the colored sheets into letters and transferred them to silk, using solvent transfer (Plate 1-19).

Betsy Nimock's compelling "Third Time Round" in Color Plate 19 is a full-size quilt using solvent transfer for the portrait. Four 11" x 17" CLC copies were required to make up the portrait. Using a b/w photo, she first ran copies in blue only and then ran them through the copier a second time to print black. She transferred (with solvent) the portrait to silk. Her transferred color matched the faded indigo of the old quilt. The silk portrait was then appliquéd over the pieced background. The original quilt was a Flower Basket design over which a Drunkard's Path was later added. Betsy revealed parts of both quilts and the portrait of Everywoman, which is her symbol for the feminine presence in handwork.

Plate 1-16: *Detail of* Minnie Beyond Her Sphere *by Holley Junker.*

A *page from Holley's fabric book includes this haunting solvent transfer portrait.*

Plate 1-17: *"Dreams of Serenity" by Gretchen* P. *Vander Plas, 18" x 24".*

*Solvent transferred images on fabric and paper are combined with thread, fabrics, and paint.*

For "Americana" (Color Plate 18), she did a charcoal enhancement of an 1870's photograph. Enlarged to life size, the photo is solvent-transferred to fragments of quilts in this powerful and nostalgic work by the quilt archaeologist. Her work is among the earliest and most outstanding of the quilters exploring this new technology, and her imagery allows us all to identify with it.

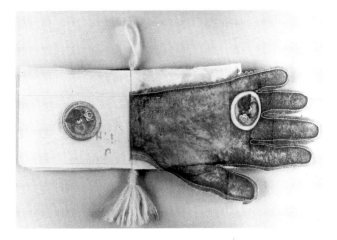

Plate 1-18: *Detail of* The Button Book *by Gretchen* P. *Vander Plas.*

*The hand is solvent transferred.*

Plate 1-19: *Detail of* The Button Book *by Gretchen* P. *Vander Plas.*

*For the blurred button on the right, the image was melted into the silk with solvent.*

### C. ACETONE

Acetone is only slightly toxic with any normal exposure, but special care must be taken to prevent any possibility of eye contact. Goggles are recommended. Work out of doors to avoid fumes and because acetone is extremely flammable. Most households have other liquids around which contain acetone (some nail polish removers, lighter fluids, cleaners, etc.), and all offer some degree of success for transfer. Plate 1-20 shows two acetone transfers rich in detail and photographic clarity.

Plate 1-20: *Detail by Jamye Donson.*

*Minute details are retained in these solvent transfers.*

### D. SOLVENT TRANSFER WITH IRONING

Some designers prefer an iron to any other burnisher, as the heat facilitates the transfer. Get an extension cord and take the iron outside. Follow general instructions and, after moistening the back of a copy with the solvent, apply heat and pressure.

### E. HEAT SETTING THE SOLVENT TRANSFERS

Fabric transfers should be heat set to help assure permanence. Let the fabric dry thoroughly, then press the reverse side with a medium hot iron. Actually, I press directly on the print, but it must be completely dry (allow a full day). If the ink is damp, it will smear.

## Transfer by Ironing (color or b/w)

Occasionally, copies can be transferred by ironing only. It's not common, but it is always worth a try. Transferability is dependent upon variables (unknown to me) and even two copiers of identical model may perform differently. Place your fresh copy face down on fabric and press with a hot iron for about 30 seconds. Lift a corner to check, and continue ironing if the image has not transferred. If you are in luck, your copies will be compatible with this method; if not, try another copier or a different method.

### Washability of solvent transfers

Hand washing of test prints has shown my transfers (made on Canon copiers) to be permanent. Other designers have found similar permanence, but a few maintain that their prints washed out completely, so the difference probably lies in the toners. If your results are not permanent, try another machine. It is important to dry the print (3 to 24 hours) before heat setting, or the iron may remove the toner. Fabric must be free of finishes for permanent transfer.

## TROUBLESHOOTING FOR TRANSFER WITH TURPENOID, MINERAL SPIRITS, OR ACETONE

Problem:   No transfer occurs.
Solution:   Try another copy or another copier.
Use fresh solvent.

Problem:   You get a runny-looking print on fabric.
Solution:   Use less solvent.
Use a faster wiping technique (the paper should not be soaked in solvent).

Problem:   You get pale prints or loss of detail.
Solution:   Use a darker or fresher copy.
Use more solvent.
Burnish with more elbow grease.
The details may be too fine to transfer to fabric, which has a more textured surface than paper. Darken areas of the original with an opaque marker. Then make a new copy and try it.

Problem:   Your print is spotty (some dark areas, some light).
Solution:   Apply solvent and burnish evenly.
Make sure your work surface is smooth.

Problem:   The image is misaligned.
Solution:   When lifting the fabric to peek, take care to replace it in the exact same position. Tape or tack the copy and the fabric to keep them from moving.

Problem:   You have general difficulty in transfer.
Solution:   Use small images rather than a half or full page.
Use a fresh, dark copy.

It requires time and effort to develop skill in copy transfer. Don't give up if you don't have immediate success. You'll develop a feel for the method, as have the many designers who have worked with it extensively and successfully. Copiers vary and the temperatures at which toners are set on the paper affect how easily they may transfer.

**[V. Transfers directly to fabric from the copier or printer are covered in Chapter 4, Direct Printing on Fabric.]**

## GENERAL INFORMATION

### Photographs (for black-and-white copier)

When photographs are used in a paste-up or collage, lines will sometimes appear where the cut edge of one paper overlaps another. Glue the edge for better contact, or set a stack of paper on top of your collage after it's placed face-down on the copy machine, to flatten it and eliminate lines. If lines persist, you may need to cover them with a correction fluid made especially for copies.

A first photographic enlargement on a copier is made directly from an original. After that, as each enlargement is made, the clarity of the print diminishes further. Originals give the clearest results, but interesting effects are achieved as the images expand. Black areas break down into patterns, as seen in Plate 3-2. If this effect is undesirable for your purposes, have a Kodalith → made or work from an enlargement of your photograph.

### Photographs (for color copier)

To use heat transfer paper efficiently, always group pictures to fill the sheet, enlarging if you like. Later the pictures can be cut apart to be used individually.

Color-copied photos can be transferred individually to fabric, or they can first be collaged and then transferred in one step. Cut up the prints, alter and re-assemble them. When the collage is ready, it can be transferred in any of several ways. Make a new color copy and use the solvent transfer method or medium transfer. Solvent will penetrate a single sheet of paper more readily than it will a double thickness. For medium transfer, you may wish to transfer the individual parts separately. A third method involves making a copy of the collage onto heat transfer paper, to be ironed onto fabric. If parts are transferred separately, the first transfers would be subjected to the heat of later additions.

### Drawings (for black-and-white copier)

Only opaque lines copy clearly. Lead pencil or blue pencil works poorly. If you wish to use a pencil drawing, trace over it with a permanent marker and try to get a dark copy. If this is not appropriate, you'll have to get a photographic copy made and then make a photocopy of that. Adjusting the copy machine to a darker setting gives a blacker line, but eventually the background begins to pick up toner. The density of the black may be affected by the age and condition of the machine, how it is set, or the toner itself. Some brands of copiers deposit more toner than others, so find the one which works best for you.

### Fabric

A transfer will carry more detail onto a smooth fabric than onto a rough one. Satin, muslin, chintz, glazed cotton, and smoothly woven fabrics give better results than nubby or textured fabrics. The filler or sizing in some glaze finishes will wash out, removing ink as it goes. All-cotton cloth works best for most transfers, but you'll need to test fabrics to find the one best for your purposes. While there is less concern over washability in wall pieces than in garments, quilts, or pillows, a test for permanence and washability is recommended. Select fabrics without surface treatments, and pre-wash.

Add color to b/w prints by using permanent markers →, transfer crayon →, or dye sticks →. Coloring or tinting prints with textile paints or airbrush inks creates very different effects.

### Printing single colors on the black-and-white copier

Colored toners are available to replace black in copy machines. They produce single-color prints, and can be transferred to fabric using the same methods as those for black toner. Some copy shops schedule colors only on certain days, so check. Brown toner gives a sepia effect to a photograph, and red-letters days are a natural. (I could make some blue Jeans? or red-eye specials? or little green men?)

A family photo, copied in black, can be fun to play with. Cut out and remove your sister's image and copy her in red. Transfer the black copy of the family to fabric, then transfer your blushing sister back into the family setting to give her special significance. Highlight your grandfather in a school picture, or include a square redneck in the family circle.

# Crayons, Dye Sticks, and Markers

A fresh box of colors with wrappers intact and sharpened points prismatically aligned seems irresistible to most of us. Inexpensive and bright, both crayons and dye sticks offer great ways to add color to our own designs or to children's drawings. Both are made permanent (on the appropriate fabrics) by heat setting, and are available in fabric or quilt shops and toy stores. The methods described here are:

I. Crayon Transfer
    A. Drawings (Crayola Transfer Fabric Crayons ✳)
    B. Rubbings
II. Dye Sticks on Fabric (Pentel's Fabricfun Pastel
      Dye Sticks ✳)
    A. Direct
    B. Stencil
III. Markers

Don't overlook the potential of these humble methods. They are great for transfers, and for adding color to other processes. Silk screen →, thermal image prints →, or copy transfers→ on fabric can be highlighted with fabric crayons or dye sticks. The transfer crayons are made to be used on paper and then heat transferred to fabric. The fabric crayons are for direct use on cloth, which is then covered with paper and set with a hot iron. It's easy to achieve smooth, soft or blended color which is permanent on the appropriate fabrics.

My first experience of crayon on fabric goes back to third grade, using plain old crayons (there were no special ones for fabric). I colored the knees of my drab, oatmeal-colored long cotton stockings. Smears of green and violet animated my knees for months and survived (to my mother's dismay) all washings. But a more dramatic use of crayons awaited me at home. My mother had taken down the monk's cloth dining room draperies and penciled in an abundance of flowers and leaves. Then, with two turkish towels in her lap, she held the iron between her knees (sole plate up), put the cloth over the iron, and colored in the designs. As the crayons heated, they melted onto the cloth, making brilliant, opaque areas of color. An old cigar box filled with broken crayon stubs had been the means of this metamorphosis which, it seemed certain to me, was nothing short of divine inspiration.

## I. CRAYON TRANSFER (Crayola Transfer Fabric Crayons)

Available in brilliant hues, these crayons are safe for children to use. They are sublimation (or disperse) dyes in a wax base. Drawings can be transferred from paper to cloth easily. If they are used directly on fabric, however, transfer crayons continue to give off excess color.

You need:
- Crayola Transfer Fabric Crayons
- Paper
- Synthetic fabric
- Iron →
- Newsprint, butcher's paper, or other plain scrap paper

### A. The process for transfer drawings

1. Draw with firm strokes on bond, typing, or other paper that has a slight "tooth" (slick paper does not hold the crayon). When the drawing is ready, remove any crayon crumbs by shaking the paper, or use masking tape to pick them up.

2. Cut fabric larger than the drawing.
3. Place fabric right side up on an ironing surface covered with paper. Place the drawing on top of fabric, crayon side down. Cover with a sheet of scrap paper.
4. Heat iron to highest setting the fabric will tolerate without scorching. Press, moving iron slowly until the drawing begins to show through the top sheet of paper. Iron carefully: if the papers slip, they may smudge or blur the images. Children must have adult supervision for this step of the transfer.

For permanent transfers, use fabric which is at least 60% synthetic. Satin acetates will be bright, while cotton and silk give a pastel effect and are less permanent.

One drawing can be printed several times, although the first print will be brighter than second transfers →. The original drawing can be recolored to make additional prints as bright as the original. Or outline pale prints with permanent markers to add definition. A child's drawings on paper were heat transferred to cotton fabric for a quilt

*Plate 2-2: Detail of "Vehicles" by Anna Laury.*

*As images reverse when they are transferred, all lettering must be reversed in order to read correctly. Results on synthetic acetate are brilliant and permanent.*

shown in Plate 2-1. The drawings are soft in color, compared to the brilliance achieved on synthetics. The two drawings were re-colored to maintain similarity in the repeats. The young artist had colored quite enthusiastically, so there were crayon crumbs everywhere. Rather than remove them, she added more to create a speckled background.

When transferring crayon drawings to T-shirts or other clothing, use padding to prevent color from bleeding through to another part of the garment. Test for washability before launching a large project.

The vehicles in Color Plate 20 were transferred to synthetic satins in this panel by a 12-year-old. The lettering appears backwards, since the drawing is flipped for transfer. In Plate 2-2 the young artist reversed her letters so that they would transfer correctly. Colors are more brilliant on this quilt than on the cotton one.

Color Plate 22 depicts exotic tropical fish created by Jessica Berman, 13. The crayon drawings on paper, shown below, were transferred to synthetic fabrics, shown above, with almost no loss of brilliance.

The fabric crayons can be used in another very interesting way. Start with a b/w copy of your original drawing. Color it as you wish. Transfer the crayon to fabric, either by heat setting in a photo (or dry mount) press for 10 to 12 seconds or by medium hot iron for about one minute. Only the color will transfer, but the copy serves as a guide for coloring.

*Plate 2-1: "Me and a Tree" drawings by Emma Laury, 40 "x 47".*

*A child's transfer crayon drawings on paper were heat transferred to cotton fabric. Pieced and machine quilted.*

Plate 2-3: *Block rubbings by Bea Slater.*
*Crayon rubbings over children's building blocks reflect intricate patterns of the carved wood. Words, dates, or initials can be spelled out in this way for use in quilts or panels.*

Plate 2-4: *Rubbing by Bea Slater.*
*Crayon rubbings over household items, such as this one from a bacon press, can be made directly onto the fabric, avoiding a reversal of the image.*

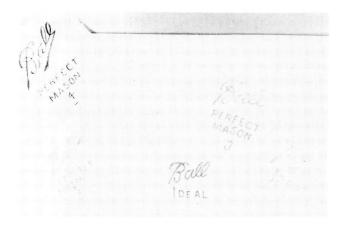

Plate 2-5: *Rubbings by Bea Slater.*
*The raised letters of a Ball Mason jar were transferred to fabric in a two-step crayon-rubbing process.*

## B. Crayon rubbings

Rubbings are made by coloring onto paper or fabric which is placed over an object that has a relief pattern. Rubbings can be either indirect or direct.

### INDIRECT RUBBINGS

The rubbing is made on paper using Crayola Transfer Fabric Crayons. The image appears reversed when it is heat set onto the fabric.

The process:

1. Select any smooth, flat object which has a relief design on the surface, such as a bowl with an incised design, an embossed glass, a child's block, or a cookie press.
2. Place a sheet of smooth white paper over the surface.
3. Color the design with crayons, as with a rubbing, going back and forth until the image is clear.
4. Remove paper and place it face down on fabric.
5. Heat set by ironing as for crayon drawings.

### DIRECT RUBBINGS

The rubbing is made on fabric using Crayola Craft Fabric Crayons. The image is not reversed.

The process:

1. Stretch the fabric and tape it over the raised surface to keep it taut.
2. Color the design with fabric crayons, stroking back and forth until the image is visible.
3. Remove the tape and lay the fabric, crayon side up, on an ironing surface.
4. Cover the colored area with clean scrap paper and heat set.

All kinds of familiar household objects can be used for direct crayon rubbings. In Plate 2-3 a child's building blocks provided the relief patterns. Words can be spelled out in this way. The bacon press in Plate 2-4 provides another good surface for this simple method. It's ideal for people who think they can't draw.

In Plate 2-5, fabric rubbings on fruit jars worked great with small (4") fabrics, but for a larger piece of cloth the curved surface proved difficult. Rubbings were therefore first made on paper, then transferred to fabric. Because the design includes letters, the reversal is a problem. To correct the reversal, the rubbing on paper was then taped to a window or light box, with the crayon side touching the glass. The design showed through enough to allow the original to be traced with color onto another sheet of paper. The tracing was then placed face side down on fabric and heat set to make the words readable in this panel for an ardent canner and jar collector.

Thorough ironing is important to heat setting. Finished pieces can be washed gently in cool to warm water without bleach. Do not place in the dryer. If you cannot locate fabric or transfer crayons, any regular crayons can be used with PAROdraw (see Chapter 3).

## TROUBLESHOOTING FOR CRAYON DRAWINGS AND RUBBINGS

Problem:   There are flecks of color over the transferred surface.
Solution:   Shake the drawing before heat setting to remove the flecks and bits of crayon which crumble off during use. Once ironed, they cannot be removed.
Consider them a natural part of the process, like freckles.

Problem:   You get a pale print.
Solution:   Use more crayon on the original.
Check the fiber content of your material: synthetics give brightest colors.
Increase the temperature of the iron.
Add color directly to cloth to brighten it, or re-color the original and try again.

Problem:   The images are blurred.
Solution:   Tape paper or cloth more securely in place over a three-dimensional object.
Work with smaller pieces of paper or fabric.
Be sure that paper does not move as you heat set.
Change paper under the fabric to avoid picking up color from any previous transfer.

## II. DYE STICKS ON FABRIC (Fabricfun pastel dye sticks✳)

Dye sticks bring out the mad artistic genius in all of us. The soft sticks in brilliant colors adhere readily to the cloth, drawing every budding Matisse into action. Paint with dye sticks on new fabrics, or color over old calicoes (the ones you thought were ideal a few years ago, and now can't imagine using). These sticks are easy to use, non-toxic, and require no additional equipment. Because they are portable and safe to handle, they are ideal for away-from-home work or projects for kids. Great for creating textures and strokes, the heat set drawings are permanent on cotton, silk or wool. They are not permanent on synthetics.

You will need:
• Dye sticks
• PFP fabric → (non-synthetic)
• Iron
• Pad of paper
• Freezer paper (optional) →

*Plate 2-6: Detail of Mother Jones's portrait from "A Tribute to American Women" by The Hamish Amish Quilters.*

*This block combines appliqué and needlework with crayons.*

## A. The process for direct use of dye sticks

1. Use light or white PFP fabric. Press and stretch it over a hard surface (pin to cardboard or tape to a board). Or iron freezer paper to the back of the fabric to add stiffness or to stabilize it. Edges of the cloth can be taped off with masking tape to retain a white mat or border, or use freezer paper for the masking.

2. Apply dye sticks, stroking evenly in one direction for smooth areas of color. The sticks are soft and can be blended with your fingertips.

3. Cover the finished design with a sheet of paper and iron with a hot iron (essential for washability).

## B. The process for dye sticks with stencil

As dye sticks are fairly soft, it is difficult to get hard or fine lines. By using them with stencils, you can achieve finer lines and sharp edges. The stencils are quick, easy, and readily controlled.

1. Cut fabric and freezer paper to same size.

2. Draw a design on the dull side of freezer paper. Cut out the design with scissors or a craft knife and re-move it. If you're doing a bird, for example, cut out the bird and toss it aside. The background shape (in freezer paper) will be the stencil; the open area of the bird is the part that will print. Cut out an eye or wing, or any other details, from the bird scrap.

3. Place the freezer paper stencil, shiny side down, on the cloth and press it in place with a medium hot iron. Be sure cut edges have adhered well, but too much heat will make the paper difficult to remove.

4. Place eyes, wings, or other details in the open fabric areas and iron into place.

5. Color the open area with dye sticks, which can be used in varying intensities from pastel to bright.

6. Carefully peel off the freezer paper, cover the drawing with a sheet of plain paper, and heat set with a medium hot iron for 30 seconds to a minute, moving the iron to avoid scorching.

Any sticky-backed or self-adhesive material can be used as a stencil. Try stickers (the ones fourth graders collect) as block-outs. Use freezer paper or tape to make lines and stripes. Once a color has been set, a new piece of tape can be added to cover a part of the first color, thus creating plaids, checks, or lines. Crayons and dye sticks are versatile and can be used to add color to other printed fabrics. Add solid color, sketchy lines, textures, or polka dots. Keep them in mind when you need to rescue a print; they're great for touch-up color! In Plate 2-6, the detail of Mother Jones from "A Tribute to American Women" was hand-drawn on muslin and colored with crayons. Appliqué and quilting complete the block.

# TROUBLESHOOTING FOR DYE STICKS

Problem:     You get a pale print.
Solution:    Use a heavier coating of dye sticks.
             Use a hotter iron.
             Use natural (non-synthetic) fabric.

Problem:     There are uneven edges where dye leaked under the edge of the stencil.
Solution:    Use more heat to adhere the freezer paper.
             Use the point of the iron to adhere edges more firmly.
             Avoid stroking into or against a cut edge of the stencil. Stroke from freezer
                paper toward the center of the open area.
             Color less vigorously.

## III. MARKERS

Markers do for fabric painting what spray cans do for graffiti: make it easy, colorful, and permanent. Anything is possible! There is a tremendous range available, so select permanent non-toxic colors. If the fumes smell obnoxious, they probably are; work only with good ventilation, and find a safer brand for the kids to work with. Markers are great for adding color to other projects, but you can also use them to draw and paint on cloth. To make drawings with markers, you will need:

- Permanent markers
- PFP fabric →
- Iron and board →

If you have used markers before, you know it's far easier to draw on fabric that has been stretched taut. Cut the fabric to working size, then staple or pin it to a board: some color may soak through, so protect your work surface if necessary. As the fabric absorbs the dye, colored areas may become saturated and colors may bleed. To avoid this, dry and heat the colors while you proceed. Always test for washability on the specific fabric, especially for a large project.

A detail of a quilt decorated with markers is shown in Plate 2-7. Designer Jackie Vermeer first dipped the background fabric in a mixture of equal parts of Sta-Puff and water. After it was dried and pressed, she drew her design with a light pencil line. She then colored it with El Marko pens in a variety of bright colors.

In Color Plate 23, Mrs. Bengel's eighth graders colored a block in their "Freedom Quilt" with Marvy markers. The students made drawings for the blocks, then librarian Jeanette Goshgarian placed the drawings in the overhead projector to enlarge them for the students to trace with pencil onto the cloth. They then colored them in. All of the brightly-colored blocks were sewn together, tied and quilted, and the finished quilt was hung in the school library.

Heather Avery's jacket (Plate 2-8) offers a wonderful way to use wide-tip marking pens. Her boldly drawn lines create the overall fabric pattern and allow for specific shapes to be used on various parts of the jacket (striped lapels, polka-dot pockets).

*Plate 2-7: Detail of "Hannah's Quilt" by Jackie Vermeer. Designs were painted onto starched fabric with marking pens, then the piece was quilted.*

*Plate 2-8: "Musician's Jacket" by Heather Avery.*

# Dye Transfer
## (Deka IronOn Transfer Paint ✳, Design Dye sheets ✳, disperse dye powders ✳, and other iron-on color transfers such as PAROdraw ✳)

The wonders of dye transfer were demonstrated to me as a teenager on a hot summer day. I sang in a small-town church choir and we occupied leather-covered chairs at the minister's side. Directly in front of me sat Mrs. Beula K., a soprano of alarming proportions. After an endless sermon on a stifling hot and humid day, we rose to sing. As Mrs. K. rose, her dress, a flamboyantly printed voile, peeled itself loose from the leather. There on the back of her dress was a perfect square of off-white fabric; transferred to the seat of her chair was a grand profusion of flowers! I'm still intrigued that heat and ample pressure will transfer color, though I'm no longer convulsed with giggles that force me to my knees (weakness, not piety). All dye transfer is accomplished in a similar way.

This chapter includes:

I. DYE TRANSFER (with disperse dyes)
    A. Deka IronOn Transfer Paint
    B. Design Dye Sheets
    C. Dye Powders
II. COLORING PAPERS (non-disperse dyes)
    A. PAROdraw Sheets
    B. Improvised Color Transfer

## I. DYE TRANSFER

Dye transfer papers are coated on one side with non-toxic transferrable colors which can be heat set → to fabric. Heat opens the fibers of the cloth, allowing the disperse dyes → and fibers to bond permanently. The papers can be purchased ready-painted; you can also apply liquid dyes to paper yourself or purchase powdered dyes and mix your own. Cut dye transfer papers into abstract patterns, constellations, or anteaters. Use them for letter-ing, apply them to natural forms ↘ (leaves, ferns, and feathers), or use them with the copier (for photos and drawings). Use the paints for watercolor effects or with stamp printing. Fabrics remain flexible and soft with dye transfer. The prints are permanent and washable on synthetics, but somewhat less permanent on cotton.

### A. Deka IronOn Transfer Paint

Deka IronOn colors come in liquid form to be painted onto paper and transferred to cloth. You can intermix the six available colors for greater variety, and thinning with water makes tints. The transfers can be graphic, flat areas of color or more painterly, with shadings, gradations, and patterns.

You will need:
- IronOn Transfer Paint
- Smooth white paper
- Bristle or sponge brush, 1" wide
- Small brushes or sponge
- Fabric on which to print (at least 60% synthetic)
- Iron and board →
- Tissue paper

1. For a graphic effect:
   a. Select smooth, non-absorbent white typing or copy paper. Apply an even coat of dye to paper, adding a second coat if necessary. A thin coat will transfer only once; thicker coats can be transferred several times.
   b. Dry the papers, then cut them into shapes or designs.
   c. Cover the ironing board to protect it and place fabric on board. Pre-heat iron to a hot setting.

d. Place cut papers painted side down on fabric. Cover the design with a sheet of tissue paper or scrap fabric and iron carefully with a hot iron for 1 or 2 minutes. Change tissue sheets as they become colored.

2. For a painterly effect:

a. Paint patterns onto paper, using a variety of colors, brush strokes, and thicknesses. A thin coat resembles watercolor and can be given visible brush marks, swirls, dots, or textures which will transfer. Dry.

b. Cut a square or rectangle from the patterned dye sheet for transfer. For an overlay effect, place one pattern face down, with another larger one on top of it. This creates an illusion of layers on the finished fabric.

c. Heat set as above. Unintentional transfers may occur if dye seeps into the protective papers and is then transferred to your fabric.

d. Or, arrange natural objects (leaves, grass), strips of cut-up patterns, or white paper cut-outs face down on the fabric, cover with a rectangle of painted transfer paper and heat set. This gives silhouette forms of the fabric color surrounded by the dye colors.

This process gives a surface texture quite different from the flat graphic use of these papers. Lura Schwarz Smith's "Mono-wing Angel" in Plate 3-1 has a face printed on opaque nylon stocking with Deka IronOn Transfer Paint. Soft lines were created by ironing only briefly before moving the cut shapes (see Color Plate 24). The "Women in Space" in Color Plate 21 are transfers from sheets painted with Deka IronOn Fabric Dye.

## B. Design Dye sheets

Design Dye sheets are available in pre-coated 8" x 10" sheets in eight different colors. The permanent dyes offer flat graphic effects, though it takes practice to avoid any migrating color in the transfer. The birds depicted in Color Plate 25 are created from sheets of dye transfer colors. Design Dyes can also be used to transfer color to other objects which can then be transferred to cloth. This indirect method can be used with natural forms (leaves, etc.) or by using Design Dyes with the copier ↘ and with stamps ↘ for unique printing effects.

You will need:
- Scissors or X-Acto knife
- Design Dye papers →
- Fabric on which to print (at least 60% synthetic)
- Tissue paper
- Newsprint
- Iron and board →

The basic process:
1. Work out your design and cut the shapes from dye papers.
2. Place tissue on pad of newsprint.
3. Place fabric on tissue.
4. Place cut-outs on fabric, color side down; avoid sliding them over the surface.
5. Cover with tissue.
6. Heat set with a hot dry iron.

Richard Daehnert's Heritage Souvenir series makes a unique and painterly use of a variety of design papers. In addition to powdered or liquid dyes and dye sheets, he has located dye sheets which are left over from the printing of polyester yardage. Available only in the proximity of textile industries, they are recycled and sold as wrapping papers, but they still contain enough disperse dye to transfer to cloth. Richard uses, in addition, powdered transfer dyes which he mixes and paints onto paper. A dry mount press at 350° provides high and consistent heat, simplifying transfer to larger areas. In "Heritage Souvenir: Mesa Verde," his initial images were made with dye transfer, then embellished by an intricate tracery of stitches laid over the color. Another in his Heritage Souvenir series features the space shuttle with surfaces richly embellished in linear patterns. See Color Plates 26 and 28.

## C. Powdered Disperse Dyes ✳ (Aljo →, PROsperse)

CAUTION ☞ Health hazards from the powdered dyes are slight, but it is advisable to avoid eye contact and breathing the dust. Wash up thoroughly after mixing or using the powders. Mix powders in a room with good ventilation, but avoid any breezes which could carry the powders.

Disperse dyes can be purchased in powdered form and are available in about twenty colors. Mixed with water, they can be applied directly to fabric, or the mixed color can be added to a thin gelatin base, which gives a consis-

*Plate 3-1: "Mono-wing Angel" by Lura Schwarz Smith, 12" long.*

*Made with a variety of techniques, including dye transfer, direct printing in copier, drawing on fabric, and other embellishments, this doll was constructed from separate stuffed parts, then assembled.*

tency suitable for painting on paper. It is available from Aljo. PRO Thick F serves as a thicker carrier for the PROsperse dyes. Dyers may have sodium alginate or mono gum on hand, and either will work. The gelatin is important if you prefer to make up your own dye transfer sheets. The mixed powders are heat set in the same way as other disperse dyes. Their primary advantages are the wide range of available colors and the cost, lower than liquids or pre-painted papers. They also allow for direct painting on paper, so that changes and overlays are possible.

## General Information for all Design Dyes

### DESIGN DYES WITH THE COPIER

Dye sheets can be used with the b/w copier in a simple and wonderful process to create permanent single-color prints. While one color is printed at a time, several transfers will create multicolored images. Follow these steps:

a. Run a good black copy of your photo or drawing. (It may help to use Letraset's Copy FX, a specialty paper for photocopiers which has a continuous tone for fine prints. But try a standard copy first.)

b. Place the fresh copy face up on an ironing surface (a cardboard on an ironing board works well).

c. Cut a piece of Design Dye paper (or a paper well-covered with Deka IronOn) the size of the copied image and place it color side down on the copy.

d. Press with a hot iron. Color will transfer to the toner, though it will be difficult to see that it has adhered. Some color will also transfer to the background area. During heat setting, there is some tendency of colors to migrate, depositing a pale color over all.

e. Cut out the area you wish to transfer. The cut shape is important, because the shape itself will also transfer. For example, if your copy is of a cat, cut a distinct shape around it (maybe a rectangle). When transferred, the linear part of the cat will be dark in color, overlaid by a pale rectangle of the same color.

f. Place copy face down on fabric and heat set. Image will be reversed. If it must be right, make a transparency → first. Fabric will remain soft and flexible.

In Plate 3-2, the upper right shows an enlarged photocopy of a portrait. It was covered with dye paper and ironed to transfer dye color to the copy. The image was then cut from the background paper and placed face down on muslin to produce the image at left. While this is a one-color print, several different pieces of dye paper could be used at one time to make a multicolored image. At the lower edge of the plate, a b/w photo copy of a drawing was transferred to cloth using the same method. This process offers wonderful transfers with a minimum of preparation.

Plate 3-2: Image by Jean Ray Laury.

*Dye transfer paper can be ironed over a photocopy to produce a heat-transferrable image. At upper right, the photocopy has been ironed over with the design dye sheet and the background has been trimmed away. At left, the same copy has been transferred to fabric. In the lower part of the photo, a drawing has been transferred the same way.*

## Other Hints

### DESIGN DYES WITH STAMPS

Deka's IronOn dye can be painted onto a stamp pad (Chapter 9 describes how to make one). Stamps can be inked on the wet pad and stamped directly onto the appropriate fabric. Cover the print with tissue and heat set.

### FABRIC

Dye transfers work best on white or light fabrics. Brilliance and permanence can be achieved with 100% synthetics, such as polyester, acetate, and acrylic. Next choice is 65% synthetic. Satin acetate's smooth surface accepts color especially well. The tissue-paper cover is especially important over fabrics that can be melted by direct ironing. Finer fabrics give more intense color than coarse fabrics, and all must withstand the heat required for heat transfer. When natural fibers are used, the effect is not as bright or as permanent. A spray solution called Fabric Prep (available with Design Dye papers) allows natural fibers to accept the Design Dyes more readily.

### LETTERING

Draw letters on the white uncoated side of dye sheets, cut them out for transfer and they will read correctly. The free-hand cutting methods described in Chapter 10 will work effectively. Use stamp alphabets, which are already reversed, for any extensive wording.

### NATURAL FORMS

Leaves, or other natural objects, can be used in two distinctly different ways. In the first, a leaf is used as the block-out, placed directly onto the fabric. A sheet of paper covered with iron-on dyes is placed over the leaf and is heat set. The leaf appears in the original fabric color, surrounded by the dye color.

In the second method, you paint directly onto the back of the leaf. Select one with prominent veining, for greater textural effect; smooth, flat leaves create a less interesting pattern. Place the leaf face down on the fabric and cover it with a tissue or cloth. Using the highest iron temperature the fabric will tolerate, transfer the leaf to cloth. It sometimes helps to press the leaf first to flatten it. Ferns, feathers, or leaves all offer interesting patterns, and even parsley and baby's breath can be ironed flat to make them printable. In order to have leaves available for winter use, printmaker Renée Auchard Ray freezes them.

Plate 3-3 shows a T-shirt which has been leaf-printed. Plastic or absorbent paper should be slipped inside the shirt to prevent paint from oozing through. The dye is painted on the back of the leaf sparingly, and the wet leaf is placed on the cloth. Clear wrap goes over the top, pressed with your hand to ensure good overall contact; or, you can cover it with paper and use a brayer. Lift the paper and leaf carefully, then heat set. This example was painted with Inkodye, but the process is the same, except for the drying. A print made with Inkodye can be hung in the sun to develop the color. To print a variegated leaf, apply several colors at the same time. When printing a series, be sure to protect one printed area before doing another, unless you want to create overlays.

*Plate 3-3: T-Shirt by Renée Auchard Ray.*
*Dye, painted directly onto the veined surface of a leaf, is heat set in three separate steps onto a shirt.*

## SECOND TRANSFERS

Shapes can be transferred more than once, but second or third transfers are less brilliant than the first. With Deka IronOn, the color intensity of the second transfer depends in part upon how heavily the coat of paint was applied. Design Dye sheets transfer well, but lighter, the second time.

## STENCILS

Work in the manner described for natural forms, but substitute your own cut shapes or stencils. Or utilize the tendency of colors to migrate by placing them colored side up on the fabric. Cover with tissue and iron with a careful, circular motion to help the colors spread to the sides. The stencil will retain the background color as dyes spread around it in a halo effect.

## STORING UNUSED PAPERS

The color from dye sheets can be rubbed off onto other surfaces, so they must be handled and stored carefully. Keep papers covered in a cool place, and separate the sheets with tissue or scrap paper. Avoid keeping colored papers face to face.

# TROUBLESHOOTING FOR DESIGN DYE PRINTS

Problem:    The color does not transfer at all.

Solution:    Use a higher iron temperature.

Dye in the sheets may be depleted by earlier use.

Problem:    Lines or spots appear in the color.

Solution:    Apply pressure and heat evenly.

Be sure to cover the shape entirely with the iron. The edge of the sole plate will make a line.

Avoid using a steam iron, as the vents may create dots or spots due to uneven heating.

To avoid streaks in hand-painted papers, mix colors thoroughly; if they are not completely blended, spots will result.

Problem:    Pale color transfers over the background, past the design.

Solution:    Migrating of dyes is difficult to control with thick layers of paint and larger shapes. Paint a thinner layer; use smaller shapes.

Problem:    You get a blurred print, or colors that bleed or spread.

Solution:    Avoid too much paint, heat, or movement of the iron.

Experiment to determine the correct heat and time for the fabric and dye paper you are using.

Use a heavier background fabric which will absorb more dye.

Use smaller shapes.

Be careful that the dye papers do not shift during ironing.

Problem:    The transfer is unclear or uneven.

Solution:    Use a finer fabric (too porous or coarse material cannot record fine details).

Use higher heat.

Reposition the paper and repeat the heat setting step.

Problem:    There are shadow images.

Solution:    Use a clean cover under the print.

Use a clean cover over the print (especially if color has migrated).

Avoid moving the papers as you iron.

Problem:    The color is pale.

Solution:    Use new paper, as color may be depleted if the paper was previously used.

Use more heat.

Be sure to use recommended fabric.

## II. COLORING PAPERS (non-disperse dyes)

### A. PAROdraw Sheets ✳

A paper just recently made available by Graffoto allows you to transfer drawings or writing permanently to fabric. Available as PAROdraw, it is a two-step process, so the cloth image reads the same as the original. It is great for children's work and appeals to adults who want to add writing or sketches to fabric. It is a one-time transfer, so a new drawing must be made for each print. The packaged papers come in sets of three, one sheet each of A, B, and a finishing paper. A full-sized sheet is a good proportion for a T-shirt, though for children's sizes a half-sheet is best, or they'll be tucking part of the design in. For other uses, the sheets can be cut up into smaller portions as needed.

You will need:
- PAROdraw paper
- Fabric (white or light-colored)
- Iron and hard surface
- Coloring materials

The process in brief:
1. Make a drawing on PAROdraw sheet A.
2. Place the drawing face-up on a hard surface and place sheet B over it, face down. Heat set at low iron temperature for 2 or 3 seconds. This transfers the drawing to sheet B.
3. Cool to room temperature, then peel the sheets apart.
4. Cut away any excess of paper B.
5. Place fabric on the board with sheet B face down on top of it.
6. Heat set on high for 2 or 3 seconds, then peel paper away while it is still hot.
7. Cover the transfer with finishing paper, and press hot.

### PAPER

While PAROdraw is relatively expensive in packets, it will soon be available in bulk sheets for slightly less. It transfers a sharp image from many kinds of color and requires only a home iron, not a heat press. It is available only in 8½" x 11" at present.

### FABRIC

Use a white or light-colored fabric for best results. Any fabric which can withstand the heat of the hot-iron transfer can be used. All cotton fabrics and 50/50 blends print well and can be washed in cool to warm water. The surface is very slightly stiffened by the transfer. If you are not using a whole or half page, attention must be given to the shape cut out of sheet B. When transferred to cloth, it will alter the color of the fabric just slightly so that, in some lights, the shape will show. Use a rectangle or square, or cut carefully around the shape to be transferred.

### IRON

Use a non-steam iron. Since most ironing boards are well padded, you'll get better results by using a table top or a board covered with a cloth or tea towel. Set the iron down in one spot and hold it there, being careful not to slide the iron, or you may smear the design. As the transfer is made from sheet A to B, or from B to cloth, there is a slight change of color just discernable through the back of the paper.

### COLORING MATERIALS

Any non-waterbase drawing tool can be used, including pencil, colored pencil, charcoal, crayon, or oil pastel. The oil pastels transfer in brilliant color. I got excellent results with Crayola's Color Works, which are very fine-line crayons similar to mechanical lead pencils (the rods of color can be replaced). But I got good results using Color Works directly on fabric, too. Old marking pens, with a xylene base, will also transfer. You can probably identify them by the smell (which is terrible and familiar). New markers don't contain this toxic solvent, but they don't transfer as well either. Plate 3-4 shows fabric with PAROdraw transfers from several kinds of coloring materials.

### COPIER

Drawing sheet A can be used in a copier, but with mixed results. Some machines will give a good image, which means you can copy photographs and hand color them before transfer to fabric.

### B. Improvised color transfer (non-disperse dyes)

Color transfer papers can be made from any heat-transferrable color, even if it is not a disperse dye. Several

*Plate 3-4: PAROdraw examples by Jean Ray Laury.*
*Drawings on the two-step PAROdraw transfer paper were made with markers and colors.*

methods described in other chapters also adapt themselves to transfer paper.

Caran d'Ache color pencils and color crayons can be used directly onto the sticky side of a self-adhesive vinyl or contact paper (e.g., Magic Cover, Con-tact, Grid-Grip). This will create a colored area which can be transferred to give a hand-colored or painted effect. It works especially well on b/w copies of photographs and drawings which have been transferred to contact paper, a process described in Chapter I. Color and copy are transferred simultaneously, though only the top layer of ink or color will be transferred. If areas of color are drawn over a line, the color will transfer, leaving the line behind on the paper. Fabric Fun Pastel Dye Sticks can be used in the same way as the color pencils and crayons. With this method, transfers can be made to cotton fabric and will not wash out.

The water-soluble Caran d'Ache colors can be brushed on with water, or the pencils can be dipped in water for special effects with a contact paper. The more coats of color added, the more intense the transferred color. When water is used, the color must dry between coats. A shape is then cut from the colored adhesive paper. If it's hard to handle during cutting, place the sticky surface against the plastic side of freezer paper. After cutting, peel freezer paper away. Transfer the contact sheet to fabric, following directions in Chapter 1.

Crayola Transfer Fabric Crayons → and Pentel Dye Sticks → can also be used to make dye transfer papers, though they are not disperse dyes. Cover part of a sheet of typing or copy paper with solid areas of color. Cut out letters or shapes and heat transfer them to synthetic fabric (see Chapter 2, Crayon Transfer.) Or draw, sketch, and

Plate 3-5: Detail of "Fabric Sale" by Jean Ray Laury.
Quilts copied onto color heat transfer paper were cut into figures and heat set to cloth.

Plate 3-6: Image by Jean Ray Laury.
Hearts and hands, cut from heat transfer paper, impose one quilt pattern over another.

scribble with crayons to create patterns and textures for transfer.

CLC copies on special transfer paper can be used for cut-outs. Keep all colored scraps from Copy Transfers, described in Chapter 1, to be used as iron-on papers; the process is similar, though the dyes are not. Make, for example, a color copy from a slide of your quilt on transfer paper. Cut it up into wild animals, letters or geometric shapes, or cut a house from your own quilt, make treetops from a Trip Around The World, or snip clouds from your own pieced patterns. Plate 1-19 (Chapter 1) shows a book in which cutout letters are transferred to cloth from one-color heat transfer prints made on the CLC copier.

In Plate 3-5 and Color Plate 27, the cavorting girls are cut from color copies of favorite quilts. It's like making teddy bears of your grandmother's quilt without cutting into the quilt. The hearts and hands, in Plate 3-6, transferred onto silk-screened checkerboards, were cut from color copies of photos of pieced quilts.

## TROUBLESHOOTING FOR PARODRAW SHEETS

Problem: Part of the color remained on sheet A and did not transfer to B.
Solution: After setting at a low temperature and cooling, pull a corner of the paper back. If the transfer is not complete, heat set again.
Use the toe of the iron to add extra pressure to stubborn spots.

Problem: Part of sheet B did not transfer to cloth.
Solution: When heat setting, turn back a corner and check on transfer. Iron again if necessary.
Peel layers immediately. Reheat the sheet before peeling.

Problem: An error was made in the drawing or writing of the original.
Solution: There isn't a good solution. Do not erase on the surface of A. If you can cover over the original, you may be able to save it. Or cut out a misspelled word and insert the new one with a separate small piece of A.

## TROUBLESHOOTING FOR IMPROVISED COLOR TRANSFER

Problem: Contact accepts color unevenly.
Solution: Dampen the paper slightly. Then coat it with colored pencil.

Problem: Some details are obscured in the final transfer.
Solution: When painting on the contact sheet, avoid adding color over the copy details. Only one layer is going to transfer to fabric, so if copy lines are covered with watercolor, they will be obscured.

Problem: Contact sticks to your hand as you color it.
Solution: Use a piece of freezer paper, shiny side down, under your hand.

3. Detail of "Babar and the Elephants" by Jennifer Robin Angus.

Copy transfer of a b/w photo is superimposed over an intricately pieced ground in this highly embellished cushion.

1. "A Tribute to American Women" by the Hamish Amish Quilters, 90" x 78".

Color heat transfer is combined with appliqué, drawing, embroidery, and other embellishments to honor 42 outstanding women.

2. "Villa Torrigiani" by Jacqueline Treloar, 5' x 6'.

Transparent fabrics with color heat-transfer images overlay the large dimensional architectural form.

4. "Ladies with Big Hats" by Jennifer Robin Angus, 24" x 35".

Copy transfers over the background are enhanced with embroidery and piecing in this large pillow.

5. Detail of "Colonial Attitude" by Jennifer Robin Angus.

The face is heat-transferred over striped fabric with richly detailed embellishments.

7. "Don't Make War So Beautiful" by Heather J. Urquhart, 74" x 54".

Color heat transfer was used to convey the reality of war in graphic, full-color scenes on cloth, combined with piecing and quilting.

6. "Colonial Attitude" by Jennifer Robin Angus, 6' x 2'.

Manipulated fabrics form the background for color heat transfers, hundreds of buttons, appliqués, and three-dimensional fabric pieces.

8. Detail of "Don't Make War So Beautiful" by Heather J. Urquhart.

Note the contrast of quilted textures and smooth transfer surfaces.

9. Detail of "A Piece of the Pie" by Wendy Lewington Coulter.

Images of our threatened environment are color heat-transferred to fabric and fragmented as the filling in "your piece of the pie." It is also pieced, quilted, and stamped.

11. Detail of "River Trout" by Jackie Vermeer.

Contact paper copy transfer was used to add fish to hand-painted fabrics.

12. "Fish" by Nancy Clemmensen, 4" x 7".

Brilliant colors were achieved by drawing with crayons on contact paper before the final transfer to fabric.

10. Detail of "Art Object" by Wendy Lewington Coulter.

With color heat transfer, "fine art" images are stitched into the traditional quilt format, confusing some generally accepted expectations of where "fine art" is to be found.

13. "Wedding Dolls" by Karen Page. Dolls approximately 10" high.

Portraits of the bride and groom were transferred to fabric using mending-tape transfer to personalize the open-armed dolls in their finery.

14. *"Peg's Quilt" by Nancy Taylor, 45" x 49".*

*The sharp and detailed photo transfers in this memory quilt were made using bottled transfer medium.*

15. *A Cautionary Tale" by Joan Schulze, 59" x 40".*

*The artist recreates an earthshaking event with photographs, transferred to fabric with transfer medium, and printed "caution" tapes from construction site areas.*

16. *"Cloud Watching" by Joan Schulze, 20" x 16".*

*Transfer medium on photographs and magazine lifts was used to create this atmospheric piece.*

17. *"Juggler Doll" by Elaine Brunn , 18" tall.*

*A stuffed and dressed doll was given a full-color face with bottled transfer medium.*

18. "Americana" by Betsy Nimock, 38" x 37".

The quilt archaeologist combines old blocks with imagery, using solvent transfer to place the enhanced photograph on fabric.

19. "Third Time Around" by Betsy Nimock, 76" x 78".

Black-and-white photos, used with the color copier, were solvent-transferred to create compelling and haunting effects.

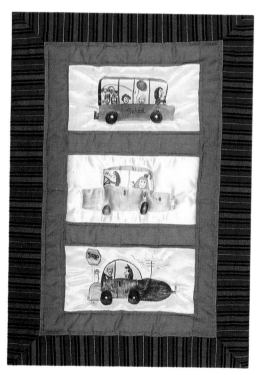

20. "Vehicles" by Anna Laury, 33" x 23".

A 12-year-old's transfer crayon drawings on paper were heat set to synthetic acetate for brilliant colors.

21. "Women In Space" by Jean Ray Laury, 21" x 25".

These free spirits were created from design dye papers, ironed onto synthetic acetate fabric and hand quilted.

23. Detail of "Freedom Quilt" by Jeanette Goshgarian and Mrs. Bengel's eighth-grade class from Fresno, California.

With an overhead projector, a small drawing was enlarged onto fabric, traced with pencil, and colored with permanent markers.

22. "Fish" by Jessica Berman, c. 8" x 10".

Transfer crayon drawings on paper (below) are shown after heat transfer to fabric (above) which reverses images. Brilliant, permanent colors result from the use of synthetic fabrics. Machine quilted.

24. "Mono-wing Angel" by Lura Schwarz Smith , 12" long.

Stuffed fabric angel combines drawing on cloth, dye transfer, and fabric run through the copier.

27. Detail of "Fabric Sale" by Jean Ray Laury.

Scrambling figures are cutouts from copy transfer papers, heat set to fabric.

25. "Birds" by Jean Ray Laury, 15" x 17".

Design Dye papers were transferred to fabric, then pieced and machine quilted.

28. "Heritage Souvenir Series: Space Shuttle" by Richard Daehnert, 8 ⅜" x 7 ⅞".

Stitched lines add an interlacing network over drawing on canvas with dye transfer.

26. "Heritage Souvenir Series: Mesa Verde" by Richard Daehnert, 8" x 9".

Drawing on canvas with dye transfer was overlaid with a linear pattern of stitches.

29. "Lovebirds" by Jean Ray Laury, 13" x 13".

Fabric was run through the copier, then colored with permanent marking pens.

30. "Lovebirds" by Jean Ray Laury, 13" x 13".

Birds were copied onto fabric by running them through the copier. Color was added by brushing on thinned textile paint.

31. "Great-grandparents' Pillow" by Jean Ray Laury, 13" x 13".

Copies of old photographs were enlarged, and the backgrounds were cut away to make up the original, which was then copied onto muslin in the copier.

32. "The Cleveland Pillow" by Jean Ray Laury, 13" x 13".

A paste-up of two photo prints and a quotation were photocopied directly onto muslin. Color was added by hand painting.

33. "Bed Pillows" by Jean Ray Laury, 6" x 11".

Faces copied onto muslin were hand-painted, combined with screened fabrics, and stuffed to make little pillows.

34. "Emma's Quilt" by Emma Laury, aged five, 36" x 30".

After the drawing was copied onto nine fabric blocks, color was added with quick-screen.

# Direct Machine Printing on Fabric

A logical and obvious next step in putting images on fabric is to dispense with transfer methods altogether and run fabrics directly through the copier, typewriter, or printer. This more direct, head-on approach is sometimes a collision course, as it becomes a matter of wills: will the machine dictate what it (and you) can do, or will you dictate to the machine. It's exciting and rewarding work, but not without risk. Having successfully run lots of fabric through my copier, printer, and typewriter, I'm pleased to report that all still function perfectly. Methods include running fabric directly through the machine (plain paper copier, typewriter, dot matrix printer), and direct transfers from the machine (laser printer, transfer ribbons for the printer).

## GENERAL INFORMATION

Know how to remove a paper from your copier or printer and understand its basic functions (or have someone at hand who does) before feeding it this unusual high-fiber diet. Some machines are sensitive to changes in page thickness, and they may reject your first efforts.

Fabric finishes affect printing and permanence, so use untreated cloth or PFP fabric →. In order to run directly through a machine, the fabric must have some body. Stabilize it by stiffening the fabric or laminating it to paper using any of the following:

1. Iron-on freezer paper →
2. Glue sticks
3. Spray adhesive →
4. Starch

1. Iron-on freezer paper, heat set to fabric, adds enough body to make the fabric paper-like. It is easily applied or removed, and it leaves little or no residue.

To use:
a. Cut the freezer paper exactly to copy-paper size.
b. Cut fabric (cotton muslin, silk, or a similar-weight light-colored fabric) slightly smaller, leaving margins of no more than ⅛". Trim off all loose threads.
c. Cover ironing surface with paper. Place the shiny, plastic-coated side of the freezer paper on the cloth and heat set with a medium hot iron, securing the edges carefully. Leave no loose threads which could be lost in the inner sanctum of the copier to play havoc with any subsequent printing. The laminated sheets sometimes curl towards the fabric side. Flatten them by running the iron over the paper side just before inserting it into the machine. This is the method I prefer: the freezer papers are re-usable.

2. Glue stick: To run fabric through a typewriter, you may need to glue only at the leading edge; for the printer, adhere by making 5 or 6 glue-stick lines across the paper. When printing in your copier, observe where the grabbers make contact with the paper to pull it through: it is essential that the paper-cloth bond be firm in that area. The leading edge and the far edge must both be well adhered. A few additional lines of glue across the central part of the sheet will be adequate.

3. Spray adhesives are more difficult to handle. Avoid breathing the spray, and work out of doors. A spray does provide good, smooth contact, and some designers prefer it.

4. Spray-and-iron starch adds enough body and stiffness to a fabric to make it printable, especially for a typewriter or printer. It's relatively easy to use, and

you can stiffen the leading edge more heavily than the rest. Part of any copy or print, however, will adhere to the starch. When you wash the fabric, you will remove part of the print with the dissolved starch. A machine which rejects laminated fabric may accept this thin, starched sheet, but it must be rigid enough not to crumple as it's pulled through.

## I. RUNNING FABRIC THROUGH YOUR COPY MACHINE

There are fabric artists (including me) who are dead set on running fabric through their copiers. The directness is exciting, but the machines reveal their prima donna hearts and get petulant. Pampering and cajoling will urge them to perform: when it works, it's great! If you own or have access to a private copy machine, you may want to try it. I've worked extensively with success. In the initial stages, my left hand was always on the electric outlet so that the machine could be unplugged instantly if a problem surfaced.

Both the permanence and washability of copies on cloth vary. I've copied onto fabric using my Canon 270 copier: the copies are permanent, even when I've run them through the washing machine with detergent (worst scenario treatment). Some designers report that their prints washed out entirely. Variables include the fabric, curing time, heat setting, the toner (which differs among machine brands, and even models), and the temperature at which the machine sets the toner. Both the Canon 24 and 25, which I leased for several weeks for class use, gave permanent prints. Esther Cheal made permanent copies on cloth with her Canon PC-7. Always test for washability, as some copiers will not give permanent results.

You will need:
- Original artwork or a good copy
- Copier
- Iron →
- PFP fabric → laminated with freezer paper or stiffened)

The Process
1. Laminate or stabilize PFP fabric. Leave no loose threads.
2. Run a test copy of your art to be sure it is clear. Adjust for size and density.
3. Feed the prepared fabric into the machine, either through the tray or by hand feed. My machine prefers the tray feed, but others accept either. Keep a finger on the Print button: the copier seems eager to expel the fabric sheet when another print is coming right behind it. It's like being pushed in line; it does keep you moving!
4. If the machine refuses to pull the laminated fabric through, try laminating silk.
5. If the laminated fabric stalls inside, open the machine and carefully pull the sheet out.
6. When the print emerges, lay it out to dry or cure for at least several hours, longer in damp weather. When dry, heat set. Then test for washability.
7. Add color with direct painting, quick printing, dye sticks, or marking pens.

Machines range in temperament from tolerant to persnickety. None of them *like* printing on fabric, and they may balk or jam when fed the laminated sheet. This is almost never disastrous. Jams most often occur after a sheet is printed but before it moves through the heat set and expulsion steps. Open the machine, reach in, pull out the offending sheet, and discard it. Take special care not to tear a sheet, leaving shreds in the machine. Being fickle, machines may accept one sheet and reject the next. Occasionally a machine will reject the laminated sheet at the feeding mechanism. If this happens, turn the sheet and try the other edge first, or press to make sure it is flat. If it is still rejected, try a lighter-weight fabric. Silk on freezer paper adds almost no weight at all and will usually sail through.

Fabric copies are rarely as black as paper copies, so be sure to work from art that has as much contrast as possible. Make several progressively darker copies until you achieve the strongest possible black-on-white copy from which to print your fabric. If you are not getting dark, clear prints, try another copier. When printing a small image, you must use a full-size piece of cloth on a full sheet of paper. If you can't bear to waste the fabric, print two small images at one time.

For the pillows in Color Plates 29 and 30, an original drawing was first copied onto a transparency. The transparent image was flipped and taped right next to the original, so that the two birds were standing face to face (dancing beak to beak?). This double image was then

Plate 4-1: Transparency for "The Cleveland Pillow" by Jean Ray Laury.

A postcard portrait, top left, was photocopied and enlarged, then duplicated and made into a transparency, shown at the bottom edge. The transparency was copied onto muslin by running the fabric through the copier.

Plate 4-2: "Bed Pillows" by Jean Ray Laury, each 6" x 10".

Direct printing on fabric with a copy machine put the heads to rest on these pillows. Bedcovers were silk-screen printed.

Plate 4-3: "Family Dolls" by Jean Ray Laury, each 12" long.

Photos, copied onto flannel and cotton in the copier, were hand-tinted and stuffed to make dolls.

*Plate 4-4: "Emma's Quilt" by Emma Laury, each block 6" x 8".*
*A child's drawing was enlarged and copied onto a transparency (at lower center) which was in turn copied directly onto fabric, shown upper left. At right the copy has been colored with quick-screen.*

*Plate 4-5: Detail of "Emma's Quilt" by Emma Laury.*
*Flipping the transparency lets the figure alternately raise her left and right hands. Blocks are pieced together with sashing and hand-quilted.*

photocopied onto the laminated cloth. Two copies on cloth were required for each pillow.

The lovebirds were hand-colored, the pale one with thinned Versatex color, the bright one with Marvy markers. For details of painting, refer to Coloring and Tinting Prints →.

"The Cleveland Pillow" in Color Plate 32 was duplicated in a similar way, so that the two heads and the quote were copied at one time. The name, at the bottom, was printed separately and pieced into the pillow top. Plate 4-1 shows the original card at left. After the background was cut away from the copy, a transparency, shown at the bottom, was made. At upper right the image is shown copied onto cloth. The fabric was hand-tinted.

Lura Schwarz Smith's Angel (Color Plate 24) was assembled from parts printed on fabric in the copier. Once printed and heat set, the figure was colored with Versatex.

My great-grandparents, in the pillow of Color Plate 31, were taken from an old photo. Background was cut away and the photo was enlarged on the copier. No transparency was needed. The enlargement was then copied onto laminated cloth and the piece was hand-painted with thinned textile paints.

"Bed Pillows" in Plate 4-2 required no transparency, and the process is simple. The faces were enlarged on the copier from old snapshots, and the background was cut away. Each face was then pasted onto a sheet of paper and copied directly onto laminated muslin. Combined with pieced silk-screened fabrics, the girls appear to recline on their pillows. The hand-painted images are shown in Color Plate 33.

Doll faces in Plate 4-3 were also run directly through the copier. One is printed on cotton flannel, the others on broadcloth. The copies were less permanent on flannel, as much of the ink rested on the fuzzy little threads of the nap without penetrating the cloth.

In "Emma's Quilt" in Color Plate 34, a child's drawing was the original image. It was enlarged, as shown on the upper left in Plate 4-4. A transparency was made (center) so that the image could later be flipped, letting the figure lean to either the left or right. At right is the print copied directly onto laminated muslin. Color was added with quickscreen, described in Chapter 5. A detail of the finished quilt is shown in Plate 4-5.

# TROUBLESHOOTING FOR FABRIC IN THE PLAIN PAPER COPIER

Problem:     The machine won't accept the laminated sheet.

Solution:    If it has curled, press the fabric sheet and try again.

              Use a thinner fabric (try silk rather than cotton).

              Keep your finger on the Print button until the next sheet comes through.

              Try another machine.

Problem:     The machine won't spit out the paper and fabric laminate.

Solution:    Open the machine and remove the reluctant sheet.

              Keep your finger on the Print button until the next sheet comes through.

              Use a thinner fabric.

Problem:     The print is pale.

Solution:    Start with a darker original.

              Adjust the machine to a darker print.

              Use fine-line permanent marker to clarify lines.

Problem:     The copy on fabric washes out.

Solution:    Let it dry or cure for a longer time.before heat setting.

              Heat set for a longer time and at a higher temperature.

              Try a different machine.

Problem:     The print is smudged.

Solution:    Laminate the paper and fabric more securely to avoid any looseness.

              Make sure the original is legible.

              Do not touch the print for several hours.

## II. RUNNING FABRIC THROUGH YOUR TYPEWRITER

With fabric run into the typewriter, you could write your entire family history on the back of a quilt! Messages and letters of every sort can be written on fabric quickly and easily. For permanence, purchase an indelible ribbon ✳. Heat set the typing after it dries (allow a couple of hours) and it will withstand washing. If you use a standard ribbon, dry and heat set the typed message, then test in cool water with mild liquid detergent. Some standard ribbons seem to give permanent results, others last through several washings, and a few wash out completely and immediately. Test yours, and remember that fiber content and fabric treatments can affect permanence. General Ribbon Corp., a major supplier of typewriter ribbons, considers all their ribbons to be fairly permanent, though they acknowledge that eventually the type will wash out of fabric. Wendy Lewington Coulter has worked out a process to stabilize standard ribbon on fabric. After heat setting, she sprays the typed fabric with a Krylon Workable Fixative, made for artists' use on rag papers. After drying and heat setting, she found the typing remained through test washings.

Stiffened fabric is easier to roll into the machine than limp fabric. Use any of the methods described earlier in this chapter, though overall lamination is less crucial for this use. A few fabrics will roll into the machine with no additional stiffening at all. The smoother the weave of the cloth, the more easily the message can be read.

You'll need:
- Standard ribbon or indelible ribbon
- PFP cloth (smooth and slightly crisp or laminated) →
- Typewriter
- Iron and board →

The Process:
1. Roll stiffened fabric into the typewriter.
2. Type your message.
3. Allow it to dry for several hours.
4. Cover the print with paper, then heat set with a hot iron.
5. Test for permanence.

Wendy Lewington Coulter's "Heirloom Quilt" in Plate 4-6 includes messages typed directly on the fabric; they overlay the traditional pattern, making the quilt personal and poignant as well as timeless. The typed quotes from abused women add visual pattern and texture as well as emotional impact to this powerful work.

Cloth envelopes, sewn to quilt blocks, were used by another designer. The flap of each envelope lifted to reveal a letter, typewritten on cloth. If washing was necessary, the letters could be removed. This would also be an excellent way to attach your quiltmaking history to the quilt. A fabric envelope could be sewn to the back of your quilt and the typed fabric document inserted.

## III. RUNNING FABRIC THROUGH YOUR PRINTER

Using your computer to prepare drawings opens a Pandora's box crammed full of possibilities. Volumes have been written about computer drawing, and it's not within the scope of this book to cover the intricacies and the various programs; offered here is a brief accounting of the process which will make it possible for the beginner to start working. My concern here is with printing on fabric. Even those of us who are not computer buffs can expand the range of our work tremendously under these guidelines.

Any dot-matrix printer which will accept single sheets can be used successfully to print fabric. The printer, like the copier, prefers stiffened or stabilized fabric, described earlier. Spray adhesives, spray starch, and sodium alginate will work, but freezer paper seems the easiest to handle

Plate 4-6: Detail of "Heirloom Quilt" by Wendy Lewington Coulter.

*Typing directly on fabric, Wendy made these quotations a permanent and integral part of the pieced pattern.*

and least likely to wrinkle or fold during printing. I like it especially for lightweight silks, though I use it as well for muslin. Once prepared, the laminated fabric is run through the machine just like a sheet of paper. Fine lines will print with clarity; the smoother the fabric, the better the detail will carry. Large dark areas print less well than linear patterns and lettering.

You will need:
- Dot-matrix printer
- PFP fabric, laminated or stiffened →
- Iron and board →

The process:
1. Write or draw on your computer the information or image you wish to print.
2. Switch the printer to manual feed. Switch the paper-thickness lever to a position that allows heavier papers to pass through.
3. Insert the laminated sheet into the paper feed, and print.
4. Dry the print for a day, or at least several hours in dry weather.
5. Cover the print with paper and heat set with a medium hot iron for a minute or two.

Ink, fabric treatments, and the specific printer affect permanence. Hand-washed with mild soap, my prints show little change. After two or three machine washings with detergent, almost all images will fade somewhat. Test for washability if you're doing quilts or clothing. Abrasion may also remove ink. For a wallhanging or book cover which is unlikely to be washed, test for permanence to handling. Manufacturers consider inks used in dot-matrix printers to be permanent, but do your own testing on cloth.

Esther Cheal runs paper-backed muslin through her printer (a Panasonic KX-P 124), then removes the paper and lets it dry. It must be completely dry before heat setting, or the ink will smear. Her prints do not bleed or wash out. She reports, "I got sort of comfortable with this and tried not using the paper. I switched it on and went to fix a cup of tea.... My attention was called back to the printer when we heard this dreadful repeating 'chalunka chalunka.' It sounded worse than it really was. The printed fabric was feeding back in, and there was a wrinkle that the cartridge got hung up on."

Printed directly on silk is Susan Migliore's "Mysteries." She made various interpretations of a single image, manipulating it from positive to negative, reversing the images, changing scale and enhancing it with drawings and stitching. Mysterious symbols are overlaid on the head, as shown in the details in Plates 4-7 and 4-8.

In her article in *Threads Magazine*, Mary Anne Caplinger describes how she ran silk scarves through her printer. The width restriction is about 9". Another designer found that with China silk she could fold the silk over the edge of the paper (lengthwise) to overcome the page-width limitation.

A quilter using a Panasonic printer found that a silk-cotton blend would go through without any further stiffening. Another designer adheres fabric to regular form-feed sheets covered with spray adhesive. This makes it possible to print a long piece of fabric and overrides limitations of the standard sheet size. Any bubbles or wrinkles must be smoothed out before printing. Many different computers and printers have been used with success.

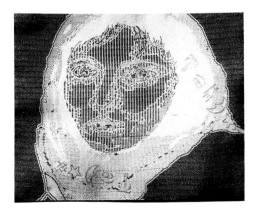

Plate 4-7: Detail of "Mysteries" by Susan Migliore.

*The figure was drawn on her computer and then varied in numerous ways. Printed faces are pieced together.*

Plate 4-8: Detail of "Mysteries" by Susan Migliore.

*Variations of the original portrait were created with the computer program to reverse the image left to right and positive to negative, and by fragmenting and altering sections.*

Direct machine printing is great for adding words, lettering, or information, especially since many fonts and sizes are available in the word processor. Computer drawings can be printed the same way. I use an ImageWriter II and have never had a paper/fabric misfire, but I have made smudgy or echo prints when the paper pressure was incorrectly adjusted.

Fred Blesse ran fabric laminated to freezer paper directly through his color printer to make "Let's Dance" in Color Plate 38. He used a multicolored ribbon, and the images are from the software he was using.

## TROUBLESHOOTING FOR RUNNING FABRIC THROUGH THE PRINTER

Problem: The prints have an echo or a double image.
Solution: Adjust the paper-thickness lever to accommodate the laminated sheet.
The page must be held firmly in place to avoid an echo print.

Problem: The printer won't accept the paper.
Solution: The laminated sheet may be too thick. Try a thinner fabric, such as China silk on paper.
Adjust the paper-thickness lever.

Problem: Prints wash out.
Solution: Dry them for a longer time before heat setting.
Heat set at a higher temperature.
Switch to a heat-transfer ribbon or a different printer.

Problem: The printer sticks or the print head stops and prints repeatedly on one line.
Solution: Prepare a smooth fabric surface on which to print. A wrinkle, fold, or rolled hem may jam the printer.
Use a thinner fabric.

Problem: Prints are pale.
Solution: Select a print mode that deposits more ink ("best" rather than "draft" copy, for example).
Use a new ribbon.

Plate 4-9: *Tunic by Esther Cheal.*
*Laser-printed fabrics turn this tunic into a personal revelation with scanned photos and computer-aided drawings.*

## IV. TRANSFER ON LASER PRINTER

Esther Cheal, in a lengthy trial-and-error process, has worked out a quick method of transferring copies from a laser printer. Her first images smeared when heat set; when she'd resolved that problem, the inks seemed to flake off. Finally, she came up with this process:

1. Run a laser print of the graphics or lettering you wish to use.

2. Cut PFP cloth larger than the image. It must be completely free of finishes.

3. Place cloth over the laser print on a smooth, hard surface. Place a sheet of white paper over the cloth.

4. Spray the stack lightly with water and heat-set with an iron on top of the paper. The image will come through to the top paper, and you will need to change to a clean sheet. When the top paper remains clean, the image is transferred. If the image is not transferring, spray and heat set again.

Plate 4-10: *Detail of tunic by Esther Cheal.*
*Using pages from her* Scattered Patches *publication, Esther Cheal combines the words with printed fabric and drawings to make up Flying Geese and Ohio Star blocks.*

This method gives a reversed image. To make it read right, have the computer flip the image on the screen, and make a print-out of that. When transferred to fabric, it will read correctly. Esther's tunic in Plate 4-9 uses transfers of words and images from her Hewlett Packard LaserJet III. See the detail in Plate 4-10.

## TROUBLESHOOTING FOR LASER TRANSFER

Problem:     You can't get the image to transfer at all.
Solution:    Try another printer which may respond at a different temperature.
             Use a finer, smoother fabric.

Problem:     The image is uneven.
Solution:    Fabric finish is interfering with the transfer. You need a PFP cloth.
             Use a smooth ironing surface.
             Spray and heat set evenly.

Problem:     Ink flakes off the fabric.
Solution:    Dry for a longer time before heat setting.
             Spray to dampen it lightly before covering and heat setting.

Problem:     The print is not permanent.
Solution:    Use a heat-transfer ribbon.
             Try another printer.

## V. TRANSFER RIBBONS FOR THE B/W PRINTER

Special heat-transfer ribbons allow you to transfer single colors to fabric from your print-outs. They expand the possibilities of including lettering (in a wide range of fonts and sizes), making fabric books an exciting prospect. Add to that the fun of computer drawings, and another world opens up.

You will need:
- A personal computer with graphics capabilities
- Dot matrix impact printer
- Heat-transfer ribbons ✳
- Fabric (at least 50% synthetic) in light or bright colors
- Iron and board →
- Foil

The process:
1. Draw your image or write your message on your computer screen.
2. Reverse the image (if possible, necessary, or desirable).
3. Turn off the printer to replace standard ribbon with a heat-transfer ribbon.
4. Print a copy of your image on paper.
5. Cover the ironing board with foil, to protect it from the transfer color.
6. Place the fabric right side up on foil.
7. Place the print face side down on the fabric. Cover with another sheet of paper to avoid scorching your fabric.
8. Heat set with a dry hot iron (cotton setting ) for 30 seconds.

Plate 4-11: "*Chicken Chicken*" *by Jean Ray Laury, blocks 5" x 7".*

*Heat-transfer ribbons in a dot-matrix printer produce an image on paper which can be ironed onto fabric. Each paper print will transfer several times.*

Plate 4-12: "*School*" *by Jean Ray Laury, 18" x 22".*

*Fish are ironed onto cloth from paper printed with heat-transfer ribbon. Each image was transferred several times, with subsequent transfers becoming lighter.*

As the print-out is heat-transferred face down, there will be an image reversal. Some computer programs will reverse your initial images on paper, and the transfer will then read correctly. If you cannot reverse the image, you'll have to accommodate your designs accordingly and do lettering by another method.

Available in several colors, transfer ribbons are permanent once they have been heat set. For permanence and clarity, use a polyester blend of 50-65%. The fabric must be able to withstand the temperature of heat setting.

Your heat-transfer copy can be made on standard print paper, but you may get a better transfer with a 16-pound erasable bond. Several print options are available, and you will need to experiment to determine which is best. Remove the ribbon when you have finished, and do not use it for normal printing (particles in the ink can wear out the print head). Store it in a reclosable bag or plastic zip-lock.

"Chicken Chicken" in Plate 4-11 was printed with the ImageWriter II and a heat-transfer ribbon. Some images were reversed so that the chickens head both east and west. Lettering was added separately, in a second color. (Extra pages of textures and patterns printed in other colors can be cut up and ironed on to any transfer.) Several fish in Plate 4-12 were printed in repeat and then arranged on the fabric.

The small designs on Bonnie Meltzer's "I Forgot" were printed with transfer ribbon and heat set to silk fabric. The face shown with her scarf is an enlargement of a student's computer drawing, heat transferred and used as the outline for a painting. See Color Plate 37.

Color Plate 35 by Susan Migliore is filled with the symbols of consumerism that confronted her on a move to Southern California. Her drawings of Rolex watches, cellular phones, and Mercedes Benzes were made on the computer. She used a full-color ribbon (three hues plus black) and a software program capable of doing color separations. (That allows for oranges, greens, and violets to be mixed.) Using a single large piece of fabric, Susan blocked off areas of fabric with masking tape and hand painted the background. She then transferred (by ironing) the printed designs to cloth. Added embellishments include ribbon, stitching, and beading.

The subtly colored "Computer Crabs" by Susan Migliore in Color Plate 36 was made using computer printer heat-transfer ribbon in black only. The images were printed, cut up and reassembled for transfer. She then hand painted the entire design, using water-base textile paints.

It will require time and patience to become comfortable with the process. Once you have mastered it, the possibilities skyrocket!

## TROUBLESHOOTING FOR TRANSFER RIBBONS IN THE PRINTER

**Problem:** Colors are not bright or strong.
**Solution:** Use greater heat.
Transfer onto white or light colors.
Check the fiber content of the fabric.

**Problem:** The image is smeared.
**Solution:** Cut the page into smaller parts and heat set one part at a time.
Adjust the print option so that less ink is deposited.
Adjust the paper-thickness lever.
Move the iron less during heat setting.
Do not let the paper slide or shift as you heat set (but don't use tape, which will be melted by the iron).
Use a clean sheet of paper under the iron. A used sheet may have absorbed some of the ink and will redeposit it.
Be sure your ironing surface is smooth.

# Quick Screen and Stencil

My first awareness of stenciling was watching the wondrous transformation of a chocolate cake. A paper doily, placed on top of the cake, was lightly dusted with powdered sugar. When the doily was lifted, voilà! Similar stenciling abounds in every household: a muddy youngster displays a patch of clean skin under a bandage. We are all familiar with ancient cave paintings in which hands served as stencils, over which colored pigments were daubed (or spat). Now we lead a luxuriously easier life, with freezer paper and Mylar to cut up for stencils.

## I. QUICK SCREEN

From design to fabric takes just minutes with this speedy variation of screen printing, which is best suited to small, simple shapes. Quick screen is a stencil process. Freezer paper →, ironed onto fabric, masks out areas which are to remain unprinted. Paint is spread over the open area of the design, either with or without the use of a silk-screen frame. Other stencil methods described in this chapter work similarly but use no screen or freezer paper.

You will need:
- Freezer paper →
- Craft or X-Acto knife
- Paper towels
- Iron and board →
- Pad of newsprint, or scrap paper
- Water-based textile paints →
- Squeegee → (or credit card)
- PFP fabrics →
- You may also want: silk-screen frame →, brush, or airbrush →.

The process:
a. Select a simple design or drawing which has flat areas of color: avoid fine or sketchy lines. On your first try, work with just one or two colors.
b. Tape the drawing to a flat, hard surface.
c. Cut white or light cotton fabric to the desired size. Allow at least a 2" margin between the edge of the drawing or design and the edge of fabric.
d. Cut freezer paper the same size as fabric. Cut a piece for each color you intend to print.
e. Place freezer paper, dull side up, over the design. Secure the edges with tape.
f. Trace all parts of the design which are to be the same color onto a single piece of freezer paper.
g. With a knife, cut out and discard the areas which are to be printed in color. Remove tape.
h. Center the stencil on fabric, on an ironing surface.
i. With a medium hot iron, adhere the freezer-paper stencil to fabric. Use a little extra pressure at the cut edges and points, to be sure they are bonded. The design is now ready for printing.

To make multiples, such as for quilt blocks, you will want designs to appear in the same place on each block. To print them identically, you need to register them. This method is not perfect for very detailed registration, but it is fairly accurate and easy to do. First center the original on a paper the size of the finished block plus its seam allowance. Cut fabrics and freezer papers to that same size, aligning the corners. Each time a stencil is to be cut, it must first be placed on the original, with the corners carefully lined up. The corner of the stencil is then aligned with the fabric when it is ironed on. That will put all the images in the same place on each block and will assist you in registering a second color. When the first color has been printed, it will show through light fabric to aid you in placing the second accurately.

To Print:

1. Place the fabric, with stencil ironed on, on a smooth work surface covered with paper.
2. Spoon a small amount of textile paint (½ to 1 teaspoonful, or the amount you estimate will cover the design) onto the freezer paper, about an inch from the exposed fabric. You can spread the paint over the exposed cloth by squeegee, by brush, with the aid of a silk-screen frame, or with an airbrush.
   a. Squeegee: Use a squeegee to pull paint evenly over small open areas of fabric. A plastic silk-screen squeegee is best, but a cardboard or a small plastering squeegee will work. Your credit card may find its best, safest use here. To avoid scraping paint directly into sharply cut corners, squeegee from the outside edge toward the center. Return any excess paint to the jar and wipe or blot the freezer-paper stencil with a paper towel. Let the print dry.

   b. Brush Printing (for blended or shaded colors): Use any stiff-bristled brush to add color, as you would in stenciling. Brushing takes longer than other methods, but it allows you to blend and mix the colors right on the fabric. Brush from the cut edges towards the center, then let dry.

   c. Screen Printing: Place a clean silk-screen printing frame on top of the open area of your freezer-paper stencil, with the mesh (or silk) side of the frame down. Put a dollop of paint on the screen over the freezer paper and squeegee it across the open area of the design. The silk helps you to spread a smooth layer of paint and prevents the lifting of intricate cut edges by the squeegee. Lift the screen to check the print. If it is not sufficiently clear, carefully put the frame back down and reprint. Remove the frame and let the print dry.

   d. Airbrush: The use of an airbrush with quick screen offers a different look — neither flat nor brushed, but soft and shaded. Use several light sprays and dry them between coats to achieve strong color. Over-saturated fabrics tend to bleed or run under the stencil. If you have one, use an artist's airbrush with textile airbrush inks, which are thin but

Plate 5-1: "Northern Lights" by Lura Schwarz Smith, 22" diameter.
Airbrushed fabrics in the outer circle are quick-screened. In the center, printed fabric is overlaid with a series of four quick screens.

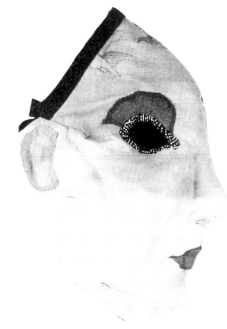

Plate 5-2: "Mask" by Lura Schwarz Smith, 10" high.
This padded, quilted, and somewhat mysterious mask has a quick-screened face and lips with hand-sewn details.

Plate 5-3: *Child's drawing for "Anna's Quilt" by Jean Ray Laury.*

A *child's drawing is enlarged and cut into a stencil for one of several animal blocks.*

Plate 5-4: *Detail of "Anna's Quilt" by Jean Ray Laury: drawings by Anna Laury, age 11.*

Outlining prints with permanent markers adds details of whiskers and noses. Blocks are then pieced, bordered, and quilted.

intense in color. Or use LetraJet Air Marker ✳, which utilizes marking pens. Dye*namite ✳ is a ready-to-use fabric dye in spray cans, which can be used in a similar way. Or an atomizer.

3. When the color is dry, remove the paper and heat set the print according to paint instructions. Truthfully, I pull the freezer paper off immediately to see the results: it's a risk but, if you're impatient, enlist a friend to hold one end of the cloth while you remove the paper. Let the fabric dry. After heat setting, a second freezer-paper stencil (for the next color) can be ironed over the printed fabric. As it is easy to see color through the freezer paper, visual registration of subsequent stencils is not difficult. Printing on dark colors is less successful than printing on lighter ones. Light paints and dyes, such as yellows, tend to get lost on dark colors. (An opaquer will help in printing light on dark.)

If the item you are making is to be washed frequently, do a test piece. Allow any print to air dry for several days before washing. Some brands recommend two weeks of air-curing, so read individual directions. Drying prints in direct sunlight before heat-setting seems to increase their permanence. A good textile paint for quick screen is Versatex ✳ as the consistency seems just right. Deka ✳ works well, as does Cloud Cover ✳. Any paint identified as water-based textile paint or color will work as long as the consistency is appropriate for screening. There are numerous brands on the market.

Lura Schwarz Smith used freezer paper and airbrush to create her "Northern Skies," Plate 5-1. Fabrics were first airbrushed to give an overall color variation to the background. It was heat set, then freezer-paper stencils were ironed on to create the bears and their tracks. Some of the bear stencils were printed with a fairly thick layer of paint for opacity; the shaded effect results from varying the thickness of the layers of paint. One stencil was used for the four bears in the outer ring, a second for the fish in the bears' mouths, and a third for the pawprints. Several different stencils were used in the center panel and on the fish, which are attached to the ribbon-like extensions at the lower edge. See Color Plate 40.

Lura's muslin mask in Plate 5-2 was quick-screened with Versatex using Niji fabric markers ✳ for details. Other details were stitched and appliquéd.

Plate 5-5: *Detail of "Animals Nik Knows" by Marilyn Judson.*
*All the animals known to two-year-old Nik are pictured on this delightful silhouette quilt,*
*using quick screen for images and words.*

Freezer-paper stencils are re-usable. Once a stencil is printed, the paper can be peeled off to let the print dry. Retain the freezer paper and wipe off any paint with paper towels. Position it on the next piece of fabric and reset it with the iron. Depending on the amount of heat applied, the stencil can be used six or more times.

"Anna's Quilt" is made from a child's drawings. In Plate 5-3 the original is in the center. It was enlarged and darkened as you see in the lower drawings, and I cut a freezer-paper stencil from the darker copy. I cut out and removed the face of the cat and ironed the background onto the fabric. The eyes, nose, and ears were cut, placed and ironed onto the fabric inside the large stencil before I applied the paint. The first color print is the one you see on the upper right. At the top is the cat with an outline drawn in permanent marker. I laid fabric over the enlarged line drawing and traced the name with marker. Plate 5-4 shows several animal drawings made up into a quilt, and in Color Plate 41 rabbits, cats, fox, and mice co-exist peacefully.

Marilyn Judson's graphic silhouetted animals in "Animals Nik Knows" (Plate 5-5) are quick-screened with Versatex and freezer paper. Then, using her computer, Marilyn typed the words she wanted to use, enlarged them to the size needed, and ran off copies on the laser printer. The lettering printouts were spray-mounted to the dull side of freezer paper. Using an X-Acto knife, she cut through both the printed paper and the freezer paper. Freezer paper was ironed to fabric and the tiny inside shapes were also ironed on. The letters were then printed using a squeegee and Versatex. French knots were added before the quilt was pieced and quilted.

The quick screen process is great for adding color to other prints. In Color Plate 34 of "Emma's Quilt," the linear drawing was copied onto muslin in the copier. All color was added with freezer-paper stencils, and no stencil had to be cut more than twice.

# TROUBLESHOOTING FOR QUICK SCREEN

Problem:   You can't see the original through the freezer paper.
Solution:  Outline the original with black marker.
           Place original and freezer paper on a light table or against a window.

Problem:   You can't easily remove freezer paper from fabric.
Solution:  Use lower temperature when ironing paper to fabric.
           Try another brand of paper, as they vary slightly and require different temperatures.

Problem:   Paint oozes under the edges of the design.
Solution:  Squeegee more gently, since paint is being pushed under the stencil.
           Use a screen frame over the stencil.
           Iron freezer paper with more heat: it must be firmly attached at the edges, but not so
               firmly that it won't peel off later.
           Use the point of the iron to adhere edges especially well.
           Use an absorbent pad under the fabric as you print.
           Use less paint.

Problem:   Fabric wrinkles as you squeegee over it.
Solution:  Select a design with smaller areas of color.
           Use the squeegee with less pressure to avoid stretching fabric.
           Press fabric flat before applying freezer-paper stencil.
           Squeegee with the grain of the fabric.

## II. STENCIL

Any object used to protect an area from the application of paint is referred to as a stencil. Masking tape, pressed over a piece of cloth, forms a stencil which can be brush painted. While the preceding examples using freezer paper are variations of stencil, "real" stencils use other materials. There are different approaches, and the following is one which fiber artists most commonly use on fabric.

You will need:
- Mylar (or other clear or translucent stencil material)
- X-Acto knife
- Pad of newsprint
- Water-based textile paint →
- Stencil brushes

The process:
a. Draw your design, enlarge or reduce it, and tape the final version to a hard surface.
b. Place Mylar, shiny side up, over the design, and tape it in place.
c. Cut out all those shapes which are to be stenciled the same color.
d. Cut a new stencil for each additional color.
e. Tape the first cut Mylar stencil, shiny side up, on fabric. Tape both fabric and stencil in place.
f. Using a stencil brush, apply color to the open, unprotected areas.

A thin Mylar will cut more easily than a thicker one. Most crafts shops stock stencil materials, such as Mylar or a similar substance. Some designers apply a coat of spray adhesive →, such as 3-M's Spra-Ment, on the back of the stencil. Use the spray out of doors and avoid breathing any vapors. This slightly adhesive backing helps hold the stencil in place as you work.

There are dozens of variations and refinements of the above process, and just as many books detailing them. This is the basic process, however, and you can adapt it to your own specific needs.

Robin Schwalb's "Gift of Tongues" (Plate 5-6) resonates with a complex intermingling of sounds. Printed with stencil processes and photo silk-screen, the varied fonts, alphabets, and changing styles tumble over one another with apparent urgency. The large, crisp-edged letters are stenciled onto a printed background. Robin uses contact paper for her stencil or block-out, covering those areas which appear patterned. Exposed areas are stenciled with white Deka paint. For letters which have no inside segments, like a V or L, she cuts a Mylar stencil; for those with

Plate 5-6: Detail of "Gift of Tongues" by Robin Schwalb.
Stenciling and photo silk-screen printing combine to form patterns, textures, and words which tumble together with spirited voices.

inside shapes, such as an R, contact paper is used so the floating centers can be adhered in place. The stenciled squares are hand appliquéd to the panel. This remarkable piece is also shown in Color Plate 43.

Mary Preston, whose stunning garments are patterned with her stencil designs, uses a thin (.003 inch) Mylar. She cuts the stencil shiny side up and, after cutting, she sprays the stencil on the dull side with an adhesive. (Some designers use double-sided clear tape for this.) This helps keep the stencil in contact with the fabric and helps prevent any color bleeding. Mary applies her paint with a dauber, an inexpensive and long-lasting tool made from two 4" squares of ¼" foam rubber, one folded inside the other. (This is a technique she learned from fiber artist Lenore Davis.) The outside piece is gathered up around the folded piece and secured with a rubber band.

Mary stencils her fabrics with Lumière ✳ (metallic) and Cloud Cover ✳ fabric paints. She finds that heat setting Cloud Cover (even though it's an air-curing paint) makes it hold up better in dry-cleaning. "Animal Magnetism" in Plate 5-7 demonstrates Mary's enjoyment of stories and myths as sources. She adds, "It also keeps me entertained as I work." Along with her imaginative stenciled animals, she adds words and tells stories using permanent-ink markers. Details in Plate 5-8 show the loose ties and ribbons which contrast with the hard edges of her stencils, also shown in Color Plate 39.

In "Tickling the Ivories," Color Plate 42, elephant-like creatures, symbolic designs, and ivory tusks adorn the jacket in lovely soft colors. Plate 5-9 depicts details of the animals, the patterned band which intersects the jacket, and the small forms scattered throughout. Color Plate 47 and the detail in Color Plate 46 show "I Like To Be Under the Sea," a stenciled and painted jacket which places hard-edged and soft lines together with lines drawn delicately in stitches and threads.

Robin Schwalb's "One View of Mt. Fuji" is startling in its brilliance and contrast. Most designers simply consider that printing light over dark is nearly impossible, and the rest find it (at best) difficult. Robin would not disagree. Her remarkable effects result from persistence in adding many layers of paint. The repeated layers were crucial to create the opacity needed. See Color Plates 44 and 45. With contact paper stencils pressed to the fabric (by hand, not by heat), Robin used Deka white paint to built up layer upon layer of thin coats. Over the white she added a tint of

*Plate 5-7: "Animal Magnetism" by Mary Preston, 32" x 60".*

*Stenciled forms of imaginary animals are interspersed with storytelling in this delightful and lively jacket.*

*Plate 5-8: Detail of "Animal Magnetism" by Mary Preston.*

*Contrasting with the crisp, clean lines of the outside, the inside of the jacket has pieced colors. The ends of ribbons and threads swing freely.*

*Plate 5-9: "Tickling the Ivories," jacket by Mary Preston, 36" x 59".*

fluorescent color; because this is somewhat transparent, numerous layers were required to develop full colors.

Katherine Knauer in Color Plate 49 combines many different processes to create her complex quilt, full of painted details, piecing, embroidery, and appliqué. In the detail of her work in Color Plate 50, stencil or block-out were used with airbrush and Deka fabric paints on cotton.

My pictorial child's quilt in Color Plate 48 was made to illustrate No Dragons on My Quilt, a children's book. From 2 to 6 stencils were made for each block. All were squee-geed directly over the fabric, without the use of a screen frame. The quilt is pieced and hand quilted.

Various kinds of brushes can be used for stenciling, but the standard stenciling brush is designed especially for this use. It has short, stiff bristles, and it is cut square at the end, so that paint is applied with the stub ends of the bristles. The stiff brush allows you to use a thick paint, as a thin one would creep under the edges of the stencil and bleed into the fabric. The dauber described above works well in this same way.

## TROUBLESHOOTING FOR STENCIL

Problem: The paints have smeared on your fabric.
Solution: The stencil may have slid or moved; an adhesive on the Mylar will help to secure it.
Brush gently, so the Mylar is not jarred.
The stencil may have been placed over previously stenciled areas which had not dried completely.

Problem: Paint has run under the edge of the stencil.
Solution: Use less paint.
Brush only until you have covered the open area.
Brush from Mylar to fabric, rather than into the stencil edge.

Problem: Painted image is too pale.
Solution: Use more paint.
Let the first coat dry, then stencil a second coat of paint.

Problem: The design areas are shaded, but you wanted a flat, graphic look.
Solution: Switch to quick print or screen printing, which produce that effect. Shading is natural in stenciling.

Problem: The edges appear uneven or ragged, lacking sharpness.
Solution: Re-cut the stencil if the edges are not cleanly cut.
There may be paint build-up on the edge of the Mylar.

# Silk-Screen
## (stencil and photo emulsion)

If some is good, more must be better — unless it's the salt in the soup. Making a few prints is exciting, while making dozens may bring on palpitations. For those of us who spend endless hours sewing one small area, multiple prints seem extravagantly productive! And this productive aspect of screen printing probably explains its appeal to many designers (including me).

Multiples are compelling, and it's particularly hard to ignore anything that is repetitious. Our consciousness of multiples was sharpened by Andy Warhol's images of Marilyn Monroe and soup cans. He increased our awareness of the repeated image, a concept familiar to most quiltmakers. My own idea of multiples runs to the Dionne quintuplets, Tweedledum and Tweedledee, 76 Trombones, and the Three Musketeers. None of the individuals is particularly intriguing: it is only when repeated that they pique our interest and take on new dimensions.

With silk-screen printing you can use snapshots, drawings, invitations, old love letters, family photographs, silhouetted cut-outs, weeds, leaves, announcements, or maps. It's easy. The simple processes given here require no special photographic equipment or darkroom facilities. Dozens of books have been written about screen printing, directed primarily towards oil-based inks on paper; the methods I describe here are for water-based paints on fabric.

In this process, parts of a screen are blocked off while the open areas allow paint to go through to the fabric, printing it with color. The block-out → stencil can be anything which will resist paint and adhere to the silk, such as newspaper, shelf paper, stickers, or contact paper. After working with those, you'll want to try photo emulsion, a process in which the silk is made light-sensitive. With it, anything opaque enough to inhibit sunlight (leaves, paper, transparency copies of photographs) can be used.

A frame, with fabric stretched over it, serves to spread the paint or ink in an even layer and to hold the stencil. Screen-printing frames are no longer actually made of silk: polyester is now used, since it can withstand the bleach required to remove photo emulsion. (Silk melts.) If you use only paper or contact block-outs, either silk or polyester can be used to cover the screen; if you use photo emulsion, a polyester-covered screen is essential. Therefore, the fabric which covers the frame (formerly the "silk") is sometimes referred to here as the "mesh."

If you purchase a screen at an art-supply store, look for a multifilament polyester in a 12xx mesh. Mesh size indicates the openness of the weave. A larger number (16xx to 20xx) indicates a more open weave. Paint can more easily be pressed through, but you get less fine detail. A 10xx mesh would offer more detail but would be harder to squeegee and would tend to dry out faster. Unless you are ordering from a supply house, you will probably have little choice. Buy a polyester screen as near to 12xx as is available.

For your first prints, buy a small screen. The smaller the frame, the easier it is to handle, and the less likely you are to have smears or problems. An 8" x 10" is a great size to learn on. However, the size of the frame limits the size of the print you can make. You will save time, energy, and probably money, by buying a frame if you need only one, or even a few. If you have an eager resident woodworker, however, the library will offer good reference for frame-building. Mesh is attached to the frame in either of two ways: by stapling, or with cord that is pressed into a channel or groove. If you have a choice when you purchase, get the corded frame; it will be easier to replace or tighten the mesh. Polyester yardage is available at art-supply stores to re-cover screens. You must clean and degrease ↘ a new screen frame.

Silk-screening was once a heavy-duty undertaking, involving films, tedious cutting, application with acetone, and the use of oil-based paints. Clean-up was messy, laborious, and probably unhealthy. We screened anyway because there was no comparable alternative. With the new textile paints and simple photo methods, it's relatively easy, safe, and simple. None of the methods described here requires a "real" darkroom, and all use water-based non-toxic paints.

Read all directions before beginning.

Three block-out methods are described here:

> I. PLAIN-PAPER SCREEN PRINTING
> II. CONTACT-PAPER SCREEN PRINTING
> III. PHOTO-EMULSION SCREEN PRINTING

The three are listed in order of complexity. The simpler methods are generally used for very short runs, while the photo emulsion can be kept on a screen permanently. Tusche and glue (last page of this chapter) is a more painterly method. For each of these methods you will need:

- Screen-printing frame →
- Squeegee →
- Water-based textile paints →
- Masking tape
- Tongue depressors ("say aaaah" sticks) or something similar
- Smooth cardboard
- Paper towels
- Newspapers
- Scrap paper
- PFP fabric →
- Empty tuna or cat-food can

## I. PLAIN-PAPER SCREEN PRINTING

The simplest form of screen printing can be accomplished using nothing more complex than a sheet of typing paper for the stencil. This is a good way for beginners to learn the process. You will need:

- Basic screen-printing supplies
- X-Acto or craft knife, or scissors
- Typing or copy paper

- Tissue paper

The basic process:

1. Clean or degrease ↘ the screen if it is new.
2. Cut a piece of fabric on which you intend to test a print. Place it on a smooth work surface over a smooth, lightweight cardboard or paper.
3. Cut a sheet of plain white paper the same size as your frame, to serve as your stencil.
4. Cut a simple shape, such as a bird, out of the center of the paper. Toss the bird aside and keep the background, which is now your stencil.
5. Place the stencil on the bottom of the frame (against the mesh) and tape it at one end. The paper will cover the entire bottom surface of the frame and no additional masking is needed. You need not tape the inside or outside edges.
6. Place the frame, mesh side down, on top of scrap paper to make a test run.
7. Spoon a small amount of textile paint into the screen over the paper stencil area. (Use the "say aaah" stick.)
8. With the squeegee, draw paint over the open areas of the screen, using a smooth, even stroke. You may have to stroke it 2 or 3 times for the first print. (See Squeegee → and Squeegee Techniques →.) The paint will make the paper stencil stick to the frame.
9. Lift the frame carefully and set it with one edge resting on the edge of the tuna can so that paint will not transfer from the silk to the table.
10. Check your first run or print. If the image is printing clearly and evenly, place the frame onto the fabric. It will take a little more pressure or more strokes of the squeegee on fabric than on paper, as the cloth absorbs more paint.
11. Clean up ↘ the screen immediately.

### Paper stencil

The paper used for the stencil will affect the character of the print. As it absorbs some moisture, it sticks to the screen. Waxed paper, for example, would not work. Hard-finish papers will last longer than soft papers, and some can be used for 20 or 30 prints. Less absorbent papers will warp, and paint may scooch under the warped edges. Tissue paper block-outs allow paint to soak through

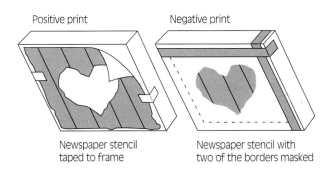

Positive print    Negative print

Newspaper stencil          Newspaper stencil with
taped to frame             two of the borders masked

and add a textured pattern. As the tissue soaks up more paint, the print become progressively more textured.

Always start with paper cut to the size of your frame. Working within that rectangle, cut or tear out the shapes you wish to print. The remaining part of the paper will mask the edge of your screen. You will make a positive print; that is, you will print the shape you have cut. (When you make a negative print, you color the background.) If a heart, for example, is torn out of the rectangle of paper, and the rectangle is taped to the back (or underside) of a frame, you will print the heart in color. If you stick the heart to the frame, however, you will print the background (make a negative print) and in that case you will need a mask at the edges, as shown in the right-hand drawing. In addition to the heart, cut a paper the size of the frame. Within that rectangle, cut out another shape which will define the edge

*Plate 6-1: Detail of sticker prints by a student of Joyce B. Aiken. Self-adhesive stamps and stickers were pressed onto the underside of the screen-printing frame. Several images include mats cut in circular, oval, or rectangular shapes.*

of your print. Your rectangle will look like a mat or a window. Be sure to allow at least 1" between the inside edge of the paper and the inside edge of the wood frame, as you will need space in which the paint can sit. Tape one end of the mask to the back (underside) of the frame. Once the mat is in place, center the heart or other torn or cut paper design in the open area of the screen, also on the back. Stick it in place with a dab of paint. Then make a practice print on paper to moisten the stencil, to keep it in place.

Another quick and easy paper stencil is a self-adhesive sticker, adhered to the back of the mesh and used as a block-out (Plate 6-1). The nine hearts were printed using the leftover background from the stickers as the stencil, giving a positive print. All the remaining examples use stickers (cat, larger hearts, rockets) as positives to print the negative area. When the background area is printed, the edge of the frame must be masked out.

"The Van Dalsem Quilt," in Color Plate 51, was made in part with paper stencils. The senator, his coat, and his tie were each cut from plain white paper and printed separately. The red neck was added with a permanent marking pen, as were most tiny details. Both the cow and the plow, like the lettering, were done with photo-emulsion screening ↘. Radishes, books, rabbit, boot, and bare foot were all paper or contact-paper stencils. The senator's obituary which appeared in my local paper inspired this piece. He felt he had been quoted out of context in regard to "barefoot and pregnant." so the quilt sets him back in context. (It was not an improvement.)

"The Burpee Quilt" in Color Plate 53 also grew out of a newspaper clipping. In the detail of Color Plate 54, the platter and steam were cut from paper stencils and the ham from contact paper, while photo emulsion was used for the parsley and the leafy background. The inebriated man in the top panel was printed from five different contact-paper stencils, while plain paper was used for the glass and another for the splashing drink. All the printed leaves were outlined with a fine-line permanent marker.

## Torn paper

A soft or deckle edge can be created with newspaper. Cut the paper the size of the frame, then (working in the center) either tear it by hand or draw on the paper with water, using a brush or your finger. When the water soaks

Plate 6-2: Detail of "Sun" by Jean Ray Laury.

*Torn wet paper was used for the block-out of the sun shape in this plain-paper screen print.*

in, scrape away the wet paper with a fingernail. In Plate 6-2 a torn-paper stencil of the sun was made this way. The sun was scratched out and discarded. The stencil (with the sun removed) became the block-out and was used to cover the background. It is a positive print. Paper stencils like this will last for 25 prints or more, depending on how hard you squeegee and the viscosity of the paint.

## TROUBLESHOOTING FOR PLAIN-PAPER SCREEN PRINTING

Problem:  The image is printed but the paint is spread beyond the edge of the design.
Solution:  Try another paper, as paint is slipping under the edge of the block-out.
Use a softer, more absorbent paper for the stencil.
Squeegee with less force.
Squeegee in the other direction, away from leaks.

Problem:  The image is pale, streaky or only partially printed.
Solution:  Use more paint.
Take more strokes, or use more pressure.
Hold the squeegee more parallel to the mesh.

## II. CONTACT-PAPER SCREEN PRINTING

A more durable and inexpensive block-out can be made from self-adhesive shelf paper or a contact paper → available at grocery or hardware stores (Con-tact, Magic Paper, etc.). Purchase a clear (not a colored) contact paper. One three-yard roll will make dozens of block-outs. Start with simple shapes and avoid detailed lines until you become familiar with the process. You will need:

- Basic screen-printing supplies
- Self-adhesive clear contact paper →
- X-Acto or craft knife
- Scissors

The process:

1. Cut a sheet of contact to the outer size of your frame.

2. Place the original design on a smooth surface and tape it in place at one edge. Outline the design with a fine-point marking pen if necessary to make it more visible.

3. Place contact paper with shiny or plastic side up on top of the original. Tape.

4. Trace the design with a knife, cutting through the plastic coating, and remove those areas which are to be printed in a color. The image will look "right" at this stage but it will print in reverse.

5. To transfer the cut stencil to the screen, peel the plastic film away from the paper. Apply the adhesive side of the transparent plastic to the mesh bottom (outside) of the frame, matching corners, and smooth it into place.

6. Place the frame, mesh side down, on a smooth surface. Working inside the frame, burnish with bowl of a spoon, so that all cut edges of the contact are firmly adhered. Contact paper now covers the bottom of the frame, except for the open areas of the design.

7. Run the first print, following steps 7 through 10 of the basic process.

## Cutting the contact paper

Work on a hard, smooth surface. The contact paper consists of a clear plastic sheet over a translucent paper sheet. Try to cut through just the plastic layer, leaving the paper backing intact. Cut in a continuous line, pivoting at the corners without lifting the craft knife from the plastic. If your cutting lines cross, the contact is sometimes dented and will not adhere well. The contact paper has some give, and it will stretch slightly if not pulled away from the paper with care.

## Reversing the image

Letters, numbers, and some drawings need to be flipped to come out correctly. To cut the contact for a reversal:

1. Put the drawing on a hard, smooth surface. You may want to use a light table or a clear window.

2. Put the contact, paper side up, over it and trace the original onto the paper.

3. Turn the contact paper with the plastic side up so that the drawing can be seen through it. Cut and complete as above. The image will look reversed but, when applied to the mesh, it will read correctly.

Contact screens can be printed many, many times. Eventually, moisture may get between the adhesive and the mesh, causing the contact to loosen. The stencils can often be re-used, so it's worth a try. Wash away all excess paint and hang the stencil to dry. (Pin it sticky side out to the wall.) I've re-used contacts as much as two weeks later. Once the stencil is dry, the stickiness seems to rejuvenate, though this varies with the brand of contact used. Eventually, it will dry out.

When a run of prints is finished, the screen should be cleaned and checked for any residue. Clean-up ↘ must be thorough.

Several burglars in Plate 6-3 were cut from contact paper, then each was adhered to a separate screen. They

Plate 6-3: Detail of "Neighborhood Watch" by Jean Ray Laury, burglars about 7" high.

*Two different prowlers were cut from contact paper and screen-printed to fabric. The yellow beam of the flashlight was printed with a second screen.*

were screened to strips of cloth which were later pieced. Separate contact stencils were made for the arcs of light from the flashlights. See Color Plate 61. In some cases, light fell across a previously printed prowler. On others, a mask was made: a single figure was printed on paper, patted dry, and cut out. The paper cut-out was then carefully placed over a printed fabric figure to protect it, and the yellow was screened right over the top. The paper figure was then removed and the prowler appeared in solid black with the light behind him. Of course, the yellow could have been printed first, but until the flashlights were in place it was difficult to tell where the beam of light would go. Windows were printed from contact cut-outs.

Barbara Carow, in "Jane's Other War," (Color Plate 58) was wonderfully inspired by a battle of the bulge and Jane Fonda's books and tapes. She chose figures from magazines to represent women of three different ages, enlarged or reduced them on the copier, then cut them in silhouette from contact paper to make positive prints on fabric. Additional figures cut from paper served to help her with the arrangement of the panel. The figures in the background were printed with dyes, and later overprinted. Using Lumière dyes, Barbara mixed colors with pearl white to print the youngest figures. Neopaque ink was used for the middle set of figures. The contact screens were washed in the bathtub and re-used, though some of the small shapes washed off and had to be retrieved and put back in place (once both mesh and contact are dry, they'll re-adhere). All the figures were printed over hand-dyed background panels. The final color was applied with cotton swabs.

The Kilauea volcano, with its exotic and tropical eruptions, was printed from a contact-paper stencil which combined the mountain and a border into a single shape, as seen in Plate 6-4. All of the details were drawn in with permanent marker and then hand-painted. (See Coloring Prints in the Additional Help section.) Lettering was added with photo-emulsion screening.

The small squares and tiny nine-patches of "Water and Ice" (Plate 6-5) are also contact-paper printed. The squares which make up the checkerboard tend to slip out of place after a number of prints; they are not attached to a larger piece of stencil. Each nine-patch was printed individually; if a square slipped off, it was dried and re-adhered.

The small squares, sticks, and squiggles in my "Two Blue Jeans and A Violet Lincoln," in Color Plates 56 and 57, are contact-paper prints.

Barbara Carow's silhouette figures in "Equinox" were printed from contact-paper stencils. Using newspaper and advertising figures as her source, she cut them from construction paper, reduced them on the copier, then traced them onto contact paper. She placed paper cut-outs of the figures on the background to determine the arrangement before screening onto her tie-dyed panels. Graduated values and sizes create a sense of space and distance. Barbara screened with Procion dyes, adding a thickener to give the dye a workable consistency. In Plate 6-6 and the detail in Plate 6-7, you can see that her quilting at the edges of the printing creates a raised effect, putting the figures in relief.

## TROUBLESHOOTING FOR CONTACT-PAPER SCREEN PRINTING

Problem: Small folds or wrinkles at the cut edges of the film let paint leak through.

Solution: Try additional burnishing to get the edge to stick flat.

Wipe the area dry; then, using scissors carefully, take a tiny clip in the fold and overlap the cut edges. Don't clip your mesh!

Squeegee away from, rather than into, the fold.

Problem: Lines printed past the edge of the design.

Solution: When cutting contact paper, avoid cutting past any corners of the design: these cut lines may allow paint to seep through.

Cover lines with cellophane tape on the bottom of the frame (not on the inside).

Problem: Small spots or blurs show up in the printed area of the design.

Solution: Your screen is not clean. Remove paint, wash and dry the mesh. Scrub away any dried paint.

Wipe mesh with rubbing alcohol, as contact adhesive may have clogged the screen.

Screen may be clogged with residue from an earlier print.

Plate 6-5: "Water and Ice" by Jean Ray Laury, 38" x 44".

Screen-printed with photo emulsion and contact-paper block-outs, the blue and white patterns merge and separate. Pieced and hand quilted.

Plate 6-4: "Kilauea Volcano Hawaii" by Jean Ray Laury, 45" x 50".

Screen-printed with a contact-paper stencil, the mountains and borders are a single color. The tropical eruptions, drawn with permanent markers, are hand-painted, then pieced and quilted.

Plate 6-6: "Equinox" by Barbara Carow, 45" x 60".

Silk-screen printed figures trudge off with great determination into the rain. Where two prints overlap, third colors are created, especially effective where the striding women appear to have wet feet.

Plate 6-7: Detail of "Equinox" by Barbara Carow.

Looped threads droop like ominous clouds over the pieced and quilted paths of solitary walkers.

# III. PHOTO-EMULSION ✹ SCREEN PRINTING

Of all silk-screen methods, the most magical is photo emulsion. It is a direct-contact method, meaning that some opaque substance must come between the emulsion and the light source during exposure. In this process, the screen itself is made photo-sensitive by painting it with light-sensitive chemicals. It is dried in a dark room, then exposed to sunlight or artificial light. Any area left open to exposure will develop and become the block-out. Those protected areas which remain unexposed will wash out, and paint will later be squeegeed through them. Exposures are made with an easy-to-assemble direct contact frame→.

Imagine that your screen is already light-sensitive. If you spread your hand out over the dry screen in sunlight, the hand would inhibit the passage of light. After a few seconds, you would rinse the screen from a garden hose or faucet to stop the developing. The area covered by the hand would be undeveloped and would wash away, but the background would be firmly set on the screen. The squeegee would spread the paint evenly through the open mesh, printing an image of your hand. Screening is a positive method. What you see (on the screen) is what you get (in the print).

Photo screening is done in one of three ways:
1. Direct emulsion
2. Indirect emulsion
3. Direct emulsion with photo enlargement

Read all directions before beginning.
1. Direct emulsion with bichromate sensitizer (among the many available are Hunt Speedball Photo Emulsion and Advance DM-888 Photo Emulsion) is a direct-contact method, a favorite of many fabric artists because it facilitates the use of photographs and allows for multiples. The process may sound complex, but it's just photo screening, an inexpensive method in which sensitizing solutions are applied to a screen. It is great for water-based textile paints on cloth. Most of the information given here refers to the bichromate emulsion, but a diazo emulsion is also available (Holden's Diazo, Naz-Dar, Speedball Diazo). Diazo contains different chemicals but works similarly: it has a longer shelf life after mixing, it can be left on the screen for a longer time before exposure, and it requires a special remover (Naz-Dar Encosol 3 or Speedball Photo Emulsion Remover). I like working with Hunt Speedball Photo Emulsion because it is relatively simple and requires only household bleach to remove it.

2. Indirect emulsion utilizes a photo-stencil film, such as Ulano. It is water-soluble and requires the use of oil-based inks; therefore, the method is not included in this book. With Ulano, exposure is made on the film which is then transferred onto the mesh of the screen.

3. Direct emulsion with a photographic projection is a method in which the screen is sensitized and a direct projection enlargement from a small-format positive film is then made directly on the screen. Either oil-based or water-based paints can be used. Anyone who has the projection and dark room equipment for this method will find materials at any large photographic supply house. All steps are identical with the process given here except for the manner in which the emulsion is exposed.

## Direct photo emulsion

For this wonderfully versatile and exciting process you will need:

- Basic screen-printing supplies
- Credit card or small squeegee
- Direct-contact frame →
- Chlorine bleach
- Positive image ↘
- Panel or board on which to print
- PFP fabric →
- Photo emulsion ↘
- Contact paper or wide masking tape

Briefly described, the steps are:
a. Prepare the original.
b. Mix the emulsion, following directions and precautions on the label.
c. Paint the emulsion onto the screen and dry in a darkened area.
d. Prepare a contact frame: a rigid board, foam pad, black fabric, and glass.
e. Place the screen on top of the black fabric, with the image, block-out, or transparency on top of the screen.

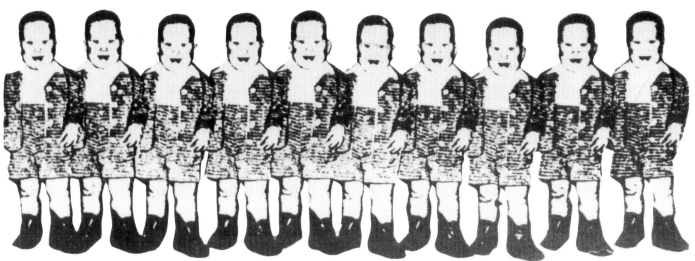

*Plate 6-8: Detail of "New Boots" by Jody House, figures 5" high.*
*To create this one-boy parade, Jody first photocopied an old family snapshot so that the images could be cut apart. Everything and everyone was eliminated except the boy, who was then duplicated and re-arranged into this band which became the border on a quilt.*

f. Put glass over the image to keep lightweight objects from moving in the breeze, and to keep transparencies from curling in the sun.

g. Exposure lasts approximately 8 to 20 seconds in sunlight, which hardens the emulsion.

h. Immediately wet both sides of the screen with water from faucet or hose to stop development.

i. Continue running water over the emulsion until the image area has washed clear.

j. Wipe the wood of the frame and lay it flat to dry in the shade.

k. When it is dry, add strips of contact paper or masking tape to the outside edges, just beyond the image to be printed. Put the sticky side of the contact paper to bottom or outside of the frame.

l. Place fabric to be printed on a flat surface covered with paper or smooth cardboard.

m. Print as described earlier in this chapter.

## Preparing the positive image

Photo-screen printing requires a positive image, not a negative. To clarify the process, start by using a few leaves, a fern, or some similar natural form as the block-out. When you have followed all the steps, your leaves will be printed in color . Most leaves and flowers will be opaque enough to produce an image, though anything that seems transparent to the eye probably lets too much sunlight through. (Some flower petals are too transparent.) Very fine stems, like the beard on wheat, will not produce a sufficiently strong block-out.

Paper cut-outs → are good for initial projects. Cut any shape from a piece of construction (or similarly opaque) paper and use it in the contact frame; a paper doll, a star, a snowflake, or any flat opaque object will do. Or use any handy opaque object: scissors, spatula, comb, etc. Remember that the area which inhibits sunlight is what will be printed. The shape of the paper doll will print, but not details of the face.

When you are ready to work with photographs or words, another step is required. The image must be put onto a clear background — an acetate or transparency →. Select a photograph which has lots of contrast, deep shadows with areas of white. Make a good b/w photocopy from your print. The copy can now be altered by cutting away background, removing any unwanted guests, or duplicating one person into an entire crowd (see Plate 6-8). Because copies can be enlarged or reduced, there are great opportunities to play with a photo or image. You might shrink your big brother (bringing him down to size) or enlarge your mother-in-law. (That's not the same as blowing her up!) The altered image is then copied onto a transparency in the b/w copier. This gives you a positive (the opposite of a photographic negative). What appears black on the transparency is what will print in color.

Since strong contrast or good black lines are important, be sure your copy is dark before you make a transparency. If the original is pale, the transparency will not be dark enough to block sunlight. Sometimes stacking two transparencies will make them more light-resistant. Make a second transparency, place one over the other, and tape them together at the edge. Since copies vary slightly in size from the originals, make both transparencies from the original. Anything you can photocopy can be put onto a transparency: an old love letter, drawings, school pictures, diplomas, announcements, traffic citations (not your own, of course), and hand prints. Hand-written or stamped words on paper can be handled similarly. After being enlarged or reduced on the copier, they can be copied onto a transparency for photo screening. See Chapter 10 for further details on lettering.

To get a stronger black-and-white image, you can have a Kodalith ✳ → made of your photo; this turns the image to black and white, eliminating the grays. It will be delivered to you as a black image on a film or transparency. You expose directly from the Kodalith (which is also referred to as a "line film positive"). This will mean an extra errand and extra cost, so first try working with your photographs as they are. You may not need a Kodalith.

## Emulsion ☛→

The photo-sensitizing solution requires cautious handling, as it contains an ammonium dichromate solution. You need not handle powders, as it comes in liquid form. The dichromate has been diluted 1 part to 8 in a liquid before you buy it. You dilute it further in a mixture of 1 part to 4 of emulsion. About a teaspoonful of the mixed emulsion will cover a small screen, so you are using a minute quantity. Working with liquids avoids any problem of breathing powders, the greatest hazard posed by this chemical. Read all precautions or warnings which come with the packaged emulsion. The substance is mildly toxic to skin contact or ingestion, so wear rubber gloves. No cookies, no cigarettes, and no kids in the work area. Goggles are recommended. Store the sensitizing liquid away from heat.

Photo-sensitive emulsion comes in two containers: a yellow, watery light-sensitive liquid and a blue, viscous vehicle solution which acts as a thickener and spreader. (Some brands may come with a third solution to add color

to the mix.) I use, and like, Hunt's Speedball emulsion, because the two solutions (yellow and blue) mix to a dull green, so it's easy to tell when the solutions are thoroughly mixed. Since it is difficult to measure the thick emulsion, pre-measure with water: For a five-tablespoon batch, put four tablespoons of water in a small jar. With a marker, indicate the height of the waterline. Measure 1 more tablespoon and again mark the line. Empty and dry the jar. When you mix the solutions, pour emulsion directly into the jar to the first line, add sensitizer to the second, and mix.

Once the two liquids are mixed, they are light-sensitive. Keep the mixed emulsion in a closed jar, covered well with foil or black plastic. It can be stored for a week or two, depending upon temperature. It'll last longer (up to a month) in a refrigerator, but don't store it there if you have kids in the house. It is best to mix only the amount needed, or to use the excess within a few days. Just five tablespoons of emulsion is enough to coat a half-dozen small screen frames. If you have a small amount (a few tablespoonsful) of leftover emulsion which is outdated, dilute it in several gallons of water, then flush it down the drain while running lots of water with it. If you have a large amount of emulsion, which is unlikely, let it dry out in the jar. Then cap it, label it, and dispose of it at your local toxic waste site.

### A. APPLYING THE EMULSION

Even though the emulsion is light-sensitive, there is adequate time for you to work. Use subdued lighting, avoid sunlight or direct light, and work at a normal pace but don't leave the whole thing while you answer the phone. You have several minutes in which to apply the emulsion.

Pour 1 or 2 teaspoonsful of mixed emulsion on the outside of the screen. Using a credit card or a small squeegee, spread the emulsion evenly over the mesh. Scrape in both directions and return any excess to the jar. Turn the frame over and scrape any excess that has oozed through to the other side. Briefly hold the frame up to the light. If you see dark areas, they indicate thick emulsion. If you see air holes, add more emulsion. The goal is to spread a smooth, thin, even coat over the mesh.

### B. DRYING THE EMULSION

Place the screen to dry in a dark area, laying it flat. It can be leaned against a wall, but if you have added slightly too much emulsion, it may run or slip to the bottom edge. The resulting unevenness may cause problems in exposure and wash-out. A windowless closet makes an adequate darkroom, but put a towel over the floor sill to prevent light from leaking in. You can use a cupboard, a drawer, or a cardboard box as a darkroom, as long as it remains free of light. Hang a towel or cloth over any cracks. Circulating air or a small fan speeds up the drying time, so obviously a closet is better than a box if time is important.

It takes anywhere from twenty minutes to over an hour to dry the emulsion mixture, depending upon its thickness, the temperature, humidity, and air movement. Optimum drying temperature is 76°. If you use a hair dryer to speed the drying, use air only, unless your dark room is cold. In that case, do not aim heat directly at the screen.

Some emulsion directions recommend the application of a second coat after the first is dry. I never use more than one coat, but if you're going into big-time production, or if you plan to keep the design on the screen permanently, a second coat will make it more stable. The single coat may eventually begin to break down or wear out if you are making hundreds of prints.

## C. EXPOSING THE EMULSION

For best results, expose the image as soon as the emulsion is dry. (With diazo emulsion, the coated screen can be left much longer before exposure.) Emulsion will look shiny when wet, dull when dry. If a sudden change of weather or the arrival of guests forces you to postpone exposure, store the dry frame in a black plastic bag in the darkroom overnight. Optimum time for use with dichromate emulsion, however, is within 6 hours. Exposure is the crucial part of a successful screen print. Once the emulsion is dry, exposure can be accomplished in either of two ways:

### Exposure by sunlight

I prefer the immediacy of sunlight, as results are known within a minute or two. Practice makes it easy to estimate the exposure time required. There is enough leeway that you can get good results while learning. Among the variables are the directness of the sun, time of day, clarity of the air, and thickness of the emulsion. On a bright, clear summer day, at high noon, I expose for six to eight seconds, which is about the least time ever needed. The most I have ever used (under an overhanging roof during a downpour) was 50 seconds. So most sunlight exposures can be done within that range. A late afternoon exposure, in summer, may take 20 seconds. In winter, the sun is at a different angle, so it'll take longer. Occasionally there's a failure, but you'll soon learn to estimate exposure time. The primary disadvantage of sunlight exposure occurs on dark wintry days, when you may have to switch to bulb exposure. And, of course, for night people there's no sunlight exposing once the sun goes down. But paint your screens at night and they'll be ready for you early in the morning.

### Exposure by bulb

You can use an ordinary clear household bulb (150 watts) or a #1 photo floodlamp (250 watts) in place of sunlight. An aluminum pie plate or tray may be used to create a reflector, to help direct the light onto your screen. Expose as follows:

| LIGHT SOURCE | FLOODLIGHT | HOUSEHOLD BULB |
|---|---|---|
| 12" from screen (small screens, 10" to 12" long) | 10 minutes | 45 minutes |
| 17" from screen (larger screens, 20" long) | 20 minutes | 1 hour, 30 minutes |

For larger screens, move the light source farther away until the light hits all areas of the screen evenly. My preference for sunlight is based on my experience that bulb-set emulsions seem harder to remove. With a bulb it is also easy to get hot spots where the emulsion develops faster. Still, some screen printers prefer the use of bulbs and consider the use of sunlight too iffy.

## D. EXPOSING THE IMAGE

While the emulsion is drying, prepare your material for exposure on the contact frame →. You'll need a rigid opaque panel, masonite or plywood, slightly larger than your screen. Place a piece of foam sponge over that and cover it with a black cloth. Place the screen, open side up, on the cloth. The mesh will be touching the black cloth. The image or positive goes directly onto the mesh and a piece of glass → goes on top to hold it in place. Exposure can be made on either the inside or the outside of the frame. I suggest using the inside, since that lets you view the image the way it will print. Nothing needs to be reversed. It also places the emulsion surface against the black cloth, ensuring that no light can get in.

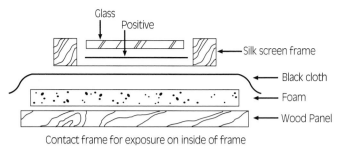

Contact frame for exposure on inside of frame

Contact frame for exposure on outside of frame

Occasionally, your positive may be larger than your screen (for example, if you are using a branch or a big transparency you don't wish to cut). Then you will have to expose on the outside of the frame. Flip the frame so that the mesh is up, fill the screen cavity underneath with a piece of foam sponge cut to fit and covered with black cloth. Place the positive block-out directly on top of the emulsion-coated screen. Glass goes on top of that. The image must make contact with the emulsion, either way. For sun exposure, use a thumb on each side of the glass if necessary to hold it secure, remembering that your thumb will also block light.

### E. WASHING OUT THE EMULSION

Immediately after exposure, spray the screen with water on both sides to inhibit further developing. You will probably see a milky version of your image where it has been exposed. It's important to wash out all the unexposed emulsion, as only the cleared areas will print. Continue to spray from the inside of the screen if your image was placed inside the frame during exposure. Tepid water is recommended, but cold works when that's all you have. I do this part of the cleaning outdoors with a spray-nozzle hose, as pressure is sometimes needed to help remove the unexposed emulsion. A faucet can be used, but a small spray nozzle will help. Water does get splashed around, so if you must use a bathroom, do the washing in the tub rather than the sink. The emulsion should disappear in all unexposed areas within a few minutes. If the design does not clear, continue spraying. Don't confuse clearing with the pale image that shows but is not yet washed out. With a stubborn screen, I've sometimes used a hard spray from a garden hose for 5 to 10 minutes, and eventually it will loosen. Hold the screen up to the light to make sure areas have cleared completely.

When the image is cleared and you can see light through all the unexposed areas, set the frame aside to dry out of the sunlight. On a warm, breezy day, this will take 10 to 15 minutes. Dry the wood frame with a towel, but the emulsion is sometimes slightly gelatinous at this stage, so be careful not to touch it.

### Printing

Once the frame is dry, you need to mask out the borders. There will be a little space at the edge of the mesh which the emulsion does not cover, and it should be blocked out, or covered with contact paper or masking tape. Then place the screen over a test fabric or paper on a smooth cardboard surface. Spoon a small amount of textile paint into the screen on a protected (emulsion) area. Draw the squeegee over the open areas to spread an even coat of paint. The angle of the squeegee determines the amount of paint which will be forced through the mesh and deposited on the fabric. Use about a 45° angle to start with. Lift the frame. If a large area was printed, the cloth or paper may stick to the frame and you must carefully peel it off. If your design is small and linear, the fabric will stay on the cardboard. Rest the frame against the edge of a tuna can (be sure it's albacore and save the dolphins). Never lay your screen flat on the table, as some paint may transfer.

Fabric absorbs more paint than does paper, and you'll soon learn to estimate the amount of paint needed. Don't put gobs of paint in your frame. Use the minimum. It eases clean-up and it's less likely to cause messes.

Whenever you smear paint, whether on your hands, the edge of the frame, the top of the squeegee, or on your work surface, stop right then and clean it up. If you don't, the problem compounds itself as it transfers from frame to hand to fabric, etc. Keep a roll of paper towels at hand.

### Registration

If you want to screen a series of identical prints (as in Plate 6-9) you will need to register them. Placement of the fabric as well as placement of the image on the fabric must

*Plate 6-9: "Home" by Jean Ray Laury, 34" x 38½".*
*Cut from construction paper, houses were arranged with paper-punched dots to provide a block-out design for the photo-emulsion process. Pieced and hand quilted.*

*Plate 6-10: "Little Boy Blue" by Jackie Vermeer, 48" x 56".*
*Outlined illustrations were printed by photo screen and colors were added with quick screen.*

be the same on each print. Some simple registration methods are described here, and hinges or clamps for screen frames make the process easier. Fabric is always more difficult to register than paper. For one thing, as fabric absorbs the water-based paint it tends to shrink or warp slightly. And just handling the fabric pulls it in one direction or another by a thread or two. If you screened a portrait on cloth and now want to make that person green-eyed, just paint the green in by hand. Registration on such a tiny detail is difficult. Keep all registered shapes simple.

For an easy registration method, place a smooth, clean cardboard on the printing area. Lay the frame on top and, with a marking pen, draw a line on the cardboard around the edge of the frame. Make a print. Lift the screen carefully to reveal your first print on the cardboard, which will serve as a guide to registration. Pat it dry with paper towels. Place your pre-cut piece of cloth on the printed cardboard. Use a light-colored cloth or muslin, and you'll be able to see the image right through it. Center the cloth over the design, then mark a line to indicate the edges or corners of the cloth. Cut all the fabric on which you intend to print to the same size as your muslin sample. Place the fabric in the marked area and place the frame back down in its original position, as marked; the next image will duplicate the placement of the first. This is a very basic kind of registration and it's all you'll need for single-color (or even two-color) prints in a small series. This simple registration method was used for the blocks in Plate 6-10.

Another simple registration method is helpful when printing on larger pieces of cloth or on garment parts. Cut a paper the exact size of the frame. Align the frame with paper, and screen a print on the paper. Blot it dry. Place the sheet of paper on your large fabric to determine where the image is to be printed. Then align one edge of the frame to one edge of the paper. Slide the paper out and print. You can cut away portions of the paper, always leaving two corners for alignment.

## Hinges

Some screen-printing frames will come already hinged to wood panels. You can use them hinged for identical multiples, or remove the hinges when you want the frame to be free. When adding hinges to your frames, use pin hinges, placing one set on your screen and a second on a wood panel. Clamps made especially for screen frames are the most convenient. The clamps are attached to plywood, the frame is slipped into the clamps and tightened into place. Two clamps go at one end of a frame and form a hinge as well as a device to hold the frame between prints. Any size frame can be slipped into the clamp, and it allows the frame to be used sideways or lengthwise. Also available for screen-printing frames is an arm which is used with a hinged frame. It holds the screen up off the fabric between prints. A simple and inexpensive arm can be made by cutting off the last 5"- 6" on your wooden yardstick. Drill the short end of the stick and screw it to the side of the frame. Now your frame has a leg to stand on.

## Drying the prints

There are various devices to hold your prints but, unless you are going into production, there is little need of them. Use a large, flat piece of cardboard for finished prints and carry it to an open space where prints can be spread out to dry. Various kinds of clamps and pins for hanging the fabrics usually take more time than they are worth. Most are designed for sheets of paper which are rigid, not for fabric which tends to hang limply and fold. Prints will dry quickly laid out on the bed or the living-room floor. As they dry, they can be lightly stacked. Even for a quilt, we rarely need over 30 to 40 prints, so drying is not a difficulty. Screened fabrics will dry within an hour or two. They should be heat set according to the paint directions, but there is no hurry to do this. Add a second color only after heat setting the first.

## Clean-up

### A. REMOVING THE PAINT

After printing, use the squeegee to remove the excess paint. Any color straight from the paint jar can go back into it. Wipe the inside of the frame with paper towels and remove masking tape or contact paper. Then wash the frame in cool water until all paint has been removed. Be certain that you remove all paint from the screen before it dries. Use a toothbrush or other soft-bristled brush if necessary. Clean screens immediately after use. If you have an emergency (must have coffee or the phone rings), put the frame under a faucet to keep it wet until you get back. The paint may stain the silk, but it should leave no residue. Wash the squeegee and clean up the area.

### B. REMOVING THE EMULSION

The exposed emulsion can be removed from the silk so that a new design can be applied. If you have done something fabulous that you wish to retain forever, the photo emulsion will last indefinitely. If you designed a quilt label with your name and photo, and you wish to keep it, remember that the screen cannot be used for anything else. But it will always be available to print a few labels as they are needed.

Be sure all paint has been removed and washed out before you start dissolving the emulsion. Cleaning is usually easy within a few hours to a day. As time passes, the emulsion gets more difficult to remove. If left too long, the image is there permanently. "Too long" is a variable, depending again on initial exposure, thickness, humidity, etc. The emulsion is removed with household bleach, readily available and easy to use. It must be a chlorine bleach. Fill a flat plastic tray, photographic tray, or cafeteria tray with a thin layer of water to cover the surface (¼" is adequate). Place the frame, mesh side down, in the tray. When the inside is wet, pour bleach directly into the frame opening. Most directions call for 2 parts water to 1 part bleach, but I don't know anybody who actually measures. If your frame is covered in silk instead of polyester, this is the process which will melt it. Soak the frame for 3 to 5 minutes, but no longer than 10 minutes. Rinse in warm to hot water; all the emulsion should wash out. If it does not, re-immerse it in bleach for a few minutes and, if necessary, scrub with a brush. If it is stubborn, continue to soak and scrub, using a little trisodium phosphate on stubborn spots.

The emulsion which has washed out and is now diluted in the bleach and water should be diluted further and flushed into the drain with lots of water. Every agency I checked with regarded this amount of chemical as negligible. However, it is important to read all precautions and observe your local and state regulations regarding disposal.

In "The Great American Coffee Break" (Plate 6-11), paper cut-outs of cups were used directly on emulsion to create photo screens. I made four separate screens, and printed each in several colors. The paper cut-out of the cup and steam, used in the contact frame, inhibited sunlight, making a positive stencil. To make the designs on the cups, I cut them out of the cup shapes. Cups were printed at odd angles so that, when assembled, the cups rattle and shake but seams remain on the grain. See the detail in Color Plate 64. I used an alphabet stamp on paper for the letters and then copied the letters onto transparencies and used them with photo emulsion. See Color Plate 63 for another Coffee Break quilt.

Various methods of screening words and letters are discussed in Chapter 10, but Jackie Vermeer's "Little Boy Blue" (Plate 6-10) uses some variations. With peel-off letters (graphic arts alphabets), all the words were spelled out onto a transparency, leaving a little space between them. A photo-emulsion screen was exposed using the transparency. To print just one or two lines at a time, Jackie blocked off large areas of the screen. A print was first made on paper. An opening or window was cut around the lettering to be printed, and the rest of the paper was used as a mask over the bottom of the screen. Each time the different lettering was to be printed, a new mask was needed.

In "Arun's War Quilt," Color Plate 52, artist Victoria Rodrigues skillfully combined a half-dozen different techniques. Using a padded table and an etching press, she followed this general procedure: with a brayer, she spread blue ink onto a sheet of Plexiglas, then repeated the process on another Plexiglas for yellow. After blocking out areas she did not want printed (the red-orange area, for example), she placed damp 100% cotton muslin on top of the ink and ran it through an etching press, then dried it. The fabric was then covered with wax paper except for the red-orange areas. Using Deka textile ink, she screen-printed those blocks. Duct tape on the screen blocked out all but the rectangles. She did the stamping with a small eraser cut in half, then cut again to leave two triangles, forming two points of the star. The stars were then stamped with Deka in various colors. Victoria both enlarged and reduced a photograph of her son, then had a negative made as well as a Kodalith (positive). Both the negative and positive were used as the block-outs on her photo-emulsion screen. The complex process yielded remarkable results.

Plates 6-11 and 6-12 both used paper cut-outs on the photo-emulsion screen. In Plate 6-13, a bride and groom were photo-screened onto white fabric with black paint, then the pair was appliquéd to the printed fabric background of a pillow. The process used to produce blocks for the record-album cover in Color Plate 62 is clarified in Plate 6-14. The first rough sketch, upper left, was enlarged,

*Plate 6-11: "The Great American Coffee Break" by Jean Ray Laury, 38" x 38".*

*Cups, saucers, and steam were cut from construction paper and used for the block-out with photo emulsion. Surrounding words were stamped on paper, copied onto transparencies, and screen-printed.*

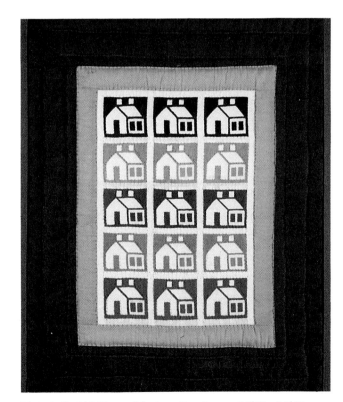

*Plate 6-12: "15 Houses" by Jean Ray Laury, 17½" x 20½".*

*Houses were printed, three at a time, from a paper cut-out for photo-emulsion printing.*

Plate 6-14: Bear block, detail from a quilt for a record album cover, by Jean Ray Laury.

Original sketch (upper left) was varied and enlarged, then inked in as shown at lower right. A transparency was made of the inked bear (lower left) to which the border and confetti squares of paper were added. The finished print on fabric, upper right, was hand-painted over the one-color print.

Plate 6-13: "Bride and Groom" by Carol Olson, 14" x 14".

A *photo-emulsion screen print in black on white was appliquéd to a black printed background for this commemorative pillow.*

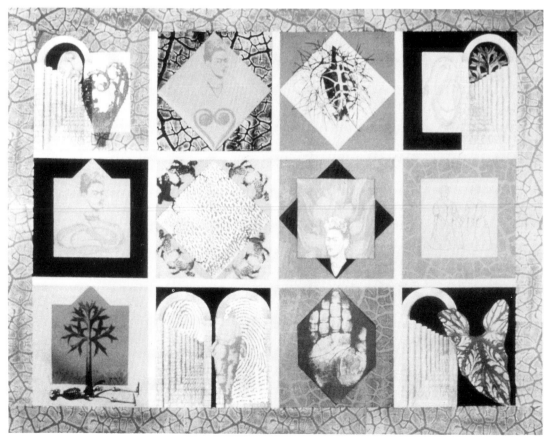

Plate 6-15: "Quilt for Frida" by Jo Ann Giordano, 33" x 42".

Architectural elements combine with portraits, plants, and human forms in these arresting combinations. Botanical patterns were printed in both negative and positive.

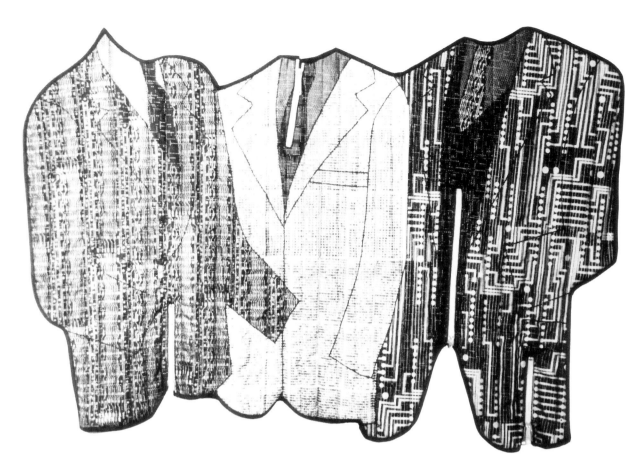

*Plate 6-16: "Computer Suits" by Jo Ann Giordano, 47" x 33".*
*The outline of the suits makes an intriguing shape for this amusing and wonderful screen-printed, collaged, and zippered piece.*

then drawn over with a marking pen, shown at lower right. The bear, a frame, and square polka dots were copied onto a transparency, lower left. The transparency was exposed on a photo-emulsion screen. Upper right shows the final print on fabric, with hand-coloring added.

Using a variety of techniques, dyes, and paints, Jo Ann Giordano screen-printed her "Quilt for Frida" (Plate 6-15). With contact stencils and photo-emulsion screen prints, she combined architectural details with portraits. The overlapping images of natural forms and leaf patterns created intriguing effects within a quilt-like format. A detail in Color Plate 66 shows the photocopied hand print, drawings, and photographs. Using Createx textile paint, she spray-dyed fabric with an atomizer. Jo Ann also screen printed on patterned fabric for the "Computer Suits" in Plate 6-16, a zippered, collaged, and quilted piece.

Joan Fisher's "Charlie" in Plate 6-17 includes a simple one-color photo image repeated for the main blocks, along with related symbols of the film world in the corner blocks. She used a photograph which was copied onto a transparency for her image. Hand-quilted stars add texture and pattern to the outline-stitched figures.

The original drawing for "Iris Garden," Plate 6-18, was copied onto a transparency and photo-emulsion screen-printed. Susan Smeltzer, whose green thumb is evident in her quilting, used a series of calicoes as backgrounds, and each change alters the print color slightly. It is pieced and machine quilted.

Designed for the cover of a record album, the images in the quilt in Color Plate 60 were all photo-screen printed on fabric. Six drawings were copied onto acetate, then screened in many colored paints onto assorted colors of fabric. Each was then hand-painted to add further color.

Three-dimensional dolls can be made up from flat screen-printed fabrics. In Color Plate 55, the boy doll is made up from just two pieces of fabric, a back and a front.

Plate 6-17: *"Charlie" by Joanne Fisher, detail of block, 6" x 8".*
*Photo-emulsion silk-screen print on fabric, combining the central*
*figure with movie props in the corner squares. Pieced with*
*reflective fabric and hand quilted.*

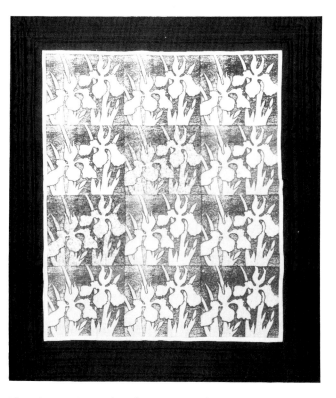

Plate 6-18: *"Iris Garden" by Susan Smeltzer, 30" x 35".*
*Printed in changing values of a single color, this quilt was given*
*variety by alternating the patterned background fabrics.*

The girl has separate arms and legs. Each leg folds down the back and, when the leg is set into the skirt seam, the toes point forward. Drawings were copied onto transparencies, then screen-printed in one color. Additional colors were added with marking pens and hand painting.

"Betsy and Ron," enlarged from a snapshot, were screen-printed onto pillowcases and sheets as a wedding gift (Color Plate 65). Photo emulsion was used for the figures, and a second screen was made for the lettering. Only the hearts were printed with contact-paper stencil.

"Hopscotch Horizon" is photo-screen printed onto many small pieces of fabric which are then joined to form the all-over checkerboards of the landscape. Color gradations are made by starting with a light color and adding consistently increasing amounts of a second color. See Color Plate 73.

The line drawing for the winged cat in the detail of Color Plate 59 is photo-screen printed in a single color on muslin. Thinned textile paints were used for the hand-colored parts. In Color Plate 60 the multicolored cats are combined with photo-screened letters, piecing, and hand quilting.

Diane E. Goff turned an old family photo into the irresistible panel in Plate 6-19. She started "Clovis Easter Morning" by taking a slide of an old family photo, projecting it onto a screen, and tracing it. The faces were enlarged on a copier until they were the size needed to correspond with the traced drawing. Then she used a transparency to develop the faces onto the photo-emulsion screen. Once they were screen-printed on fabric, the faces were appliquéd, as were trees, grass, clothing, and hats. Piecing and hand quilting completed the composition. Diane's

Plate 6-19: "Clovis Easter Morning" by Diane E. Goff, 35" x 46½".

*Silk-screened faces help to recreate this charming family photo. Along with the appliquéd Easter bonnets are areas of pieced background, pictorial appliqué, and quilted drawing.*

Plate 6-20: Detail of Quilt San Diego's "Jubilee Quilt," designed by Donalene H. Rasmussen.
*Photo-screen printing of an architectural drawing is combined with hand painting, appliqué, and quick screening.*

Plate 6-21: Detail of "Picture Start" by Robin Schwalb.
*Graphic images of perilous and memorable moments were photo-screened and combined with piecing and quilting.*

choice of prints for both clothing and background adds wonderful texture, but her selection of patterned fabrics for arms and legs is especially charming and effective.

A detail from Quilt San Diego's "Jubilee Quilt," designed by Donalene H. Rasmussen, shows the photo silk-screened Reuben H. Fleet Museum, in Plate 6-20. Donna printed the planets and stars using quick print (with freezer paper), along with hand painting and appliqué, to produce this wonderful collage celebrating the city. Another detail of the quilt is shown in Color Plate 69.

In "Projectionist Please Focus," Plate 6-22, Robin Schwalb has pieced together fragments of images which she photo silk-screened on fabric. Pictured at upper right are the projectionists (including the artist) and a remarkable collection of images and words related to film. The light from the projector, printed in yellow, is both stenciled and pieced to create the illusion of light filling the

space. Robin screen-printed with Deka, using a light-sensitive photo emulsion (Holden's Diazo) with Kodaliths and transparencies. She exposed her frames on a vacuum table using fluorescent lights, a process similar to but more sophisticated than the sunlight exposure described earlier. The work is pieced, quilted by hand and by machine.

"Picture Start" in Plate 6-21 includes black-and-white lettering along with both positive and negative images. Robin Schwalb uses words in extraordinary ways. In her panels, the symbolic value of words is as critical as content. Fragmented words hint at layered meanings while creating textures and patterns. Robin printed white letters on black in Color Plate 43 of Chapter 5. The small text was photo silk-screened and heavily printed to achieve the opaque white letters. She first flooded the screen with paint, then squeegeed over it only once. Any additional strokes would have deposited too much ink and tended to blur the images.

Plate 6-22: "Projectionist Please Focus" by Robin Schwalb, 59" x 45".

The artist, also a projectionist, used the photo-emulsion screen process with Kodaliths for the fragmented text and the images or "flicks" related to the world of films.

# TROUBLESHOOTING FOR PHOTO-EMULSION SCREEN PRINTING

Problem:    The print is spotty or unclear.

Solution:    The screen may not have been properly degreased. Clean it again, then add emulsion.

Dust may have settled on the wet emulsion, creating spots.

Paint or emulsion from an earlier print may be blocking the mesh.

Problem:    The print is light or unclear.

Solution:    Use more paint, flooding the image before squeegeeing.

Paint or emulsion was left in the mesh from a previous print. Try rubbing alcohol (70% isopropyl) to remove any old emulsion.

Paint may have dried during printing. Try applying a lot of pressure on the squeegee to force the mesh open, working over scrap paper.

Problem:    The image looks smeared.

Solution:    Take care not to slide or move the frame while screening.

Clean the back of the frame to be sure no paint has been picked up on that surface.

Use less pressure.

Check the emulsion to be sure the image is clear.

Tighten the mesh by changing the staples or the cord.

For a stapled screen, tighten the mesh temporarily with a few ½" x 4" strips of hard cardboard slipped between mesh and wood inside the screen-printing frame. A few strips at the ends or sides will tighten the mesh enough for you to finish your printing.

Problem:    The image washed out entirely after exposure.

Solution:    The screen was underexposed: increase the exposure time.

The emulsion may have been old: use mixed emulsion within a few days.

Problem:    It is difficult to get the emulsion out of the screen after exposure.

Solution:    Use greater pressure with the water.

Hose for a longer time.

The screen may be overexposed. Remove emulsion with bleach and try again.

Problem:    Emulsion cannot be removed from mesh with bleach.

Solution:    Try using bleach full strength, directly on mesh.

Soak it for a longer time (up to 10 minutes).

Scrub with a brush.

If all of these fail, emulsion may be in the mesh forever. You can replace the mesh.

Silk-screened images combined with piecing, quilting, painting, and three-dimensional objects all form parts of Kathy Weaver's complex compositions, Color Plate 70 and a detail in Color Plate 67. In "Panama — Been There Before?," a painted picture-postcard-like center is surrounded by stark images of war. Appliquéd flowers lure us with their tropical beauty and belie the images they overlay.

Construction paper, cut into pickets, fenceposts, and houses, was used as the block-out for the photo screens in Color Plate 74. Letters stamped onto paper were copied onto transparencies and photo-screened. The polka-dot falling debris was stamp-printed using a pencil eraser. Before I printed a quilt square, I placed a sheet of paper on it to block the printing area partially, so only half a house was printed. A second half was printed the same way. Paper cut-outs were used over photo emulsion for the fence and houses.

In "The River Quilt," Color Plate 71, an oak tree was printed many times in several colors, each print overlapping the last. The strips of trees were then cut into lengths and re-assembled for the border. Drawings of local flora and fauna were all exposed on photo emulsion from transparencies.

## General Information for Silk-Screen Printing

### CLEANING OR DEGREASING A NEW SCREEN

All new frames must be cleaned or degreased to remove any substances which are resistant to paint or emulsion. Wet the screen and sponge on a solution of trisodium phosphate (1 tablespoon TSP to 2 cups of water). Laundry detergent can serve as a substitute. The polyester is strong and can resist the scrubbing. You can use a household cleanser but, as it is somewhat abrasive, its use should be limited. Rinse thoroughly, then wipe with household vinegar. While this step is not always crucial, it is recommended. This cleansing precludes problems of the mesh rejecting the emulsion.

### USING THE SQUEEGEES

It will take some experimentation and practice to become adept at handling the squeegee. When it is held more horizontal, more paint is forced through the screen; held more vertical, less paint goes through. To start with, hold the squeegee at a 45° angle. Smaller squeegees are easier to work with and can be pulled over an image several times .

### OTHER CONSIDERATIONS

Avoid leaving paint sitting on the open areas of the screen, as it will affect the print. To remove the paint, angle the squeegee slightly and scrape excess paint to one end before lifting the screen.

If you get sick of the navy blue you've been printing and decide to switch to pink, it will be necessary to wash out the screen, dry it, and start all over with new block-out at the edges. If, however, you are printing with yellow and decide to switch to green, add the new color to the screen and make a few prints on paper to get the paint mixed. It's easy to move from light to dark and to colors adjacent on the color wheel (orange to red, green to blue, red to violet, or light blue to medium blue). It is also possible to put 2 or 3 colors side by side in a screen to get a multicolored image. Eventually they will mix, but they'll stay clear for a few prints.

### TUSCHE AND GLUE

Another method of creating a block-out is used less often than the photo-emulsion screen: you paint directly on the screen. The tusche-and-glue method has special appeal, therefore, for anyone who enjoys a direct, painterly approach. Traditionally tusche, which is actually a lithographic ink, is an oil-based liquid which you paint onto the mesh. When it has dried, you paint over it with a water-based liquid, such as thinned glue, which is resisted by the tusche. When this second liquid has dried, you remove the tusche with a solvent, leaving the glue in place and the painted areas open. You print with oil-based ink, creating a positive print of the original painting. The liquids used have changed over the years, but the term "tusche and glue" has stuck.

For the water-based paints we use on fabric, the process is reversed, starting with a water-based resist. Companies which market screen-printing supplies sell the needed liquids, such as Hunt Speedball Drawing Fluid and Screen Filler.

1. Paint the design with a water-based drawing fluid on either side of the mesh, and let it dry.
2. Paint screen filler on one side of the mesh to cover the design and let it dry.

3. Wash out the drawing fluid, using a toothbrush if necessary on stubborn spots.
4. Mask the edges and print.
5. Clean up the paint.
6. Remove the filler.

## PAINTING THE DESIGN

Place the frame flat, to keep the drawing fluid from running. If you paint on the inside of the frame, your image will not reverse, but you will need to prop the frame up off the work surface. If you paint on the outside, you will print a reversal. Use a small to medium brush, depending upon detail. Brush strokes and fluid lines can be reproduced.

## REMOVING FILLER

Follow the directions for the particular filler you purchase. It may be removed at a different temperature than the drawing, or it may require another solvent. For example, Hunt Speedball Drawing Fluid is removed with cool water, while the Screen Filler is removed with hot water and detergent. Remove all traces of both materials from the screen.

# Thermal Imagers (Copiers)
## (Thermo-Fax, Apollo)

As trucks deliver new copy machines and computers to schools all over the country, the older thermal imagers are often put into retirement. They were used in schools and offices to produce stencils, thermal copies, and spirit masters for multiple copies; we fabric artists can use them to create detailed stencils for thermal screen printing.

Although thermal imagers are still being made, many of the old ones can be purchased very reasonably. My somewhat ancient machine, a Thermo-Fax, was purchased from a somewhat ancient retired schoolteacher, and it was one of my wiser investments. Watch want ads or check with school equipment suppliers for a used machine. If you work in a school or office which has a thermal imager, for heaven's sake try it out.

Thermal imaging, while known to many teachers, is one of the best-kept secrets in surface design. It's a great way to add lettering, photographs, sketches, or linear designs to cloth. Without chemicals, solvents, or knives, thermal imagers make stencils for screening, and the images are not reversed. Using a thermal imager, the design is etched or burned onto a special plastic film (the thermal screen). This stencil is attached to a frame and is screen-printed with a squeegee. After printing, you can save the screen and use it again.

In addition to thermal imagers, there is the Gocco

*Plate 7-1: Detail of "Birds" by Jean Ray Laury. Birds are 6" high. The drawing for this bird (center) was copied onto a transparency which was flipped to reverse the image. The paired birds, heading both east and west, were then imaged on the thermal imager.*

printer, a small machine which works similarly. Exposure is with a flash bulb, and thermal screens can be imaged in the Gocco. It requires a special paint, and the machine produces the print. There are limitations in the printing, and I recommend using the thermal imager for greater versatility.

Plate 7-1 shows a drawing of a bird (center) which was thermal-imaged and then screened onto fabric; the prints were then hand-colored. In Plate 7-2 a face cut from a photocopied snapshot was glued to a sheet of paper, then a drawing of a kimono was added to complete the figure. After thermal-screen printing the blocks, I added line drawings (with fine-line permanent markers) and painted them. The full piece is shown in Color Plate 75.

A great advantage of thermal-screen printing is its simplicity. Once you are familiar with the process, it's a matter of just minutes from drawing to print. Thermal screen is more costly than contact paper, but you do not need to buy a wood screen frame for this process. A thermal-screen stencil will last through many printings, and I have yet to wear one out. The results are thought to be less durable than photo-screen printing, but in each case it depends upon the exposure. You will need the following materials:

*Plate 7-2: Detail of "Japanese Fairy Godmothers" by Jean Ray Laury.*

*Thermal-screen printed images include a photo and drawings. All were hand-colored, pieced, and quilted.*

- Access to thermal imager
- Thermal screen ⬎ ✳
- Plastic mat or frame ⬎ ✳
- Double-faced tape
- Squeegee → (a credit card will do)
- Water-based textile paints → ✳
- PFP fabric →

The process in brief (with details following):

1. Place your original drawing face up, centered between the two layers of the thermal screen.

2 Expose it by inserting the three layers (screen, artwork, and backing) into the machine.

3. Set the imager to Medium and press the On button. The layers will be drawn through the machine and will emerge with the design burned onto the surface of the screen.

3. Remove the original, carefully peeling the screen away.

4. Use a plastic mat, or make a cardboard one. Adhere double-faced tape to all four edges of the frame, next to the window.

5. Attach the screen to the cardboard by pressing it onto the tape. The smooth surface of the screen should be down and in contact with the frame. Keep the screen taut (but not bowed).

6. Place the fabric on a flat, smooth surface.

7. Place the frame over the fabric.

8. Spread a small amount of water-based textile paint on an unimaged part of the screen and squeegee it over the design.

## Original

The heat in the imager responds to carbon, so the original must have carbon in the drawn lines if they are to be etched onto the screen. A photocopy will work, or the original can be drawn with India ink. Most pencils, ballpoint pens, and felt markers do not have adequate carbon to image clearly. Computer print-outs, press-on letters, snapshots, signatures, and paste-ups should all be photocopied.

## Thermal screens or stencils

Packaged thermal screens consist of two layers, a backing sheet and the stencil (usually blue). The stencil is a fine layer of polyester bonded with a film. When the stencil is placed over a drawing and run through the imager, the drawing is etched into the thin layer of plastic but not through the fine fabric mesh. This leaves open areas in the mesh through which the paint can be pressed or squeegeed, much as in photo-emulsion screen printing. Leave the two sheets of the thermal screen connected at the top end so that they will travel through the machine together. You discard the backing sheet after exposure.

Thermal screen is also available by the roll, which is less expensive per print but has a higher initial cost. You can cut the length or size needed. You need not print a full-size sheet. You will be limited in size only by the page-size capacity of the thermal imager, which is usually 8½" x 11". You can run a longer sheet through, but not a wider one. The second size limitation is that of your plastic frames. The frames are available with the screens.

## Imaging

To expose or image your screen, you will need to have three layers: the backing, the original, and the thermal screen. If you are using sheets (not the roll), slip the original, image side up, between the backing and the blue stencil, which are already stacked correctly for imaging. If you are cutting thermal screen from a roll, cut off a piece which fits your frame and allows a margin of about 2" on each side of your original. Cut a backing sheet the same size as the thermal screen. Then put the thermal screen, mesh side up, on top of the original and the backing. (The smooth or shiny side touches the original.) The screen must come in contact with the copy.

In order to be sure the sheets travel through the machine together when you are using screen cut from a roll, fold over and sharply crease about an inch at the front end of the backing sheet. Slip the screen and original into this fold before running the set through the imager. (When an original is on a full page, it can also serve as the backing and you can eliminate the bottom sheet.) It is best not to use tape to attach the screen to the backing sheet, as it can be melted by the imager.

When making your first thermal image, set the adjustable heat dial just past the midway point, going towards dark. After running your screen through, carefully lift a corner to check the quality of the stencil. Don't disturb the rest of the sheet. The design should be etched into the screen so that only the mesh remains over the image. You can see light through the etched areas. If the design does not show, it was inadequately heated and the stack can be run through again at a slightly higher temperature setting. If the design was overheated and the screen is partially melted to the original, you must start over with a lower heat setting. Experiment until you determine the perfect setting. Mark that spot on your dial.

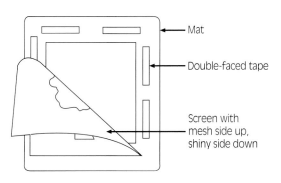

Mat

Double-faced tape

Screen with mesh side up, shiny side down

## Print Frame

A print frame is needed to hold the screen taut and make it easier to handle. In contrast to the sturdy wood of a silk-screen frame, this method uses a lightweight plastic frame which has some flexibility. Frames are available with a printing area of 7½" by 10", which can easily be managed. Large pages can be handled after some practice, but half-

sheets are easy, and smaller designs will be a snap. The plastic frames are very convenient, but you can also make one. Cut a cardboard, such as the back of a paper tablet, to the size of your stencil or slightly larger. Cut a window out of the center, so that you leave a border at each edge 1½" to 2" wide. The window is for your screen. Apply the screen with double-faced tape, as described earlier. You will save time by purchasing re-usable plastic mats.

## Screening

Always run several tests on paper or scrap fabric. These tests can be cut out and used in determining the placement of prints. Spoon a small amount of textile paint onto an area that is unimaged. Use a squeegee as wide as the image. (I often use a smaller one, requiring two strokes, but you must avoid leaving excess paint in the open areas of the screen.) Draw the squeegee, held at about a 60° angle, lightly but firmly over the image. Use a single stroke. Lift the screen carefully off the fabric, and let the fabric air dry. Follow instructions that come with your textile paints for air drying and heat setting →.

## Screening without a frame

At times you will be tempted to print without attaching the thermal screen to a frame. (I do it all the time.) If you are very careful — or in a big hurry — it's worth a try. Place the screen on fabric and dab a minimum amount of paint onto an unimaged area. Hold the screen down at one end and squeegee from that end to the other. It's especially helpful to have an extra pair of hands to hold the edges of the screen down while you print. (The edges tend to curl under.) You can usually get a few prints made this way if you keep the amount of paint to a minimum and are very careful. If you need only 2 or 3 prints, try it this way; if you need a dozen, you'd better use a frame. Larger prints require the use of a frame to prevent shifting that would blur the print.

## Reversals

If you wish to reverse an image you are screening, trace the original in reverse and make a second screen. Or, you can simply flip your (cleaned) screen and frame so that the mesh side will be down with the frame on top. This is not the recommended method, but you can with care get good prints this way. You can also make a reversal by imaging from a transparency to create a reversed thermal screen.

## Clean-up

When printing is complete, remove excess paint from the screen, using the squeegee as a scoop over scrap paper. Paint can go back into the jar. Place the screen over newspaper or paper towels, and wipe off remaining paint. Then wash both the screen and the frame under running water, cool to lukewarm. Remove tape. The screen is reusable, though it tends to curl as it dries. So store the screens flat in a file folder.

## Storing

Keep new screens in a dust-free area (the box they come in will do nicely), as dust particles may affect the image. Store away from direct sunlight and heat. In hot weather, keep them in an air-conditioned room.

## Multi-colored prints

A print of two or more colors can be made in any of several ways. First, you can separate the colors on your original. If you have a picture of a redhead wearing a blue hat, one screen can be for the red and one for blue. You image each color on its own screen and then register them as you print. Read about Registration in Chapter 5.

You can also image the entire design, then block off portions which you want to reserve for a second color. For example, if our redhead and her hat are on one screen, you first need to make a print on paper. From the paper print, cut out only the area which contains the blue hat. Leave all areas which are to be red. The paper print becomes a stencil or block-out. Place it under the screen, aligning it with the stencil; the window must be aligned under the blue hat. Tape it to the edges of the frame. Print the blue color, then follow the same process for the second color by making another paper print from which a stencil can be cut. It will cover the area of the hat and open the area for the redhead. This is difficult to do for very precise registration: don't count on getting the pupils into the middle of the eyes. But it's relatively simple for shapes which do not have to fit perfectly, such as a flower on a stem.

It is also possible, with some careful maneuvering, to use several colors of paint at one time. You'll need a small plastic squeegee for each color (just 1" or 2" lengths will do). Put a small amount of each color on the screen near the area to be printed in that color. Go over each area with a separate color and squeegee. Try to keep one color from invading another's territory. When parts of the design are separated, this will work more easily. For ex-

Printing two colors on a single screen

 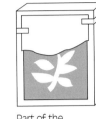 

Design block-out on screen — Part of the design exposed — Remaining part exposed

ample, three stars on one screen can be printed in three different colors.

A rainbow effect can be screened if you spoon various colors, one after another, at one end of the screen. Squeegee across with one stroke to get a rainbow effect; no two prints will be identical. They'll eventually blend and you'll have to start over to retain the effect. Always squeegee in the same direction to keep colors from mixing.

The "Dancing Ladies" in Color Plate 72 were drawn on paper, photocopied, and run through the thermal imager to make a stencil. They were screen-printed onto fabric with black paint. Once a figure was printed, it was covered with a piece of paper towel so that the frame did not get placed on wet paint. The next print could be made without waiting for the first to dry. It's always best to let prints dry, but impatience is the mother of invention, and you'll find a way.

The "Birds" in Plate 7-1 started with a line drawing of one bird which was copied onto a transparency. When the transparency was flipped, it was placed with the original to make a pair, letting them dance beak to beak. A copy of the pair was made and used in the thermal imager. A transparency can be used as the original, but the thermal screen may lift ink from the original as it images. The ink can be washed out of the screen and you can get a good clean screen print from it. The transparency, however, may be damaged, so you'll have to decide how expendable it is. Since thermal screens produce good details and lettering, they are great for labels, name tags, and text on fabric.

Susan Magretta used Day of the Dead images for her multi-colored scarf in Color Plate 68. Thermal-image screen prints on rayon were layered over similar prints on muslin, creating a double-image transparency. In another of Susan's pieces, in Plate 7-3, scenes depicting the same holiday were screened onto white fabric, and the fabric was then

36. "Computer Crab" by Susan Migliore, 22" diameter.

With black transfer ribbon in the printer, the images were printed on paper and then transferred to cloth. The crabs and other areas were hand-colored.

35. "Prayer Rug" by Susan Migliore, 42" x 28".

Using a program with color-separation capability, all the drawings were printed on paper, then transferred to a hand-painted background fabric.

37. "I Forgot" scarf by Bonnie Meltzer.

Using heat-transfer ribbon in the printer, single-color print-outs were ironed onto the silk scarf.

38. "Let's Dance" by Fred Blesse, 11" x 8 ½".

Computer graphics were printed directly onto laminated fabric which was run through the printer.

39. "Animal Magnetism," jacket by Mary Preston, 32" x 60".

Imaginative stenciled animals caper amidst ribbons, symbols, and lines from stories.

41. "Anna's Quilt" by Jean Ray Laury, 55" x 39"; drawings by Anna Laury, age 11.

Four favorite animals were quick-screened to fabric and outlined with markers, then pieced and machine quilted.

40. "Northern Skies" by Lura Schwarz Smith, 22" diameter.

Quick screen on hand-painted and printed cotton with markers and airbrush.

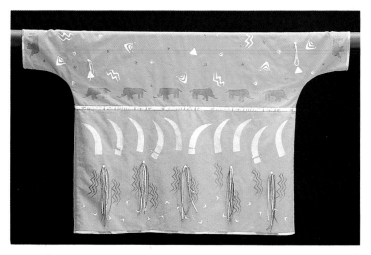

42. "Tickling the Ivories," jacket by Mary Preston, 36" x 59".

Soft colors and stenciling make a handsome jacket covered with elephants, tusks, and symbolic designs — a gentle plea for the environment.

44. "One View of Mt. Fuji" by Robin Schwalb, 54 ½" x 44 ½".

Images of travel in Japan, along with recollections of amusing language discrepancies, inspired this extraordinary stenciled work.

43. "Gift of Tongues" by Robin Schwalb, 98" x 54".

In this large quilted panel which reflects her father's facility with many languages, the artist combined quick screen and photo silk-screen into a lively visual pattern.

45. Detail of "One View of Mt. Fuji" by Robin Schwalb.

*Robin Schwalb achieves clear, sharp images of light over dark through repeated applications of stenciled colors.*

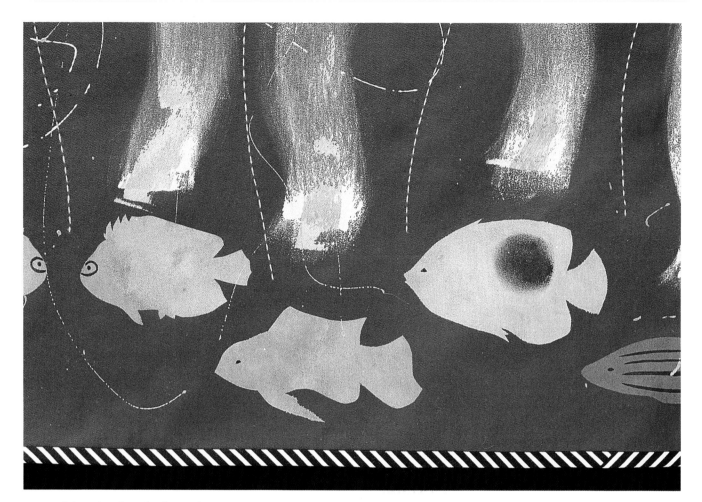

46. Detail of "I Like to be Under the Sea" by Mary Preston.
Stitched lines offer a delicate contrast to flat, graphic fish.

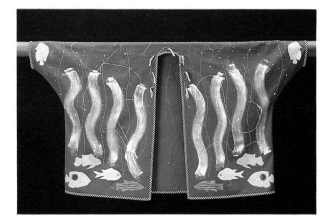

47. "I Like to be Under the Sea" by Mary Preston, 32" x 59".
Sharp-edged shapes contrast with soft lines in a jacket which evokes a sense of another world.

48. "No Dragons on My Quilt" by Jean Ray Laury, 54" x 46".
Freezer-paper stencils on fabric were quick-screened without the use of a screen printing frame

49. "A Boy and His Frog" by Katherine Knauer, 67" x 64".

*Piecing, painting, embroidery, and appliqué were combined to produce this complex collage of painterly and patterned elements.*

50. Detail of "A Boy and His Frog" by Katherine Knauer.

*Hand-painted fabrics and superlative airbrush techniques add lifelike realism to this unique work.*

52. "Arun's War Quilt" by Victoria Rodrigues, 22 ½" x 27 ½".

*Both positive and negatives images, varied in size, were used to create these evocative photo-emulsion screen prints. Various printmaking and stamp-printing techniques were combined in this compelling wall piece.*

51. "The Van Dalsem Quilt" (or "Barefoot and Pregnant") by Jean Ray Laury, 44" x 44".

*Paper block-outs, contact stencils, and photo-emulsion screen printing were combined in this cartoon-format quilt, with additional drawing and painting. It was pieced and hand quilted.*

54. Detail of "The Burpee Quilt" by Jean Ray Laury.

A polka-dot background fabric was screen-printed over paper, contact paper, and photo-emulsion stencils. Printed areas were outlined with fine-line permanent markers.

53. "The Burpee Quilt" by Jean Ray Laury, 62" x 55".

The quotation, credited in a newspaper column to David Burpee, invited a visual interpretation. Screen-printed using paper, contact paper, and photo-emulsion screens, it was then detailed with permanent markers.

55. Dolls by Jean Ray Laury, 12" high.

Just a front and back were printed for the boy doll. The girl was made with separate arms and legs. All were colored with permanent markers.

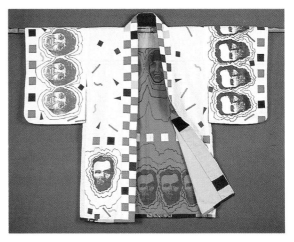

57. Detail of "Two Blue Jeans and a Violet Lincoln" by Jean Ray Laury.

Paints blended in the screen offer two-color images outlined with permanent markers.

56. "Two Blue Jeans and a Violet Lincoln" by Jean Ray Laury, 36" x 47".

Pieced checkers edge this colorful kimono printed with contact-paper stencils and photo-emulsion screening.

**58. "Jane's Other War" by Barbara Carow, 35" x 51".**

Silhouetted aerobic dancers were printed from a series of contact-paper stencils. The horizontal bands of hand-painted fabric were pieced together with contrasting colors and quilted.

**59. Detail of "Flying Wallendas" by Jean Ray Laury.**

The cat was screen-printed in one color on muslin, using a transparency for exposure with emulsion. All other colors were hand-painted. This detail shows hand quilting which echoes the feline form.

**60. "Flying Wallendas" by Jean Ray Laury, 41" x 41".**
Lettering was screen-printed in color. Panel is pieced and quilted.

**61. "Neighborhood Watch" by Jean Ray Laury, 45" x 46".**
Burglars, their beams of light, and open windows were screen-printed on muslin with contact-paper stencils. The watching eyes were also cut from contact paper, but the lettering was photo-screen printed. It was pieced and hand quilted.

62. Album cover for "Marcia Berman Sings Lullabies" by Jean Ray Laury, 68" x 75".

Drawings on paper were copied onto transparencies, then exposed on photo-emulsion screens. All the one-color prints were made on colored fabric, and additional colors were hand-painted. The panel at the top was for the record title.

63. "The Great American Coffee Break # 3" by Jean Ray Laury, 39" x 39".

Cut-paper cups and saucers provided block-outs for the photo-emulsion screen prints. Caffeine jitters obviously affect the cups as well as the words, which are photo-screened from contact letters.

64. Detail of "The Great American Coffee Break #2" by Jean Ray Laury.

Paper cut-outs combine with stamped and screened letters to detail the alarming effects of coffee drinking.

65. A wedding announcement pillowcase was printed with photo screen in three separate prints, one for each color, and the hearts were added by quick screen.

Plate 7-3: Detail of apron by Susan Magretta.
Day of the Dead images were photocopied, thermal-imaged, and screened onto fabric. The fabric prints were then appliquéd to another panel with lace, crochet, embroidery, and sequins.

Plate 7-4: "Here Kitty Kitty" by Jean Ray Laury,  34" x 34".
Cats were drawn on paper, photocopied, then etched onto a thermal screen for printing. Lettering was screen-printed, pieced, and hand-quilted.

appliquéd to a larger panel. It includes lace, crochet, and embroidery.

In "Soweto Suite, Part II: Greed," the thermal imager was used to prepare stencils for screen printing. Kathy Weaver's powerful piece in Color Plate 79 includes a collection of faces (at top) which were copied from ads, then altered and printed on fabric. The screen-printed rands were appliquéd. Other parts of the quilt were hand-painted, and three-dimensional objects were attached with Velcro. Other fabric pieces, coated with Aleene's Fabric Stiffener (a hobby-shop item) were also set in place with Velcro. Bomb-blast images at left and right were screen-printed, and the burned edges of polyester and satin add a delicate and eerie touch. See a detail of this piece in Color Plate 80. Kathy used the inviting softness and warmth of a quilt to draw the viewer to study her messages — strong, unsettling comments on inequality, war, homelessness, and the environment. Regarding the quilt as personal history, Kathy says, "This 'remember me' legacy has a particular poignancy when the subject matter questions the conditions of the world we are passing on to the next generation."

In "Here Kitty Kitty," I imaged a single cat onto the screen and printed it to make a center unit, Plate 7-4. To aid in registration, I arranged a few paper prints on the cloth. Pressing light folds into the cloth will also help to create a guide for placement. The lettering was done with photo silk-screen.

"Endangered Species" has two different drawings of figures, Color Plate 76. They were drawn on paper, copied, and run through the thermal imager. Screened with a single color onto printed fabrics, the figures were then hand-painted to create an effect of many colors.

# TROUBLESHOOTING FOR THERMAL IMAGING

Problem:     Paint dries in the screen.

Solution:    Work faster, so paint has less chance to dry.

Cover paint with plastic wrap if you must leave it for more than a few minutes.

Add medium to textile paint to slow the drying time.

Problem:     The print is smeared, or the paint appears to have run.

Solution:    Stencil may be burned (overexposed) from too much heat. Readjust the heat control and try a new stencil at a lower setting.

Too much paint is being forced through. Squeegee with less pressure or hold the squeegee more upright.

Try another brand of paint.

Problem:     The print appears light and sketchy, or parts of it are lost.

Solution:    Stencil may be underdeveloped. Readjust heat control and try again at a higher setting.

Too little paint was used. Apply more paint, squeegee it with more pressure, and hold the squeegee less vertical, letting it lean over closer to the screen.

Problem:     Pinhole spots of paint appear on the fabric where it should be clear.

Solution:    Block off any leaks with cellophane tape on the back side of the screen (the side that touches the fabric). Or block off with nail polish.

Keep thermal imager and screens dust-free, as small particles on the screen may also be etched.

Check belt, glass cylinder, or glass plate for dust particles. Clean belt or roller with alcohol.

Make sure copy doesn't have spots of toner.

Problem:     Some areas which were meant to print do not.

Solution:    Sometimes areas which have not opened up can be loosened. Use a sewing needle and prick or scrape out the plastic from the threads.

Image the screen again with increased heat.

Problem:     The screen tears when separated from the original.

Solution:    The screen was burned, so use less heat to image the design onto the thermal screen.

# Light-Sensitive Prints
## (Cyanotype or blueprint, Van Dyke or brownprint, Kwik-print, Inko print)

Fabric artists with an inclination toward sleight of hand will particularly enjoy the four methods described in this section. It's exciting to see images emerge, somewhat magically, on exposed fabric. Watching your great-uncle materialize on cloth will transform you into an eager alchemist. The methods covered here are:

CYANOTYPE (blueprint)
VAN DYKE (brownprint)
KWIK-PRINT
INKO PRINT

These photo processes involve the use of sensitized fabrics which, upon exposure to ultraviolet light, develop their full color. You've experienced this kind of exposure in a swimsuit on your first tanning of the summer. Stripped, the next day, you appear to be wearing a flesh-colored suit, and all areas exposed to direct contact with the sun are "fully developed" in red. This is essentially the process utilized in all four methods. A block-out or negative, placed in direct contact with the fabric, interrupts the light in the same way that your swimsuit interrupted the would-be tan. This is a contact print.

A photographic negative ↘ used on sensitized fabric produces a positive photographic image. Those areas which look dark on a negative will prohibit light from penetrating and will appear white (or fabric color) in the finished print. A negative produces a photograph; an opaque object or block-out → produces a photogram →. Whatever inhibits the flow of light will preserve the original fabric color.

All light-sensitive processes are particularly inviting because of the quality of the images they produce. The fabric photographs are detailed and rich, especially with halftone negatives. With natural forms →, the characteristic variation of intensity is especially alluring.

CAUTION ☞ Sensitizers (or light-sensitive chemicals) are toxic, so they must be handled and stored with extreme caution. Read all labels and information carefully. Wear protective gloves. When using powders, wear a mask and work outdoors with a safe-box or a hooded vent. Allow no food, drinks, children, or open flame near the solutions. Read the Hazardous Materials → entry in Additional Help.

The following step-by-step directions apply to all four methods. Read each specific method for variations. Restrain yourself and hold still long enough to read all of this section before proceeding to the specific method that has you intrigued,

## GENERAL DIRECTIONS

Before starting, collect the following materials (utensils are to be reserved exclusively for this work):

- Small glass bowls (for mixing and painting)
- Brown or amber bottles for storing solutions
- Plastic mixing spoons
- Gram or ounce scale
- 2 sheets of glass (one on which to paint the fabric, one for the contact frame)
- Direct contact frame →
- Darkroom →
- Paint brush or sponge brush
- Plastic clothesline (to dry fabric)
- Fabric, cut slightly smaller than the glass
- Safe-light →

## Darkroom

A darkened area is needed for painting and drying the sensitizer on fabric. To produce clear images, you must prevent light exposure during application, drying, and preparation, though there is some leeway. You have a few minutes in which to work in subdued light, or you can use a safe-light →. The drying requires darkness, since it takes the longest time. Working at night eases darkroom concerns, and "night people" prefer this. Their fabrics are then ready for printing at sun-up (if you can get them out of bed). Do not pursue this work in your kitchen. A closet, garage, or shop can be converted to a temporary darkroom. If you have no space, work at night and cover the dry sensitized fabric before daylight hits it.

Your darkroom will also need a plastic clothesline on which to dry the fabric. Unless you have concrete floors and absolutely no qualms about how they look, you'll need to protect the floor under the drying area. Use a sheet of plastic with newspapers spread over it (take care not to go into a banana-peel routine by slipping on the plastic). If you use a bathroom, hang a line over the tub (with a travel clothesline or suction cups). Either line it with newspaper or add an inch or two of water to catch any drips and make cleaning easier. See Darkroom in the Additional Help section for further information.

## Sensitizing Solutions ☞

Each process uses specific chemicals or dyes which make the fabric light-sensitive. Handle these carefully, observing all directions and warnings from the manufacturer. Read Hazardous Materials in Additional Help. Use pre-mixed liquids when possible. If you must mix dry ingredients, wear rubber gloves and a long-sleeved shirt, use a safe-box ↘ and a face mask while mixing. Work in a well-ventilated area, but not where a breeze can pick up powders. Leave your cup of coffee (and your cigar) out in the kitchen, and NO nibbling on a cookie while you work. Before starting, read labels and familiarize yourself with the correct procedures for first aid.

To avoid mixing dry chemicals, use pre-treated fabric for cyanotype and purchase the ready-mixed liquids for Kwik-print and Inko prints. All light-sensitive solutions have limited shelf lives, and solutions or pre-coated fabrics will have expiration dates stated. Mixing the chemicals yourself, although more hazardous, assures their viability.

Most chemicals needed for light-sensitive prints are available through photographic, scientific, or craft suppli-ers, listed in Sources ✳. Also check the yellow pages for a wholesale chemical company: you will have to buy a larger quantity, but less expensively. However, just four table-spoons of solution will coat from 1 to 3 photo-sized pieces of fabric, so don't buy pounds of it. Caution must be taken in the care and storage of these materials, and it is safer to keep only a minimum amount on hand. The specific amount used will be determined in part by the weight of the fabric and the degree of fabric saturation.

Reserve all bottles, bowls, and tools for light-sensitive solutions only. Do not re-use them to feed the cat or to mix paint, and never let them find their way back to the kitchen. A strip of red friction tape will readily identify them as off-limits for other use.

Carefully estimate the amount of solution needed, to avoid having any left over. That eliminates problems of disposal. To dispose of any excess, refer to Disposal in Additional Help. Always clean all work areas with sudsy water after you have finished. Keep materials in a locked cupboard where children have no access to them. Do not allow small children in your work area.

Safe-box for mixing chemicals

## Safe-box

To assure the safe handling of dry chemicals, you may prefer to work in a safe-box similar to one used in medical labs. This consists of an empty cardboard or wooden box with holes at each side into which your hands (wearing rubber gloves) can be inserted. The top of the box is covered with a transparent wrap or glass, taped at all edges. The bottom of the box can be partially cut out so that you can set the box over your jars of chemicals, or you can set the jars inside, and then cover the top. Use paper on the bottom of the box. The safe-box protects your work from breezes (or sneezes), important since you must avoid breathing the powders. Work outdoors or in a well-ventilated area. Reach into the box to do all mixing of the dry chemicals, and remove the solutions after they are mixed. While the solution must still be handled with care (and rubber gloves), the greatest hazard is from the dry chemicals. Be careful also in handling the gloves later!

More elaborate scientific safe-boxes have long protective gloves attached at the hand holes. You put the gloves on by reaching into the box, and they are never removed from the interior work area. Staple your own long rubber gloves in place and you'll have a similar set-up. I made a simple but workable safe-box out of a cardboard carton with plastic wrap over the top, two hand-holes and a doorway cut in one end, so the jars could be set inside. All jars are recapped before I remove them from the box.

## Negatives →

The print you make will be the same size as the negative you use. If you want a larger print, you'll need a larger negative. Negatives can be made from any positive transparency (slide), photograph, print, or tintype. Check with blueprinters and photo labs in your area, as prices vary considerably. If you already have negatives, make a test print. Those with strong contrast give the clearest images on fabric. Order negatives only if you need to increase the contrast or size; most of the time you will be able to work with the negatives you already have. If you do order, get halftone negatives, which will result in sharper images in your prints. If the halftone negatives are not clear enough, you will need to get high-contrast screened negatives or Kodaliths →, which eliminate gray areas and reduce patterns to black or clear. Store all your negatives carefully to avoid scratching the surface, and they can be used over and over.

## Transparencies →

Used for all methods of light-sensitive printing, the transparency is an acetate sheet to which opaque paper cut-outs, transfer letters, permanent markers, etc. may be applied. See Transparencies in Additional Help.

## Block-outs →

Any designs or objects which are opaque enough to prevent the passage of light may be used in light-sensitive exposures. See Block-outs in Additional Help.

## Drawings and Words

A drawing can be copied onto a transparency, but the lines must be opaque enough to inhibit light. If the lines become too sketchy or light, make a photocopy and re-draw them with heavier, darker lines, or adjust the copier for a darker print. Copy machines vary, so shop around to find one that gives good prints.

To print words with any of the light-sensitive print methods, you will need to have a block-out of opaque letters. These can be used either on a transparency or directly on fabric. The copy on transparency works most effectively, but you can also apply self-adhesive letters directly to acetate or glass. Even marking-pen letters on plastic bags will work, but it's more difficult to manage a flexible surface than a more rigid sheet. Placed directly on fabric, cut-outs are arranged and glass goes over the top for exposure. If you have only a few cut-outs, you can do this. If the number of letters is extensive, it will require too much time to arrange them; it would be better to have them already stuck to glass or copied on a transparency. Letters can be made from any opaque material, placed directly on the fabric and under the glass, and exposed. In this way, lettering can be printed in conjunction with negatives. Chapter 10 is packed with additional ideas.

To embellish a photo with added lines or drawings, first place your photo negative on a sheet of white paper or over a light table, so you can see the image. Then place a transparency over the negative and add your drawing to it. In this way you could inset a halo over your own head, or sketch smoke coming out of your brother's ears, without damaging your negative. You could superimpose a map of your hometown over a photograph of the family home, or add frames, shooting stars, pointing hands, or arrows. The two transparencies (the negative plus your drawing) are stacked and exposed simultaneously. By removing the drawing transparency with the drawing part-way through the exposure time, you could give it a shadowy effect.

## Contact Prints

Objects can be placed in contact with the sensitized fabric to make a photogram. The flatter the object, the better it eliminates the light and the clearer the print will be. A leaf, therefore, works well if it is as flat as paper. But a pine cone will give a sharp image only in the small areas of contact, with fuzzy images where light slips under the edges. Shadows can be used effectively, but they require

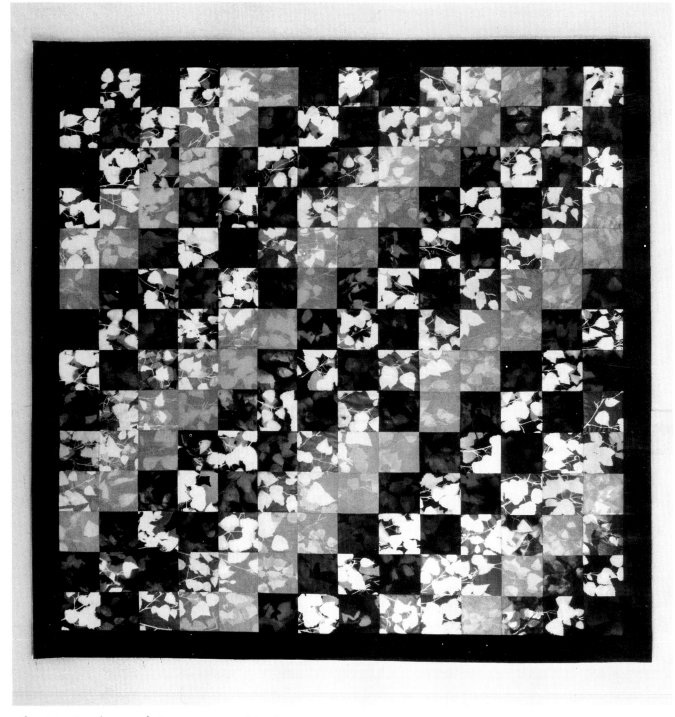

Plate 8-1: *"Sea of Leaves" by Berry Ferguson, 64" x 64".*
*Sunlight appears to filter through the leaves in this arboreal quilt. Cyanotypes were developed to*
*varying intensities of blue, then cut up, assembled, and quilted.*

some experimentation. A rubber ball will block light only in the small area of contact, but the shadow will make a light print. Paper cut-outs, ferns, silverware and scissors, objects of all kinds can be used. If they will cast a shadow, you can usually get a print. If you are printing your great-grandmother's photograph, consider including a print of her gloves, a pressed rose, or her comb. Tools of trades and hobbies can enhance the personal character of a piece. A stethoscope, calipers, eyeglasses, or pocket knife may convey a more complete portrait than the photograph alone.

At times you will prefer not to use the contact frame. When objects are not pressed flat, gradations of blues are printed. A branch of leaves, for example, will let some light pass where leaves are slightly curved (Plate 8-1). Occasionally, a breeze will move your block-out. That gives you double prints, usually with one darker than the other. This can be used to advantage, and you may want to move objects deliberately during exposure.

## Textures

Along with drawings, letters, and three-dimensional objects, textures add pattern and variety in light-sensitive exposures. They can serve as a unifying element in a series of unrelated objects. Metal or plasticized screens of various sizes produce linear checks. Dotted nets add delicate patterns. Scattering rice, confetti, spaghetti, or dried peas directly on fabric adds overall texture or pattern to your design. Try pennies or dimes, ribbons, lace, strings, weeds, and seeds. Those which can be easily manipulated, like strings, can be used to create simple drawings. If all this is too undisciplined for your usual way of working, place objects on a copier to print textures, then make transparencies of them. Use the transparencies over negatives or other block-outs.

## Ultraviolet light

All contact exposures with light-sensitive methods require ultraviolet light, and sunshine provides the best source. Choose a clear, sunny day for printing; should it cloud over as you are working, additional time will be required for exposure. I have made prints on misty, rainy days by exposing the fabric in a covered walkway for a longer time, but the results are more predictable and colors are brighter with sunlight.

If incessant rains interfere with your printing, use a sunlamp (GE sunlamp uv).The light source must be at a distance sufficient to give an overall even exposure and to avoid hot spots. A general rule for this distance is 1½ times the diagonal measurement of your print area. Never use a carbon arc light as your light source.

## Fabric

Each light-sensitive method is best suited to specific fabrics. Check individual directions and the Techniques Chart on pages 10-11. Cut fabrics to size, 1" to 2" larger than your negatives or transparencies but not larger than the glass on which you will paint them.

To expose larger fabric pieces, select objects that won't move, or pin everything in place, or incorporate planned movement (blurred or shadow-like images) in the design.

## Sensitizing the Fabric

1. To prepare the fabric for exposure ↘, you must make it light-sensitive. Wear rubber gloves and work in a darkened room with a safe-light →.
2. Mix the sensitizing ingredients according to the instructions. Read carefully and note all precautions.
3. Combine the sensitizers into a single solution, according to directions.
4. Smooth the fabric onto a sheet of glass and paint the fabric with the chemical solution.
5. If you are sensitizing only one piece of fabric, let it dry on the glass. For several, carefully lift the painted fabric by the corners and hang it to dry, keeping the painted surface towards you. Repeat for several pieces of fabric. The fabric is now light-sensitive. Let no unnecessary light reach it.
6. Now wash your hands thoroughly (also wash the gloves), and go have a cup of coffee. Or several cups. You could even go out and buy a pound of coffee beans, as it will take the fabric a while to dry. Warm air and a fan will speed up the drying.

## Exposure — The Contact Print

Stack the contact frame → (wood, foam, black cloth, sensitized fabric). Place the design (transparency, negative, natural forms, or whatever you are using) on top of the fabric. When using a photo negative, place it on the fabric with its shiny side up (so it looks "right"). Place a sheet of clean glass over the top (not the one you painted on, as it'll have sensitizer on it). This makes a sandwich.

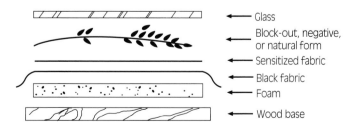

Glass

Block-out, negative, or natural form

Sensitized fabric

Black fabric

Foam

Wood base

The glass holds the layers flat, assuring good contact. The sun's heat may curl a transparency, ruining an exposure. Glass holds in place any lightweight leaves, feathers, lace, or paper cut-outs which might otherwise shift or disappear entirely with a slight breeze. On a perfectly still day, pebbles or leaves placed on the fabric would stay put without the glass.

If you wish to print images of pebbles on a breezy day, they must then go on top of the glass, removing them a fraction of an inch from the fabric surface. This will not produce as sharp a line as when the pebbles (or block-out design or object) are in direct contact with the fabric. Pins or tape can be used to secure the edges of the fabric so that a three-dimensional object can be placed directly on it without glass. Use a sun lamp and you won't have to contend with the breezes. Best of all, find a protected area where you can enjoy direct sunlight without breeze.

Once the materials sandwich is ready, place it out in direct bright sunlight for about 10 minutes. The length of exposure will vary with the time of day, time of year, clarity of the air, and the process used, ranging from 2 to 30 minutes. With practice you will get a feel for the right timing. The changing color of the fabric is your best guide. If you are using a sun lamp, allow 30 to 40 minutes exposure time. When the exposure is complete, remove the fabric from sunlight and rinse in running water for up to ten minutes, until the rinse water is clear. Heavier fabrics will take longer. Hang the fabric to dry. The dried print can then be ironed.

### Oversize Pieces

An alternative method, which works well for larger shapes, is to place the wet fabric out for exposure. This means that a glass cannot be used over the top, as moisture will condense and interfere with exposure. The wet method solves the difficulty of drying large pieces of fabric. Use a large, smooth surface under the fabric, such as foam core or a foil-covered board. For garments, the pattern parts can be cut and exposed individually before assembly. Consider making large panels in sections. Barbara Hewitt, for large pieces, uses 4' x 8' insulated board covered with foil and then butcher paper.

Blueprinting a T-shirt is not a project for the beginner, who will be better off to purchase a pre-treated shirt or to make smaller prints which can be sewn on to a shirt. If you must try it, however, stretch the sensitized fabric over a rigid surface (foam core or covered cardboard) and expose one side. Then turn it over and expose the second side before rinsing.

### Colorfastness and Care

It is important to test your prints for colorfastness. Many variables in the process (the age and proportions of the solution, degree of saturation, fiber or fabric content and treatments, and the amount of light that penetrated during drying) will affect permanence in washing. Always hand wash cyanotypes and Van Dyke prints. Use only a teaspoon of a mild washing product per gallon of cool water. Too much soap, or soap poured directly on the print, will cause fading. Never use any product that contains phosphates or bleaching agents (chlorine, borax, or soda): these products will cause the brilliant blues to turn yellowish. While manufacturers state that the prints are washable, some artists maintain that color brilliance is lost in washing, and they limit their work to wallhangings or panels. Others claim to have had excellent permanence. It is because of these variables in the process that the test prints are important.

Light-sensitive prints are safe for dry cleaning. Constant exposure to bright sunlight may fade the images, but they'll revive if returned to the dark for a resting period. Blueprints may be rejuvenated by exposure to moisture: hang them in a steamy bathroom, or give them a dipping in tea.

## CYANOTYPE

Cyanotype (Greek for blueprinting) takes its name from the color of the finished prints. The color can range from a light blue-green to deep blue. The process is similar to blueprint on paper: a piece of fabric, saturated with chemicals to make it light-sensitive, is exposed to ultraviolet light. Areas protected from contact with the sun retain the original fabric color, while exposed areas develop to blue. Cyanotype works best on natural PFP fabrics →: cotton, linen, or silk. Betty Ferguson likes chintz (for a faded, soft image) as well as cotton sateen and sheeting. Flannel gives soft, rich detail and a deep blue. Muslin, with its yellowish cast, turns prints greenish. Barbara Hewitt likes silk, which works beautifully.

## Ready-to-go Blueprint

Pre-treated fabrics, available in squares (great for quilt blocks) or in yardage, offer a great way to get acquainted with this process. Along with blue, fabric treated to produce a magenta or turquoise background is also available. (Yes, like green oranges, we now have magenta blueprints.) Commercially available pre-treated materials preclude the mixing of toxic chemicals and simplify the process, especially for the beginner (see Blueprint fabric ✹). Once you have become familiar with the blueprinting process, you can better determine your need to purchase chemicals. To expose pre-treated fabrics, follow the directions given earlier for all light-sensitive prints, as well as instructions which come with the fabrics. Remove fabrics from their light-fast packets only in a darkened area when you are ready to expose them.

## Preparing Your Own Blueprint

Re-read the section on Sensitizers in the General Directions and read Hazardous Materials → in the Additional Help. Note all precautions. While cyanotype is considered to be only "slightly toxic," it is important to wear rubber gloves and a face mask. You may wish to cut the recipe in half for a trial run. Prepare the following in the safe-box:

Mixture A: Dissolve: 2 ounces (60 grams) of ferric ammonium citrate in

- 8 ounces (1 cup or 250 ml) of distilled water, using a small glass bowl and a plastic mixing spoon.

Mixture B: Dissolve: 1 ounce (30 grams) of potassium ferricyanide in

- 8 ounces (1 cup or 250 ml) of distilled water, using a second small glass bowl and plastic mixing spoon.

Solution C (in a darkroom): Combine:

- Mixtures A and B. The solution is now light-sensitive.

Mixtures A and B should be kept in separate amber or brown bottles, to be mixed together in equal amounts just before using. If you turn really enthusiastic and make cyanotype prints frequently, one artist suggests that you keep adding to the same mixture: store any leftover solution in a brown bottle in a dark place. The next time you print, add equal additional amounts of mixtures A and B

to the remaining solution C . Other artists recommend using the solution within six hours. Obviously, there is some flexibility there! Stored separately, the mixed chemicals have a shelf life up to six months. (Dry chemicals can be kept indefinitely.)

In the darkroom, paint your fabric directly from the bowl in which the solution is mixed. Half of the recipe, a total of one cup, is ample for many cyanotype prints. The exact amount will depend upon fabric weight and saturation.

When the fabric is dry, place it over the contact frame with the block-out and glass on top, as described earlier. Put the stack in direct bright sunlight. The exposure time will vary from 10 to 30 minutes. When the material turns a charcoal blue, remove it from the sunlight and rinse it thoroughly in running water until the rinse water is clear. Then hang the fabric out of direct sunlight. When dry, it can be pressed.

A fixing bath is recommended by some blueprinters, but others advise skipping that process and avoiding the handling of another chemical. They report no adverse effects on prints. Obviously there is little general agreement as to whether or not the fixing bath is important to permanence and color retention and it is probably related to some unspecified variable. I prefer to avoid it, since I have not found it to be necessary, and it's one more chemical.

Clean all work surfaces with hot, soapy water. Wash and dry the rubber gloves. Store all materials as directed. Discard any leftover chemical mixtures following manufacturer's recommendations and read Disposal in Additional Help. Label any unused chemicals clearly and keep them away from heat and light in a locked cupboard.

## Brown Cast

To alter cyanotype to brown, or to rescue one that has turned yellow or is an uneven blue, dip the print into any of several common household mixtures. The new color will never be more intense than the blue. The following recipe was suggested by Barbara Hewitt:

1. Dissolve 1 tablespoon of soap (containing phosphate) in 1 cup of very hot water, or use 1 tablespoon of trisodium phosphate (TSP from the hardware store).
2. Add cold water to make the temperature comfortable. This is enough for 1 or 2 small pieces of fabric. Save any excess for later use.

*Plate 8-2: Detail of "Sea of Leaves" by Betty Ferguson.*

*Complex patterns were created by overlays of color, achieved in part by making changes part-way through the exposure. After part of the exposure time had elapsed, some leaves were removed and others were added, creating the many shadings.*

*Plate 8-3: Detail of "B.W. & Co. on Pratt Rd." by Tafi Brown.*

*A cyanotype image, printed with its mirror image, creates a familiar yet unsettling new image. Prints are pieced into rows with horizontal bands of patterned fabric.*

3. Soak the cyanotype until blue fades to yellow. You will still be able to see the image. Rinse under tap water.

4. Drop 2 bags of Lipton's Tea (orange pekoe and pekoe-cut black) into 1 cup of boiling water. Steep for 10 minutes to extract the tannic acid, then remove the tea bags. Add cool water.

5. Pour tea liquid into a flat container (a glass cake pan works well) and place the yellow print face side down. Soak for at least 30 minutes.

6. Yellow areas will turn brown. If the contrast is not strong enough, repeat the tea bath with a stronger solution.

7. Rinse well. Hang the fabric to dry. Solutions can be re-used several times.

8. Wash by hand. The color will not run or bleed, but may fade slightly. Press.

## Violet Cast

Betsy Benjamin-Murray suggests that you soak the blueprint in a cold borax solution for a violet cast. She creates a brown tone by using a saturated solution of sodium bicarbonate and tannic acid in equal amounts, soaking fabric in the mixture to the desired color.

The cyanotype prints can be dry cleaned, but they may lose color when laundered. When exposed to sunlight or continuous daylight, the colors will lighten. Giving them a rest in the dark restores some of the color.

Blueprinting must be a compelling pursuit. Once involved in it, some fiber artists never stray. Among those is Betty Ferguson, who has been teaching and exhibiting her cyanotype work for years. In Plate 8-2 her "Sea of Leaves" uses dozens of cyanotype prints in varying intensities. The sense of scattered light through leafy patterns is deftly combined with a traditional pieced pattern. You can see the overprinting and quilting.

Tafi Brown's cyanotypes are uniquely identifiable. Plate 8-3 and Color Plate 78 show the wonderful rhythmic mirror-image pattern we often associate with her. She photographs her subjects, then carefully selects which images to work with. In "B.W. & Co. on Pratt Rd.," mirrored images intertwine and contrast with the feathery softness of natural forms. In "May Flowers," Plate 8-4, Tafi made photograms → directly from the flowers, so that delicate transparencies are captured on the fabric.

Along with teaching and creating her own work, Barbara Hewitt has Blueprints-Printables, a company which

Plate 8-4: "May Flowers" by Tafi Brown, 47" x 47".
Leaves, fiddlehead ferns, and translucent wildflowers are sun-printed for this quilt which captures the fragile delicacy of blossoms and buds.

Plate 8-5: Dress by Barbara Hewitt, 42" long.
Grasses and weeds, along with transparencies of sea life, were used to blueprint this underwater scene. To complete her visual comment on how we treat the water, Barbara added the can of sardines, sinking to the bottom.

supplies ready-for-exposure fabrics as well as garments for printing (PFP). The sea life in her dress, Plate 8-5, was exposed from transparencies. For the sardines she used a halftone negative and made a visual pun on the fish at the bottom of the sea (as well as a comment on pollution).

In Plate 8-6, Barbara made an environmental statement about water use. An architectural structure at a major reservoir, the Hetch Hetchy Water Temple, is printed beside a map of the San Francisco water district. Also included in the panel are the flooded valley and schematic drawings of the pipes used to carry the water. Overlaid on both is the meandering pattern of evergreen. Because of its large scale, Barbara secures her work with pins in preference to using the glass in a contact frame. Both fabric and block-outs are pinned to the large panels described earlier before she takes them into the sunshine for exposure.

The samples in Plate 8-7 illustrate different kinds of block-outs. Clockwise from upper right, a drawing copied onto a transparency makes a reversal (not of direction, but

a dark/light reversal). The resulting print is sharp and clean. Next, the use of a natural form, followed by a photographic negative, then a transparency from an ink sketch.

In Color Plate 86 Betty Ferguson has blueprinted from an old negative, showing the clarity achieved with this process. At times, however, she prefers less distinct lines, as seen in Plate 8-8. Sunlight eased under the tips of curled leaves, and only where stacked leaves kept the sensitized fabric free from exposure is the print really white. A few leaves appear to have moved slightly in the breeze, making multiple prints. In Color Plate 85 of "Blue Storm," she printed the leafy images, then used the prints like fabric, cutting them into patterns of dark and light so that the leaf pattern is elusive.

A panel to commemorate the birth of a child is shown in Plate 8-9. Barbara Hewitt used old family photographs and combined them with baby's breath and an inscription from the birth announcement in this variation on a family tree.

Plate 8-6: Panel detail by Barbara Hewitt.
The Hetch Hetchy Water Temple was blueprinted along with a map of the San Francisco water district in this environmental statement about water use. Partially overlaying the negatives is a trailing branch of evergreen.

Plate 8-7: Test panel by Jean Ray Laury.
Blueprints show different kinds of block-out. The cat drawing was copied onto a transparency, so black lines (resisting sunlight) remain white, creating a reversal of the image. Another photogram of leaves is also a reversal. The portrait was exposed from a photo negative, and the eagle from a transparency copy.

Nancy Halpern hand-picked the maple leaves she blueprinted for her lively "Maple Leaf Rag," Color Plate 88. Her leaves, some double-printed, are combined with pieced maple-leaf quilt blocks as well as bars and bands of patterned fabrics. See the detail in Color Plate 87.

In her handmade book shown in Color Plate 83, fiber artist Holley Junker utilizes cyanotype and copy transfer to recreate some ancestors. On the opposite page is a mirror-image outline of the women in embroidery.

## VAN DYKE OR BROWNPRINTING

Except for the startling difference in color, the Van Dyke process and appearance are similar to cyanotype. It produces a print from deep rich brown to a light pale brown. The natural color gives a special added depth to portraits.

Follow the procedures for cyanotype. One manufacturer recommends mixing chemicals in a sink, but you can also use the safe-box. In addition to adequate ventilation,

a face mask or goggles, and rubber gloves, are a must. Pre-measured chemicals are available which must be mixed into solutions, but their use avoids handling and weighing. Avoid skin contact and inhalation and be particularly careful of your eyes. The resulting prints from this process are stunning and will be worth all the care which must be taken. Read the Hazards section in Additional Help, as well as all instructions and precautions. Mixtures 1 and 3 must be used with special care, as both are toxic and can cause burns.

The formulas vary slightly from one company to another. Follow directions which come with the chemicals you buy. Some companies (Rockland, for example) sell chemicals already in solution. If you purchase the chemicals separately, use the following recipe. You will need separate containers for mixtures 1, 2, and 3. They are not light-sensitive until combined.

Mixture 1: Dissolve 3 ounces (90 grams) of ferric ammonium citrate (green) in

- 8 ounces (1 cup or 250 ml.) of distilled water in a brown bottle. ☛

Mixture 2: Dissolve ½ ounce (15 grams) of tartaric acid in

- 8 ounces (1 cup or 250 ml.) of distilled water in a brown bottle.

Mixture 3: Dissolve 1¼ ounces (37½ grams) of silver nitrate ☛ in

- 8 ounces (1 cup or 250 ml.) of distilled water in a brown bottle.

Solution 4: Add mixture 2 to mixture 1, stirring well.

- Slowly add an equal amount of mixture 3, stirring continuously.

The final solution will be 1 part each of mixtures 1, 2, and 3. Try to estimate the amount you will need, to avoid having leftover chemicals.

The exposure process is identical to cyanotype, but the exposure time is much shorter. In full sunlight, 2 minutes may be adequate. Rinse up to 10 minutes. The final step, which turns the image brown, is a rinse in the hypo clearing agent.

While the fabric is rinsing, mix the following:

- dissolve 1 ounce of sodium thiosulfate in 20 ounces of water.

Dip the rinsed print in the hypo clearing agent for 15 seconds. When it turns brown, rinse in clear water for 15 to 20 minutes. Dry away from bright light. When dry, it may be ironed. Dispose of leftover chemicals by washing them down a drain with copious amounts of water. Never dispose of the chemicals in a wastebasket!

Photographer Helen Nestor made a "Family Tree Quilt" using Van Dyke prints of family members. The brown sepiatone seems especially appropriate for the old photographs. Helen has developed her own method of adding permanence to her Van Dyke prints. She uses a gold toning wash (available at some photographic suppliers) and dips the finished Van Dyke print into the wash. This suffuses it in rich color and extends the life of the print. She here used halftone negatives to expose the fabric, then added appliqué and quilting. See Color Plate 84.

Holley Junker's *Circumambulation* book in Color Plate 82 uses a combination of Van Dyke print and photo transfer (with solvent). The lettering in this silk book is

Plate 8-8: *Branches by Betty Ferguson.*

*Cyanotype of branches with leaves shows a gradation of color: white indicates where little or no sun came through, while the grays, at the curled tips of the leaves, indicate some exposure. Dark areas were fully exposed.*

Plate 8-9: *Detail of "New Baby" by Barbara Hewitt.*

*This is from a silk panel which depicts baby's breath, along with photos of the new baby and the family that welcomed it. Vital statistics are printed in the center of the panel of this announcement quilt.*

rubber-stamped. In another of her books, Holley has used both fabric and paper. Color Plate 81 shows a page from *Precocity*, one of a series of delightfully satiric books about perfect parenting and perfect children.

## KWIK-PRINT

Kwik-print's advantage is its availability in a variety of colors that can be intermixed to get a full range. Several colors can be painted onto a piece of fabric at one time in a marbled, mottled, blended, or striped effect. It works best on synthetic fibers, especially acetate and polyesters. While it will print on cotton, silk, rayon, or blends, it may leave a slight residue of color in the light areas after rinsing. An advantage of Kwik-print is that it is unnecessary to mix any chemicals. The pre-mixed emulsion consists of a light-sensitive solution in which colored pigments are held in suspension. Its primary disadvantage is its cost, which is greater than that for other light-sensitive methods. Follow all directions and precautions. The light-sensitive solution is toxic and must be handled carefully. ☛

Follow the procedures given for cyanotype. Wear rubber gloves, observe all precautions, and read all the information that accompanies the materials you buy. Read about Hazardous Materials in Additional Help. Since Kwik-print is available in liquid form, no measuring or mixing of dry ingredients is required. Even so, no food or drink and no children in the work area.

Have fabrics well-pressed and prepare them for exposure in a darkroom. Brush the Kwik-print solution first in one direction, then at right angles to give thorough coverage. The color of the solution is identical to what the print color will be.

Exposure is faster than with cyanotype. Here is a general guide:

Bright sunny day: 2 to 3 minutes
Gloomy day: up to 20 minutes
Sunlamp (at 14" to 15"): 8 to 15 minutes

Exposure time varies from one color to another, and may also depend upon the density of the negative. A test piece is recommended.

After exposure, rinse in cool water. Unexposed water-soluble chemicals will wash out and the image will begin to emerge. Add a few drops of liquid detergent to the surface to hasten removal of undeveloped pigment.

Finally, rinse in hot water.

Fixing solution:
- Mix $\frac{1}{2}$ ounce of 28% ammonia in 1 gallon of hot water.
- Rinse the print in the mixture to fix it. Then rinse in clear water and iron dry. The finished Kwik-print can be washed or dry-cleaned without affecting the printed image. It is colorfast and fade-resitant.

The assemblages of Erma Martin Yost juxtapose quilt patches with drawings, fetishes, and light-sensitive prints in panels of ceremonial impact and remarkable beauty. Working with diverse influences as well as wide-ranging methods, she brings all into a harmonious focus. In "Origins," Color Plate 89, fabrics printed with cyanotype and Kwik-print form a backdrop for linear patterns of hand painting, quilting, and machine embroidery. She adds pattern and line with acrylic and metallic paints, iridescent pigments, fabric pastels, and markers. "Cumulus 2," Color Plate 91, and the detail in Color Plate 90, use all of these methods with Inko prints as well. Pictographs from ancient cave walls are made permanent on fabric in both positive and negative form, made from Kodaliths. The complexity of patterns contributes a rich surface, further embellished with stitching and objects.

## INKO PRINT

Since this is available in liquid form, no measuring or mixing of dry ingredients is necessary. However, care must be taken in handling the dyes. Observe all precautions and read all manufacturer's warnings. Wear rubber gloves and allow no food, drink, or children in the work area. Read Hazardous Materials in Additional Help.

Inko print is similar to Kwik-print in that a wide range of colors is available. It is a light-sensitive process in which color develops as it is exposed to ultraviolet light (or, with Inkodye, to heat). These vat dyes work best on pre-washed natural fabrics: cotton, linen, and rayon. Inkodyes are light-sensitive and suitable for contact printing. They should be handled in a darkroom or in subdued light, and they come in brown bottles for storage. The shelf life is up to two years. To make Inko prints:

Working under subdued light or in a darkroom, paint the Inkodyes onto fabric, following the directions given for cyanotype. Wear rubber gloves and observe all the precautions. Dry the fabric in a darkroom.

Exposure time varies from color to color:

| Bright sunlight | 10 minutes |
| --- | --- |
| sunlamp (14" to 15" away) | 25 minutes |

Sunlight will give deeper and more brilliant colors.

After exposure, rinse in cold, soapy water until no further color rinses out. Dry on a flat surface. Iron on the reverse side of the print. Color will darken as it is ironed, and the dye will fume. Iron until all fuming ceases. The vapor given off during fuming is non-toxic, but it is sometimes irritating to the mucous membrane. Good ventilation and a face mask help, but ironing outdoors is best.

There will be some residue in the light areas, which varies from color to color. A white fabric, painted red, will have a reddish tinge in all the unexposed areas. Some color develops even without exposure to sunlight. If this seems unsatisfactory to you, switch to one of the other light-sensitive methods.

The wide range of colors available makes this a versatile process. As with Kwik-print, you may paint several colors onto a fabric at one time. Inkodye is permanent to any kind of washing or cleaning. I once tried removing an Inkodye print by soaking it in a strong bleach solution, and the color never budged!

In Color Plates 89, 90, and 91, Erma Martin Yost combines Inko prints with myriad other techniques. Identifying them is a little like trying to catch the flavor of the eggs in a cake. The prints are so totally integrated that there is little sense of particular techniques in various parts.

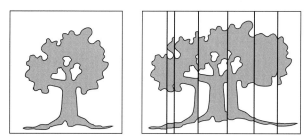

Using several prints of one image, reassemble a new design from strips. Or cut strips from several prints of one image and reassemble.

## LIGHT-SENSITIVE VARIATIONS

Making photographic prints offers a way to record and document on fabric. The process itself is intriguing; it is essentially another tool with which you can work. What you do with the prints is what is most important. To begin playing with your prints, consider breaking up the printed images. Cut them into strips or squares and reassemble them. Using several prints of one image, join them to stretch the images, elongating or shortening them. Alternate slices of identical prints in different colors. Play with them and re-create them. Coloring or tinting prints → adds a variety of hand-painted hues to single-color prints and opens a Pandora's box of possibilities. Print your images on patterned fabrics, on polka dots or on stripes.

All light-sensitive prints offer ways of making special and personal fabrics, each one-of-a-kind. What you do with that fabric is as exciting as producing it. Sometimes using an unusual fabric in a very conventional way offers startling results. Using an unusual fabric in a very UNconventional way may be even more exciting!.

# Stamp Printing and Embossing

Stamp printing is used effectively in grade B movies to show bloody handprints on white walls. Driver's license fingerprinting or birth certificate footprints are stamp processes with which we're all familiar. Jelly-covered toast, dropped face down on the floor, transfers color and shape in the same way that muddy feet leave their imprints. Stamp printing is a simple, basic concept which can be used on fabric in a hundred inventive and personal ways. This chapter includes:

I. Stamp Printing

II. Embossing

If you grew up next door to Terri Johnson, it hardly matters that now her business card says "Theresa," and she's very dignified. In your mind, she's still Terri. Our first impressions and old habits die hard. She'll always be Terri, and stamps will always be "rubber stamps" to us, even though they are laser-cut on plastic (like silk-screen frames made of polyester).

## I. STAMP PRINTING

Stamping on fabric requires the following:

- Stamps ↘
- Stamp pad ↘
- Inks ↘
- PFP fabric →
- Iron for heat setting →
- Optional: brayer → and brush

The process:

1. Coat the stamp with paint or ink — by means of a pad, a brush, or a brayer.
2. Press the wet stamp onto fabric, using some pressure.
3. Lift the stamp carefully, and let the fabric dry.
4. Heat set → the fabric, if necessary

Anything that can pick up and transfer a layer of ink can be used as a stamp. Your fingertips are a great starter. (You've already done lots of those!) While great commercial stamps abound, you'll also want to make your own, which is at least half the fun.

### A. Making Your Own Stamps

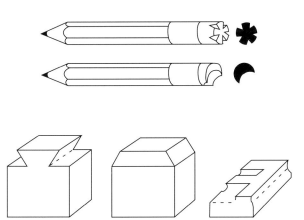

Undercut, on left, is likely to crumble more than the stamps on its right.

#### 1. ERASER STAMPS

The eraser end of a pencil makes a perfect small stamp for polka dots or tiny designs. Cut stars, moons, squares, or half-circles from them. I've seen these little erasers carved into hexagons for miniature Grandmother's Flower Gardens and squares for Triple Irish Chains. For larger stamps, many designers particularly like the Staedtler Mars Plastic Grand erasers or Staedtler's carving block, about 3" x 4". Among other favorites are Rubkleen, Magic Rub, and artgum erasers. Any white vinyl eraser works well. Pink Pearl erasers carve well, and a very large eraser (for big mistakes, apparently) is available. (It's considered a novelty item, so it's more likely to be found in an airport gift shop than at a

Plate 9-1: Detail of"Nosegays" by Jean Ray Laury.
*Artgum eraser stamps of the flower and leaf were printed into bouquets, then pieced and quilted.*

Plate 9-2: Stamps by Nancy Clemmensen.
*A snake stamp, 3" long, carved from a Pink Pearl eraser, and a star from Fun Foam are easily made and printed on fabric.*

stationers). Artgum erasers are easily carved and work well for simple shapes. They have a tendency to crumble, so they work less well for detailed designs.

The "Nosegays" quilt in Plate 9-1 is made from artgum eraser stamps. I carved square erasers, one for the flowers and two for the leaves. I used a long eraser on edge for the stems. Since stamp designs are limited in size, stamping in clusters makes large-scale designs possible. After stamping, I cut the squares, then pieced, assembled, and quilted them as shown in Color Plate 96.

Nancy Clemmensen carved a large Pink Pearl eraser for her snake in Plate 9-2. It and the star, cut from Fun Foam, were glued to foamboard → to make them easier to handle.

Plate 9-3: Tree stamps by Betty Davis.

*Incised designs decorate the upper two Christmas tree stamps, and the third has cut shapes glued to its surface.*

## 2. STICKY-BACK STAMP SHEETS

Thin layers of stamp material with self-adhesive backings are sold as flexible printing plates, available under such names as Sure-Stamp, Flexi-Cut, and Poly Print. They are easily cut with scissors or knife and are available in page-sized sheets. Poly Print is soft enough that a ballpoint pen or pencil can be used to incise details, while Sure-Stamp requires a sharper tool. Fun Foam, while not adhesive, has a good stamping surface and can be glued to

foamboard to make a stamp. Betty Davis cut Sure-Stamp into the tree shapes of Plate 9-3. She glued the trees to wood blocks, then carved the details with wood-cutting tools. One stamp has small shapes glued on top to create a pattern. Nancy Clemmensen's foot stamp in Plate 9-4 was cut from Sure-Stamp and glued to foamboard using Yes glue. Lines were then incised, and the print shows how well the line is transferred in stamping.

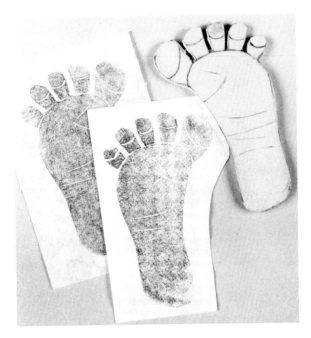

Plate 9-4: Foot stamp by Nancy Clemmensen, 3" x 5½"
The artist stamped her foot (quite literally) using a flexible printing plate which she incised to create a linear design.

Plate 9-5: Tree by Jean Ray Laury, 10" high.
Color is added to this large foamboard stamp with a brayer. The foamboard can be incised to add texture, as on the leaves at top.

In Color Plate 95 you see Karen Felicity Berkenfeld's remarkable work. She develops her intricate patterns through the use of many techniques, among them the use of a pliable Flexi-Cut printing plate. She adheres it to Plexiglas for inking and printing. Using this process, along with stenciling, sponge painting, and linoleum block, she makes up all the fabric from which she creates her vibrantly patterned quilts.

In an alternate process, any sticky-backed cut-out design can be placed (sticky-side down) on a flat surface, such as a table, glass, or masonite panel. It is inked with a brayer, and fabric is laid over the inked design to print it. Light pressure by hand or brayer transfers ink to cloth. Fun Foam is thicker than Sure-Stamp or Poly Print, so unwanted printing of background areas is less likely. A double layer of the stamp material lifts the design further, to help in making clean prints. Fun Foam is most suitable for simple shapes, as details cannot be easily carved.

### 3. FOAMBOARDS

Any kind of foamboard can be used as the stamp material itself, so don't relegate it to being only the base. In Plate 9-5 a tree, cut with a mat knife from foamboard, is stamped on fabric. The paper surface of the foamboard,

Plate 9-6: Foliage stamp by Jamye Donson, 6" x 12".
A collection of leaves cut from Fun Foam was applied to an adhesive foamboard to make this grand stamp. Printed fabric is shown at left.

which picks up the ink, is firmly bonded and doesn't loosen. Leaves are also printed from the board and, at the top, incised lines make a vein pattern.

Jamye Donson used lightweight and easily cut Fun Foam (from hobby or craft shops) for the stamps in Plate 9-6. The design is reminiscent of a feather plume quilting pattern. Each cut shape was placed on sticky-backed foamboard. You can use either a brayer or an improvised stamp pad for inking.

### 4. MODELING CLAY

Modeling clay, Super Sculpey III, or Fimo can be shaped into stamps and baked for permanence, or they can be used as they are. Nancy Clemmensen rolls Sculpey into a smooth, flat piece, bakes it at 275° for 40 minutes, then carves the surface with linoleum-cutting tools. Sanding the baked stamp helps to level the printing surface. Betty Smith's modeling-clay fish in Plate 9-7 was used for printing without baking. It remains softer and can't be sanded, but the incised designs show clearly in the prints. Be sure to read the directions for the medium you are using.

Using a clay gun (Klay Gun by Kemper Tools) to extrude ropes of modeling clay, Jamye Donson drew her designs shown in Plate 9-8. The designs were first run through the b/w copier, placed face-down on a piece of foamboard, and transferred. She used a cotton ball lightly dipped in nail-polish remover or acetone → (read precautions on the acetone container and use out of doors) and wiped it

*Plate 9-7: Fish panel by Betty Davis, 20" x 34".*
*The fish, carved from modeling clay, has incised scales and fins.*

*Plate 9-8: Stamps by Jamye Donson.*
*The designer applied a fine rope of Super Sculpey III to self-adhesive foamboard in order to create the flower stamp at the top. A similar block was made for the prints at the bottom, which were stamped with embossing ink and sprinkled with embossing powder. Color was added with permanent fabric-marking pens.*

over the back of the copy to transfer it to the foamboard, which was then cut just larger than the design. The thin ropes of Sculpey were pressed on the lines. In the upper right, the clay-rope stamp (with parts of the drawing showing through) is shown with a print. At the bottom are finished prints from another clay-rope drawing. All the prints were hand-colored. Placing the newly made rope stamp face down on glass will smooth the printing surface. The transfer method described works especially well for letters or numbers, as the transfer will reverse the image on the stamp. When printed, the final result will read correctly.

### 5. SPONGE FOAMS

Insoles, such as Dr. Scholl's foot pads, make great stamps and are easily cut.

One version comes with tiny air holes that make polka dots when printed. The rabbit in Plate 9-9 was cut from insole and glued to a wood block for printing. Use the rubbery side for printing, the silky side to adhere to a block. The insole holds paint nicely, but if you let it dry out it will be difficult to rinse later.

Thin sponge is also inexpensive and easily cut. Use either a kitchen sponge or a finer textured foam sponge. If you are working with children, it will help to pre-cut the foam sponge to fit a wood block. Then have the children cut designs into the sponge. In Plate 9-10 a sponge block, glued to wood, has been printed on fabric. Vella Draughon carved a cellulose sponge for two calligraphed K's in Plate 9-11. Sponges of different densities produce different effects. She used insole for another letter and erasers for two others.

### 6. INNER TUBE

An inexpensive source of rubber-stamp material is an inner tube. With scissors the rubber cuts like butter, so it's a natural for children. Avoid the raised seam lines (which will transfer), as well as those areas from the inside curve of the tube, which refuse to be flattened. You can get dozens of stamps from one old inner tube. (Well, you can get just as many from a *new* inner tube, but most garages will give you an old one free.) Take a paper grocery bag with you to carry it home. Hose it down thoroughly before bringing it into your work area. A soapy-water wash will then prepare it for cutting. I usually cut a tube up immediately and throw away all unusable parts. Cut the rest into half-page-size pieces which are easy to handle and store. One

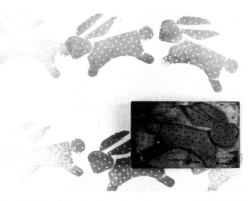

Plate 9-9: *Rabbits by Jean Ray Laury, each about 4" long. Foam insole shapes, glued to wood, produce polka-dot stamps.*

Plate 9-10: *Stamp by Jean Ray Laury, 3" block. A ½" foam pad was cut with scissors and glued to wood, then printed as an overall pattern.*

Plate 9-11: *Stamps by Vella C. Draughon, each about 2" high. These hand-made stamps were used to print the pillow shown in Plate 9-22. They were cut from kitchen sponges, insoles, and erasers.*

Plate 9-12: *Stamp by Jean Ray Laury, 3".*
*An inner tube can be cut with scissors to make a stamp that'll last for years. Here, glued to wood, it adapts to various repeats.*

Plate 9-13: *"House" by Jean Ray Laury, 15" square block.*
*The house and its surrounding checkers were stamp-printed from inner-tube cut-outs glued to wood. The stamps were printed in clusters of four squares alternated with four blanks.*

Plate 9-14: *Detail of "Maple Leaves" by Jan Myers-Newbury.*
*Maple leaves, painted with acrylic, were stamp-printed light-on-dark as well as dark-on-light. Each was hand-pressed to painted fabric.*

tube will suffice for many classes. Stamps from rubber will work best if they are glued to wood.

In Plate 9-12 a small inner-tube stamp is shown, along with prints made from it. Inner-tube stamps were also made for the house and checkerboards in Plate 9-13. Fabrics were printed and then pieced.

### 7. VEGETABLES AND NATURAL FORMS

All that cutting you did on potatoes in the third grade is still a valid way to make a stamp — especially if you like casual, imperfectly printed designs. Carrots, potatoes, and turnips work well, as they are inexpensive, firm, and can be carved. They also have built-in handles. Apples make nice prints (just cut in half), and a cross-section of cabbage is great for texture. Watery fruits or vegetables print less well. A clean, smoothly cut surface is essential for a good print, so use a sharp knife and don't saw at it. Vegetable stamps don't last, but a baggie will keep them usable for hours. Once vegetables begin to dry, they curl, making a good print difficult.

An elegant use of a natural form is seen in Jan Myers-Newbury's maple leaves, Plate 9-14. She painted the veined side of a leaf with various colors, giving the print a mottled, multi-colored autumnal effect. By printing onto hand-painted fabrics, she achieved a complex overall pattern. Where light was printed on dark, the leaves have a photo-graphic quality. She used only a thin layer of acrylic paint, so the fabric remains flexible and easy to sew through. See Color Plate 97.

### 8. FOUND OBJECTS

All kinds of household things can be used for print-ing. Corks are the most obvious: use the round ends as they are, or carve into them. Anything else that will hold some paint can be used. The rims of jar lids, or cookie cutters, will make shapes, though they are rarely ideal, as water-based paints won't stick to metal. Flat rubber bowl scrapers or even jar rings can be used to stamp. The rubber pads used in sinks may have patterns or textures that will transfer. Cut shapes from them, and be sure to try printing both sides. Look around your own kitchen with a beady eye for printing materials.

### 9. PAPER AND CARDBOARD

Even plain old throw-away paper scraps can be used for stamps. In Plate 9-15, both the positive and negative images are printed. At the top the hands are shown stamped

Plate 9-15: "Hands" by Jackie Vermeer, each hand about 9" long.

Paper cut-outs, placed on fabric, were painted with a brayer, which was rolled past the hands in all directions. With papers removed, the silhouetted hands appear in fabric color. At the top, the painted hands were placed paint-side-down and, with a clean brayer, rolled to transfer the paint.

Plate 9-16: "Self Portrait" by Kathy Miller, 12" x 20".

A slide projected onto paper was traced to make a pattern for this huge paper stamp, shown at right. At left is the self-portrait printed from it.

from inked cut-outs →. Use hand pressure on the back of the paper to ensure a good transfer, or cover the stamp with a sheet of paper and roll it with a brayer for a positive print. For the negative print, hands were placed on cloth and an inked brayer was run well past the paper cut-outs. This makes the alternating positive and negative from one paper stamp.

A print made with butcher's-paper stamps is Kathy Miller's self-portrait in Plate 9-16. She projected a slide onto paper, outlined it, traced the features in pencil, and cut out the silhouetted shape. Face, hair, arm, and dress, also cut from paper, were glued to the silhouette, with features added last. The whole paper was inked with a brayer, flipped and pressed onto cloth. The stamp is at right, the printed cloth at left. Each cut and each added layer of paper creates another line. In Plate 9-17 Kathy's portrait of her son was made the same way, using butcher's paper. Raised areas and edges create the most distinct lines.

Plate 9-17: "Portrait of My Son" by Kathy Miller, 19" x 28".

Cut-paper features are glued to a larger cut-paper head, then the entire piece is painted with a brayer and

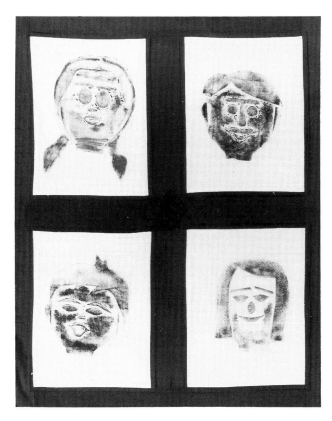

Plate 9-18: *"Friends" by Jackie Vermeer, 24" x 29".*
*Collaged cardboard portrait stamps, printed on fabric, make a*
*quilt full of a child's friends' faces.*

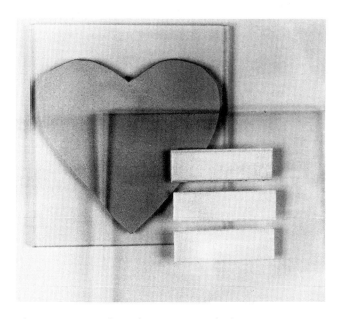

Plate 9-19: *Stamp by Jackie Vermeer, 3" high.*
*Clear plastic makes a great background for hand-made stamps,*
*allowing you to see through for accurate placement.*

Using lightweight cardboard, Jackie Vermeer made a series of portraits of a child's friends, Plate 9-18. Each was made from back-of-the-tablet cardboard, with all hair and features cut out and added. The amount of ink pressed onto the cards with the brayer determines the degree to which color is transferred. In the upper right, for example, a heavier paint layer was used. At lower right, less paint covered only the raised areas.

### 10. HANDLES

Stamps are easier to use if there is a handle or a convenient way to grasp them. The pencil eraser has a built-in handle which makes it fun to use. Put small stamps on spools or wood blocks. Most eraser stamps are thick enough to be be picked up easily. For larger flat shapes, adhere the stamps to foamboard or to clear plastic boxes. In Plate 9-19 the two stamps shown are glued to easy-to-grasp plastic pieces which, because they are transparent, make it easy to align prints. Small wood scraps, often available from cabinetry shops, work great.

### B. Commercial Stamps

#### I. GRAPHIC STAMPS

Thousands of funny and wonderful stamps are available through mail-order catalogues and in stamp shops. The possibilities in working with them are as limitless as any stamper's imagination. Kata Patton's "Love A Cow" vest has stamped cows heading home, as moooo's stretch out to fill the spaces (Plate 9-20). Using permanent black ink on white fabric, she also stamped a few pointing hands (in case we miss the message). The hands are a commercial stamp, and the cow is hand-carved. The vest is hand-quilted.

Danita Rafalovich uses a great variety of graphic stamps, all black on white, in her "It's a Wonderful Life" in Color Plate 93. The very effective use of stamps is enhanced with quilting, which covers the piece. A detail is shown in Color Plate 94. Wendy Lewington Coulter's "A Piece of the Pie" has stamp prints tucked into the pie filling, Color Plate 9.

Plate 9-20: "Love a Cow" by Kata Patton, vest 16"long.
Cows from a hand-carved stamp line up nose to tail around this quilted vest. Pointing hands and letters are commercial stamps.

Plate 9-21: Name tag by Jean Ray Laury, 8" x 18".

A *rubber-stamp portrait was commercially made from a photo, and it is here combined with alphabet stamps. Lettering was outlined with a fine-line permanent marker.*

Deeply etched stamps work best on fabric. Some commercial stamps are cut very shallow, which is fine for paper but less satisfactory on the soft surface of cloth, since fibers may wick the ink into the lines of the design.

You can have rubber stamps made from your own designs. Check the yellow pages for ads and compare prices and sizes. You'll need camera-ready art work, meaning it must look exactly as you want it made, and must be in black and white. Be sure to ask if they can reverse your work, if that's important in your design (otherwise you must do the design backwards to have it print correctly). Photographs, lettering, and drawings can all be laser-cut into a flexible plastic material. Plate 9-21 shows a name tag I made for a quilt conference in Honolulu. The stamp was made from a b/w copier print of a photo, and letters were stamped from a child's alphabet set.

## 2. ALPHABETS

Many commercial alphabet stamps are available, and they range greatly in size, font, and price. Check toy stores, airport gift shops, garage sales, and thrift stores. Some printing companies carry alphabets, and stamp companies usually carry a variety of individual letters and alphabets. Calligraphers enjoy carving their letters from any of a

Plate 9-22: Pillow by Vella C. Draughon, 16" x 16".

A *calligrapher's hand-carved designs were stamped onto hand-painted fabrics, then pieced and quilted.*

Plate 9-23: Monogram by Vella C. Draughon, 1½" square stamp.

*Carved in reverse on a plastic eraser, the calligraphed monogram reads correctly in the print.*

Plate 9-24: "Quilting Witch" by Kata Patton, 36" high.

*The witch Vještca has a stamped face, wristlet, and pin. Commercial alphabet stamps convey messages on her skirts.*

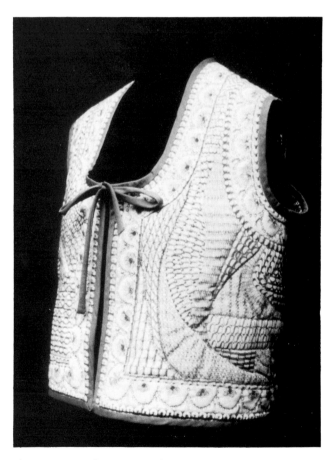

Plate 9-25: Vest by Carol Voulkos, 18" long.

*Letters of the alphabet, used row upon row, create new overall patterns as the O's, X's, or Y's merge.*

variety of erasers which carve easily with an X-Acto knife and retain sharp edges. Vella Draughon's calligraphic pillow in Plate 9-22 utilizes a checkerboard pattern for her stamped motifs. Her stamps are carved from cellulose sponges, insoles, and Staedtler Mars Plastic Grand erasers. To ink the sponge, she adds paint with a beveled foam brush. A piece of wood (or a commercial stamp pad) slightly larger than the sponge is placed on top and even, shortly sustained pressure is applied. One of the carved eraser stamps is shown in detail in Plate 9-23.

Kata Patton's doll, grinning toothily at us in Plate 9-24, wears her various alphabet stamp messages. Her features are also stamp-printed. Carol Voulkos makes extraordinary use of alphabet stamps in her vests, Plate 9-25 and Color Plate 92. She cuts out the pattern parts, stamps with permanent laundry ink, then assembles the vest. Individual letters are aligned and overlapped until they lose their identities and form entirely new patterns. Additional information about alphabets will be found in Chapter 10 .

## C. Stamp Pads

Stamp pads can be purchased or improvised, but all need to absorb and retain ink on a level surface so it can be picked up on a stamp.

### 1. COMMERCIAL STAMP PADS

The commercial pads in lidded tin boxes work fine and retain their moisture well. If you purchase them uninked, you can add your own textile color. Size is often a limitation with purchased stamp pads, though larger sizes are becoming more available. Co-motion stamp pads contain pigments and come in a wide range of colors. Stamp shops are a good source for the uninked pads, and for a wide range of inks.

### 2. IMPROVISED STAMP PADS

An advantage to making your own stamp pads is flexibility of size, which is important if you are also making your own stamps. Changing colors and paints is then a simple matter, and pads in which colors become mixed or which dry out can be tossed away, since improvised pads are inexpensive.

To make a stamp pad, first put down a layer of aluminum foil, a plastic plate, or anything non-porous. A great variety of materials can then be used. Try felt, first wetting it and squeezing it nearly dry. Stack several moist layers,

then brush water-based textile paint onto the pad. Some stampers prefer to add a layer of muslin over the top so that no lint is picked up. Two or three layers of heavy Pellon fleece, or other non-woven material, makes a good pad, and no muslin layer is necessary. Fun Foam has an excellent surface for a pad. Sponges offer a coarser texture but can be used. They tend to stiffen somewhat as they dry. Fashion Stamp Ink Pads (from Tulip Productions) are pre-cut pieces of a light foam-like material which work well. Cover all pads with plastic wrap or a sandwich bag when not in use.

### 3. APPLYING THE INK

Tap the stamp on the inked pad with a slight pressure to assure that all areas of the stamp are inked. With practice it'll be easy. The pad helps to distribute the color evenly, giving the print its characteristic look. Ink can be brushed onto each stamp, but this tends to clog the open areas of a stamp and the prints are not usually as detailed. For larger, hand-made stamps (usually simpler in shape), a beveled foam brush will work. Experimentation will help you determine the right consistency and amount of ink. Felt-tip pens (such as Niji or Marvy markers) can be used directly on the stamps and allow you to change colors for multi-colored prints. Direct coloring is best for small images, as larger areas dry out before the inking is completed.

## D. Inks

You can stamp your fabrics with just about any permanent ink, such as Carter's (purple or black) or Sanford's (black). The bright colored IMPRINTZ and Pelikan inks are permanent and, being thin, they print finer detail than the thicker inks. Transparent inks, however, will not appear bright. Daisy Kingdom has an ink especially made for rubber stamping on fabric, and Tulip has fabric ink and stamp pads in a wide range of colors. Niji's Color Cubes are great for inking hand-made stamps, as they are forgiving of slight differences in level and can accommodate to any size.

You can also use water-based textile paint for stamping. Try the textile paints you have on hand to start with, and branch out from there. Airbrush inks offer intense but thinned color and have a good consistency for stamping. Use a brush to apply textile paint to a moist stamp pad, or pour airbrush ink directly onto a pad. Most textile paints will need some thinning. You will need to experiment to find just the right consistency — thin enough to print easily and heavy enough to show the color. Liquitex is somewhat more opaque than Deka or Versatex, though all work well. Delta Fabric Paints come in handy squeeze bottles, great for inking pads, and they also come in metallic colors. With all textile paints, the stamps will need to be cleaned occasionally, as paint tends to clog the open areas of the stamp.

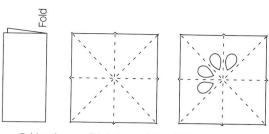

Fold and crease fabric to provide guidelines for stamps

## E. Fabrics

Smooth, shiny fabrics (satin, chintz, polished cotton) give clearer impressions that coarser fabrics, with muslin being a good middle ground. For permanent prints, your fabric must be free of surface treatments and must withstand the required heat setting. A wall piece which will not require washing offers flexibility in fabric choice. Fabrics which can't withstand the temperature required for 30 seconds of heat setting should be ironed with a paper over the top to the maximum heat that they can tolerate.

Stamps printed on white or light colors will be most vivid. On darker fabrics, the colors show less contrast and brilliance. Inks or thinned textile colors work like dyes, so background colors come through. It's not possible to dye a blue fabric yellow, so the addition of an opaquer or the use of opaque acrylic paint will be necessary to get a light color to print over dark. Opaquers will help cover darks, but they are less satisfactory for printing. Add only the amount of opaquer required for coverage. If you plan to wash your printed fabrics, let them cure for a day or two after heat setting. It will sometimes be necessary to heat set one color before adding another, as when shapes touch or overlap. Press on the reverse side of the fabric, or cover the design with paper.

## F. Printing Your Designs

Small stamps work well in repeat units to produce larger designs, though producing yardage is very time-consuming. To print repeat units or quilt blocks, cut fabric pieces first (with seam allowance at each edge) and stamp directly. Fold the fabric in half both ways, and crease slightly. (If you iron the folds in, you'll want to lightly press them flat again.) Creases will still show without interfering with the stamping. The folds serve as a guide in centering and in printing multiples. For circles, fold fabric in half and press lightly. Fold in the opposite direction and press again. Continue forming wedge shapes in the cloth to serve as a guide.

Then make several stamp prints on paper, cut out the paper images and place them on the fabric to determine your arrangement. The bears in Plate 9-26 were printed this way, using the folds as guidelines. For garments, you will also want to stamp images on paper first. Cut these out and arrange them on the garment parts to determine your final placement and color. Another way to align your design is to cut a window the size of your stamp in a sheet of paper. When you have determined where the print is to go, place the window over that area and place your inked stamp into the window. In Plate 9-27 the pieced diamonds themselves made guidelines for the stamps.

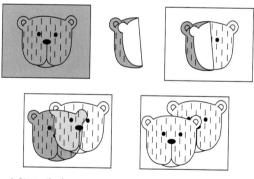

1. Stamp the image on paper.
2. Cut out the image.
3. Stamp the image on cloth and cover it with the paper cut-out.
4. Stamp the second image on cloth, overlapping the paper.
5. Remove paper, and the second image appears behind the first.

The cut-out stamped papers are also valuable in making multiple overlapping images. For example, if you want to see an entire chorus line of yourself, first print one image on paper and cut it out carefully on the lines. Make your first print on fabric, place the cut-out over it and make the second print, which can overlap it. The second image now appears to be behind the first.

Check out what's going on in stamp printing. There are wonderful books and subscription magazines, as well as shops which are a great source of inspiration and information on exhibitions. It's another whole world.

## G. Care and Cleaning

Dried paint on a stamp can interfere with subsequent prints. Always clean stamps with sudsy water immediately after use. A soft-bristle toothbrush will remove any paint that gets caught in crevices. For other than water-based paints, follow the cleaning directions that accompany the inks.

Permanent inks can be cleaned off with water which has a few drops of dishwashing detergent in it, scrubbing lightly if necessary. Once you have printed a stamp on fabric, immediately press the stamp down firmly on a scrap piece of paper or cloth to help remove any excess paint or dye. To prevent their drying out during use, place stamps face down on a moistened pad. If you must run off on an unavoidable errand (picking up the kids at school, or you've run out of coffee), slip the stamps in a baggie and seal it shut. They'll be fine for hours.

It is supposedly better not to store stamps with the printing surface down and in contact with paper. However, alphabet sets usually come in a box with slotted areas to keep the letters in alphabetical order. It'd be chaos to locate individual letters without storing them this way. I have never had any problem storing stamps face down, but I use a piece of clean paper or clear wrap under the letters.

## H. Adding Color

Even though stamp prints are essentially one-color-at-a-time, additional colors can easily be added in a number of ways. Fill in areas with permanent markers, which are fast, colorful, and easy to use. In Plate 9-28, Pele Fleming is shown adding color to stamped fabric for a miniature quilt. To paint over your images, read Coloring or Tinting Prints →. Other chapters describe the use of transfer dyes, crayon transfers, and dye sticks, all great for coloring stamped images. Embellishments with thread add texture as well as color, and French knots are especially effective. Also, dark colors on light fabrics may be cut out and appliquéd to dark materials. Work on a protective sheet of butcher's paper, or anything similar, when adding color. Working on your ironing board is convenient, but invisible bits of color can later be picked up and transferred to other fabrics where you won't necessarily want them.

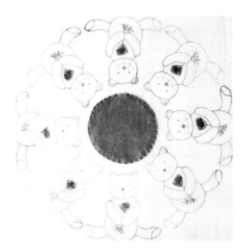

Plate 9-26: *Bears by Jean Ray Laury, 9".*
*Bears stamped in a ring surround an appliquéd circle for a quilt block.*

Plate 9-27: *Quilt block by Jean Ray Laury, 8" square.*
*Printed on the six-pointed star after it was assembled, the stamps form circular patterns.*

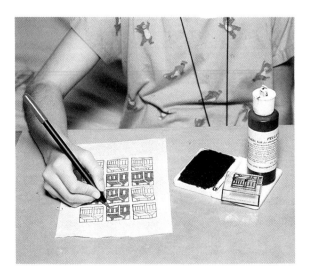

Plate 9-28: *Pele Fleming uses a marking pen over a single-color stamp print for her miniature quilt.*

## II. EMBOSSING

Embossing adds a glossy, relief pattern or sparkle to fabric in much the same way that it does on paper. Its slick finish adds a professional look. In this process, inked images are embossed through the use of a heat-activated powder. The embossing can be done over stamped prints or over prints from copier and printer.

The process is simple. You will need:
- Stamp
- PFP fabric →
- Ink ↘
- Embossing powder ↘ (transparent, opaque or glitter)
- Sheet of paper
- Soft-bristled brush
- Heat source ↘

The process:
a. Fold a clean sheet of paper lengthwise. Open it and, with the folded edge down, place your fabric on top.
b. Print your stamp on fabric, using ink described below.
c. While the ink is still wet, sprinkle with embossing powder.
d. Shake excess powder off onto paper. The fold helps you collect and pour excess powder.
e. Heat the powder to melt and set.

Embossed images are never quite as detailed as the original stamp prints, so the simpler stamp designs are preferable. The best images are made on a smooth fabric, so silk, sateen, and fine weaves work especially well.

### A. Ink

It is important to use an ink that will remain moist while you add the powders, and most ink soaks into the fibers readily. The thicker liquid of glycerin or a Niji ink pad will work well. An advantage of glycerin is that, being clear, no ink color shows through the embossing, but that also makes it more difficult to see your stamped image. Some stamp shops sell glycerin pads as well as small bottles of glycerin for inking your own stamp pad. Color Box pads by Co-motion are especially good for embossing, since they are thick and slow-drying. This company also makes an embossing pen which will stay moist for up to an hour.

### B. Powder

Available in small containers, these powders (granulated nylon) are non-toxic but abrasive, so they can cause irritation in the eyes. The opaque and transparent powders work better on fabric than does the glitter, which tends to wash out. The powder must cover the wet ink thoroughly, and any excess is then shaken onto the folded paper. All flecks, unless removed, will melt into the cloth and become permanent. Tap the back of the cloth and then use a small brush or a piece of masking tape to help remove any excess powder.

### C. Heating

The embossing powders must be heated enough to melt them but must be removed from the heat before they bubble. The process requires careful watching. A high temperature is not necessary, and a lower, steady heat is better. Some designers hold stamped fabrics over a toaster or a light bulb, while others place the fabric on a foil-covered cookie sheet in the oven at 325°. Another method uses an iron set in a towel-covered bread pan, the sole plate facing up. That way the cloth can be pulled taut and gently drawn down over the edge of the iron. A hot plate, cup warmer, or heat gun will also work; If you really get into it, use a heat gun for speed. Read directions which come with the embossing material, though most directions refer to paper and not cloth. Plate 9-8 shows embossed stamp prints on silk.

### D. Care

Most finished pieces will fade slightly on the first washing, and will be permanent after that. Hang to dry, or use a cool dryer setting. Do not iron directly on the embossed area.

### E. Embossing with the Copier or Printer

To be embossed, a printed image must remain moist for a short time. Therefore, any moist inks from a printer or copier can also be embossed. While the results are best on paper, success with fabric is possible. A thin, smooth silk is most likely to run through the machines easily.

To emboss with the copier, first photocopy a small image onto fabric using the freezer-paper method described in Chapter 4. Immediately sprinkle embossing powder over the copied image, but do not remove the freezer paper. The powders will stick to the moist print and any excess powder is shaken off or removed with masking tape. You then heat the image in any of the several ways already described to complete the embossing. Not all copiers deposit the same amount of ink, and some use a higher temperature, which dries the ink more. It will be important to experiment. Whether or not the freezer paper must be removed before embossing depends on the temperature of your heat source. If the freezer paper is sticking too tightly, use a lower oven temperature over a longer period of time for embossing.

To emboss with the dot-matrix printer requires a ribbon which deposits an ink that remains slightly moist. The embossing powder adheres to the wet ink. If the ink is not wet enough or heavy enough, the powder will not adhere. To get more ink deposited on the surface, use a fresh ribbon and print bold, large lines or letters. Laminate the fabric as described in Chapter 4 to run it through the printer. Once you have the print, leave the laminated paper and fabric together while you finish the embossing. It will be much easier to handle the stiffened fabric and to shake off excess powder.

## TROUBLESHOOTING FOR STAMP PRINTING AND EMBOSSING

**Problem:** Stamped fabric prints are incomplete or have flaws.

**Solution:** For colored prints, touch up flaws with Niji markers or Pigma Micron pens.

For a black ink print, touch up with any permanent marker, such as Pilot SC-UF or Sanford's Sharpie.

Make sure the printing surface is smooth.

Use more pressure on the stamp.

**Problem:** Corners of the stamps get inked and transfer to cloth.

**Solution:** Ink the stamp carefully, then use a cloth to wipe corners clean before printing.

A worn-out stamp pad has a depression in the center which lets the corners of the stamp touch the pad. Use a flat pad.

If it's a hand-made stamp, cut the corners away.

**Problem:** The embossing is scattered beyond the edge of the stamp print.

**Solution:** After adding powder, shake the cloth harder or try using a kneaded eraser to pick up bits.

Use a smoother fabric which will not catch the embossing granules.

Handle the fabric carefully, as oil attracts the powder (no peanut snacking).

**Problem:** The printer images do not emboss evenly.

**Solution:** Some of the ink may have dried out. Try a very small image so there is less time for it to dry.

Print in a mode that puts more ink on the paper (letter quality rather than a draft copy).

Use fresh ribbon and cover the print immediately with powder.

Try another copier.

**Problem:** After embossing with the copier, the freezer paper backing seems permanently adhered to the fabric.

**Solution:** Use a lower oven temperature for embossing. A lower heat for a longer period of time with eventually melt the powder.

Try a different freezer paper.

Remove the freezer paper from the fabric before embossing.

# Letters and Words

Words, when found on old quilts and textiles, pique our curiosity and interest us above all else. They are personal revelations of importance which tell us something of the writer. A date, a name, or a quotation are vital clues, often leading to further discoveries. In words we find values summarized (Peace, Freedom, Liberty), the urge to be remembered (Made by Mother), a sense of time and place (Illinois, 1892) and humor (a big "bow wow" issuing from the mouth of a tiny dog). "When this you see, Remember me" makes the writer unforgettable.

With words and letters, you convert fabric creations into documents, announcements, and personal commentary. Expressive possibilities expand as quotes from the famous (and infamous) keep company with their portraits. And don't overlook the dictums with which you were reared. Mother's admonitions continue ringing in our ears: "If you can't say something nice about her, don't say anything at all"; "What will people think?"(let alone what they'll say) has made its way into more than one of my works.

There are dozens of ways to integrate words into the overall design and color of a fabric piece. Many of the processes have been described earlier. Here are some others (as well as references to the lettering used in photographs in other chapters).

## PENS AND MARKING PENS

The most obvious and direct way of getting words on cloth is simply to pick up a permanent-ink pen and write. Quiltmakers have used pen and ink on fabric for many generations, and their messages always captivate us. The limitation in working with a pen is the delicate and small scale of most of the letters.

Permanent felt-tipped markers in varying widths expand the scale of handwritten letters. Always test markers on fabric, as some finishes inhibit the absorption of dye, while others tend to let the ink run on the fibers. Use PFP fabrics. Select only markers which are identified as permanent, and heat set whether required or not. Move the pen at a steady pace for even lines. A heavy paper under your fabric will prevent any ink which goes through from lettering something unintentionally. Very simple lettering is sometimes more effective if it is outlined.

Work with pens in either of two ways: draw directly onto fabric, which is free and spontaneous but risky, or draw onto another surface first. By drawing the words or messages on paper, you can then cut them out and lay them on the fabric to determine placement, color, and scale. When you are satisfied with the arrangement, the paper can then serve as a guide.

---

*Imagery On Fabric*   143

Plate 10-1: "Musician's Jacket" by Heather Avery.
Permanent markers on white cotton fabric give this jacket
a bright, clear, jazzy appeal.

Plate 10-2: Lettering detail by Jean Ray Laury.
Handwriting was enlarged by drawing around each letter to fatten
it. The expanded scale makes it readable from a greater distance.

Opaque markers can be used directly on an acetate sheet for very fluid lines or signatures. It may be easier to write on plain paper and enlarge or reduce the writing in a copier to get the right size and density. The copy can then be re-copied onto a transparency → for use with photo silk-screen, cyanotype (and other light sensitive methods), or copy transfer. This method is great for calligraphy, children's first written words, or your own handwriting.

Mary Preston (Plate 5-8) wrote on her jacket with markers so that drawings and letters were integrated into a single composition. Heather Avery's jacket, Plate 10-1, was drawn with black and brightly colored broad-tipped permanent markers. It's a perfect blend of message and design. The bold and simple letters are easily and clearly read.

## COPYING SCRIPT

There are times when you'll want to copy someone's script, such as a signature or a handwritten message, in a piece. Suppose, for example, you want to use an old love letter or a recipe from your grandmother, and you particularly want the handwriting. First photocopy the entire text onto paper. Darken the copy if necessary to get the letters very black. Then it can be copied again, directly onto cloth

(as described in Chapter 4) or run through a thermal imager → to be screen-printed (see Chapter 7). By copying it onto a transparency, you can use it with any light-sensitive method. All of these methods reproduce the original; but, if it is somewhat delicate, the print may not be easily read. If necessary, try tracing a bolder line over the paper copy to make the message more legible.

To convert longhand script from a line to bolder areas of color, first write your word or name on paper. Enlarge it if necessary on the copier. Then make a second line around each letter, so that it is as plump as a sausage. This shape can be cut out and used as a block-out → for contact prints, just as the single letters are used. Plate 10-2 shows words from a quilt enlarged in this way.

## CONTACT LETTERS

Sticky-back alphabets and transfer letters can be adhered directly to a sheet of transparent acetate (or any clear material, even glass) and used in all light-sensitive processes. A transparency need not be made in the copier since, by applying an opaque letter or block-out to a clear surface, you are in effect making the transparency.

My favorite alphabet is an inexpensive one, available on a self-adhesive shelf paper or contact paper →. Letters

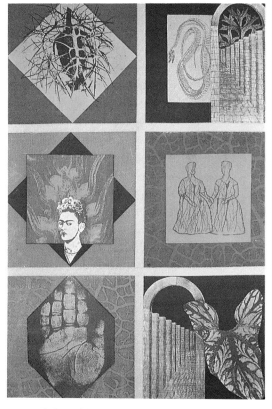

66. Detail of "Quilt for Frida" by Jo Ann Giordano.

*Rich colors and a complex combination of images were printed from contact-paper stencils and photo-emulsion screens.*

67. Detail of "Panama — Been There Before?" by Kathy Weaver.

*Richly detailed ocean blues and greens are interrupted with war slogans, and toy planes animate the camouflage and targets.*

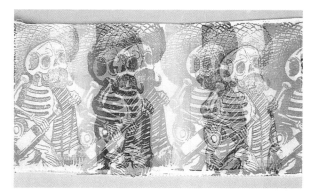

68. Scarf by Susan Magretta, 8" x 34".

*Using stencils made on the thermal imager, Susan printed bright colors onto transparent fabrics which overlaid opaque fabrics, screened with the same images. She created an illusion of space in this repeat pattern.*

69. Detail of Quilt San Diego's "Jubilee Quilt," designed by Donalene H. Rasmussen.

*Screen-printed trees, architectural details, and an airplane are incorporated into the pieced block featuring the California Tower.*

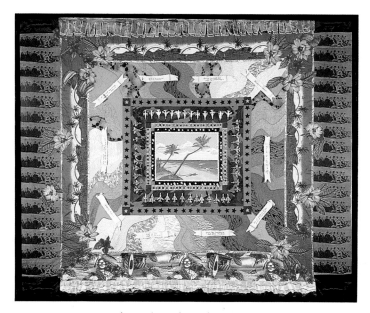

70. "Panama — Been There Before?" by Kathy Weaver, 92" x 108" x 3".

*Disturbing images of war contrast with inviting tropical picture-postcard scenes. The screen-printed and painted piece is stitched, appliquéd, quilted, and collaged.*

71. "The River Quilt," designed by Jean Ray Laury, assembled by Bea Slater, Susan Smeltzer, and Bev Karau, and quilted by friends, 76" x 66".

This fund-raiser quilt was screen-printed in small pieces and assembled into horizontal bands. Photographs on transparencies allowed for image reversals on the landscape prints. Hand quilted.

72. Detail of "Dancing Ladies" by Jean Ray Laury. Figures are 6" high.

Linear designs of the dancing ladies lend themselves to thermal-image screens. Single-color prints, in black, were hand-colored with Marvy markers.

73. "Hopscotch Horizon" by Jean Ray Laury, 30" x 32".

Each color was printed separately, then the colors were pieced together into gradations to make up the composition.

74. "Coalinga Earthquake Quilt" by Jean Ray Laury, 42" x 42".

Positioning a sheet of paper to block the printing area resulted in the broken images.

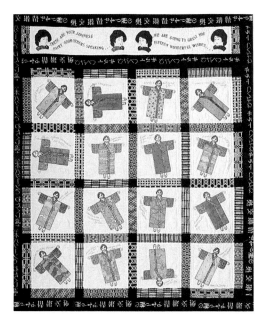

75. Detail of "Japanese Fairy Godmothers" by Jean Ray Laury, 48" x 41".

Free-floating, kimono-clad figures, made up from drawings and photocopies of a snapshot, are thermal-imaged and combined with Japanese printed fabrics.

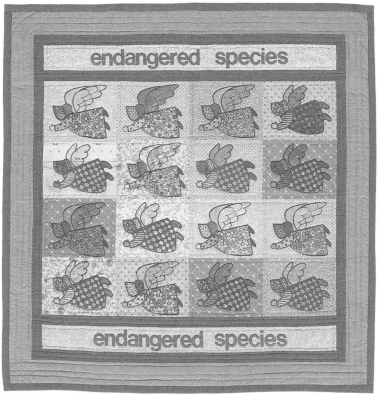

76. "Endangered Species" by Jean Ray Laury, 37" x 37".

The endangered figure, winging her way west, is familiar to all quilters. Thermal-screened onto printed cottons (her natural habitat), she is pieced and quilted.

77. "B.W. & Co. on Pratt Road" by Tafi Brown, 76" x 55".

Cyanotype prints and photograms are pieced with accents of solid-colored fabrics in this rich and complex panel. It is also appliquéd and quilted.

78. Detail of "McCarty-Norlander Raising" by Tafi Brown.

The spirit of barn-raising is captured in this cyanotype panel, in which photographs are repeated and used in mirror image. It is at once familiar and abstract.

80. Detail of "Soweto Suite, Part II : Greed" by Kathy Weaver.

*The textural richness of quilting creates a contrast to the smooth printed surfaces of photo images. Words run throughout the piece, adding both commentary and pattern.*

79. "Soweto Suite, Part II : Greed" by Kathy Weaver, 76" x 76".

*Thermal screening and photo screening are combined with more traditional quiltmaking techniques in this extraordinary work.*

81. Precocity *by Holley Junker, 10" x 7" closed.*

*A wonderful tongue-in-cheek attitude lets the artist toy with the concept of raising perfect children.*

82. Circumambulation *by Holley Junker, 8 ½" x 9 ½" closed.*

*Van Dyke print, copy transfer, and stamped letters combine in this delightful silk and paper book. Over the circular photographic brownprint, other images merge and overlap.*

83. Before Goodbye *by Holley Junker, 10" x 10" closed.*

*A textile book, inhabited by images from the past, is printed with cyanotype and copy transfer (using solvent). The silk pages are detailed with embroidery and piecing in silk.*

84. "Family Tree Quilt" by Helen Nestor, 111" x 80".

*Working with Van Dyke printing from halftone negatives of family photos, some over 100 years old, a photographer created her family tree.*

85. Detail of "Blue Storm" by Betty Ferguson.

Pieced blocks in a quilted panel utilize a rich range of blues. Leaf patterns were created with cyanotype, then fragmented and reassembled.

86. Detail of panel by Betty Ferguson.

Cyanotype print from an old negative in the artist's collection is beautifully detailed on white sheeting. Nautical motifs, blueprinted separately, surround it.

87. Detail of "Maple Leaf Rag" by Nancy Halpern.

The pieced maple-leaf block is juxtaposed with its double-printed natural counterpart. The quilted pattern reflects the leafy forms.

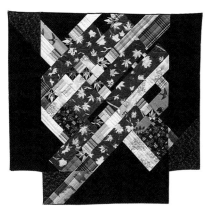

88. "Maple Leaf Rag" by Nancy Halpern, 71" x 74".

Cyanotype prints are combined with commercial prints, plaids, stripes, and piecing in this wonderful melding of natural forms with geometrics.

89. "Origins" by Erma Martin Yost, 32" x 40".

The richness of hand-painted and hand-printed fabrics is enhanced with machine embroidery, quilting, and acrylic paint on duck and Mylar.

**91. "Cumulus 2" by Erma Martin Yost, 40" x 54".**

Billowing clouds, printed with cyanotype, Kwik-print, and Inko print, are pieced into a composition reflecting the timelessness of mountain and sky. The linen panel is hand-painted and machine-embroidered.

**90. Detail of "Cumulus 2" by Erma Martin Yost.**

The traditions of quilting are taken in new directions with hand-painted fabrics and photographic printing, including Kwik-print, cyanotype, Inko print, and photo transfer.

**92. "Stock Market" vest by Carol Voulkos.**

A stock-market vocabulary is stamp-printed between rows of paper dolls cut from the financial pages. Dollar signs and pointing fingers identify the "bottom line" and symbolize Wall Street.

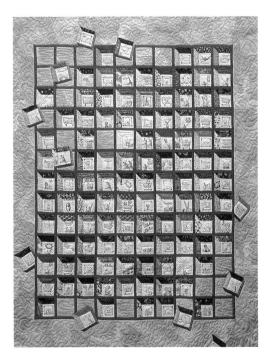

**93. "It's a Wonderful Life" by Danita Rafalovich, 68" x 54".**

Rubber-stamped designs fill the windows in this pieced quilt, and the images float away with the falling windows.

**94. Detail of "It's a Wonderful Life" by Danita Rafalovich.**

An unlikely view from these attic windows, in which stamping is combined with piecing and quilting.

95. "The Black and Blinded Birds of Night" by Karen Berkenfeld, 64" x 55".

Stamp-printed shapes, cut from flexible printing material and adhered to Plexiglas, are combined with linoleum cuts, stenciling, and sponge painting to create this powerful and energetic piece.

96. "Nosegays" by Jean Ray Laury, 34" x 34".

Artgum eraser stamps were used to create bouquets in this pieced and hand-quilted panel.

97. "Maple Leaves" by Jan Myers-Newbury, 12" x 18".

Stamp-printed maple leaves create elegant overlapping patterns of foliage.

**99.** *Detail of "Talismanic Garment II" by Jo Ann Giordano.*

Screen-printed silk organza, light and delicate, is given the power of words from advertising promises and slogans. Images are copy-transferred.

**98.** *Detail of "Gift of Tongues" by Robin Schwalb.*

Both the meaning and beauty of the written word are celebrated in this pieced and quilted panel. Letters are photo-emulsion screen-printed.

**100.** *"The Bread Quilt" by Jean Ray Laury, 36" x 45".*

Alphabet stamps used with India ink on fabric spell out tasty adjectives which were appliquéd to the blocks.

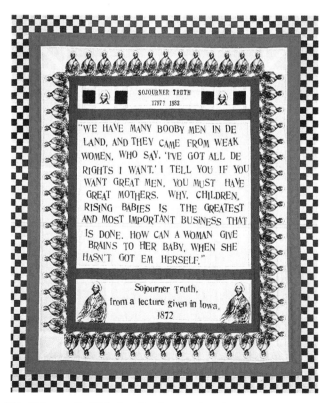

**101.** *"Sojourner Truth" by Jean Ray Laury, 46" x 40".*

Several different alphabet stamp sets, used first on paper, made up the text in this quilt. Lettering and portraits were photo-screen printed, pieced, and hand quilted.

Plate 10-3: *Detail of "Little Boy Blue" by Jackie Vermeer. Self-adhesive letters applied to a clear acetate sheet made the transparency for the words in this quilt. They were screened in blue.*

are printed in both upper and lower case in several sizes on a clear background. Rolls of this paper can occasionally be found with other shelf papers, but the best source is a school-supply house. One inexpensive three-yard roll lasts a long time, though of course you'll run out of E's and T's first. Using an X-Acto knife, cut a rectangle around each letter and peel to remove it from the page. Press it into place on an acetate sheet. The letters are black enough to block sunlight. Letters can be peeled off the acetate sheet for a second use, although when dry they will be permanently stuck.

Similar alphabets are available in art supply stores, to be either cut out or rubbed off onto another surface (Letratone, Formatt, and Geotype). They are available in a wide range of type styles, and you can apply them directly to acetate if the size is right. If they are too small, you can transfer your words to plain paper and then enlarge them before making a transparency. They are considerably more expensive than the contact paper.

Contact letters were used to print "Coalinga Earthquake" in Color Plate 74. The irregularly placed letters were adhered to clear acetate which was then used as a block-out. "Neighborhood Watch" in Color Plate 61 and

"Kilauea Volcano Hawaii" (Plate 6-4) utilize the same technique.

Any self-sticking letters can be used, as long as they are opaque. Those with water-based glues (that you lick and stick) can be used on paper and copied to a transparency, but they will not adhere well directly to transparencies. In Plate 10-3, two different sizes of stick-on letters were put directly onto acetate. They come on flat sheets of alphabets available at craft shops. The letters are similar to those used on mailboxes, but the hardware-store variety is heavier than you need and more expensive.

## COPIER

The copier plays a role in many of the methods described. Use it to enlarge or reduce lettering from magazines, announcements, newspapers, or ads. Paste up an original with which you will work. The original can be traced for freezer-paper or contact-paper cut-outs, used to make photocopies directly onto cloth, or made into a transparency for any light-sensitive method.

The making of transparencies is one of the great advantages of the photocopier. Robin Schwalb used one in exposing her photo-emulsion screen for "Gift of Tongues" (Color Plate 98). Some of the text areas are screened with opaque white, while tumbling letters are appliquéd in overlays. The "Talismanic Garment II" of Color Plate 99 is screen-printed in opaque white and color on organdy. For the bands of colored images, artist Jo Ann Giordano used a photo-transfer method.

Running fabric through a copier as described in Chapter 4 is a great way to print an extensive amount of lettering. Arrange the lettering first (whether it is stamped, cut from contact alphabets, hand-written, etc.) and, when you have a finalized copy in strong b/w contrast, copy it onto cloth. In Plate 10-4 the copy machine title strip was drawn on paper, enlarged, and run through the machine. The cat and rabbit identifications in "Anna's Quilt," Plates 5-3 and 5-4, are photocopied directly onto cloth.

## COPY TRANSFER

Lettering done with any copy-transfer method (with the exception of PAROdraw) will be in reverse. For the words to read correctly, you can either make the original lettering in reverse or make a transparency which can be flipped. From it you'll get a backwards copy which, when transferred, will read correctly.

Plate 10-4: *Title strip by Jean Ray Laury.*
*All processes detailed in this book are used to create the letters for their own title strips.*

In Joan Schulze's "A Cautionary Tale" in Color Plate 15, a construction-site tape provided the lettering from which a transparency was made. She flipped the transparency, using the method described above to reverse the image.

In Plate 10-4 the "Copy Transfer" title was cut from scraps of leftover transfers. Along with using scraps, it is possible to print colors with no image used in the copier. This will print a sheet of solid color. These colored sheets can be cut up and used to make lettering. Always do your sketching on the white side of the paper so it will read correctly when transferred.

## CUT-OUTS

Letters cut quickly and easily from paper can be used with most of the processes described in this book. Construction paper is opaque enough to eliminate ultraviolet for light-sensitive processes and will give good clear prints. Use this same cutting technique for freezer-paper letters, ironing them to fabric as stencils. Or cut letters from dye paper or leftover heat-transfer copies. In Plate 10-4, both the "Dye Transfer" and "Copy Transfer" title strips are made from letters cut by the following method.

To cut letters freehand, first determine the height of the letters needed. Trim a strip of paper to that height, so that every letter now has a top and bottom (they're half-finished!). Next, cut off a section for a letter. For an L, for example, cut a rectangle and envision the letter sitting on the bottom edge with its sides touching the sides of the strip. You need only trim away a smaller rectangle. A little practice will make this easy. For an A or D, cut through the letter to remove the center. Some letters (W or M) require larger rectangles, others (j or i) smaller ones. Take the same block letter and vary the line widths to create more interesting shapes. Or add extensions to simple block letters. Place the letters at haphazard angles to create a playful, casual look (and avoid toeing the line).

When cutting letters from dye transfer paper, work with the uncolored sides of the sheets facing you. That way, when you iron them on, the lettering will not be reversed. Words can be assembled from letters of assorted colors.

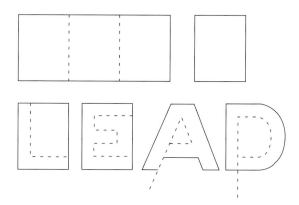

## FREEZER PAPER

Freezer paper can be used for cut-outs over which color can be added in a variety of ways. Cut letters as described for cut-outs and heat set them to fabric. (Again work from the paper side and they will read correctly on the fabric.) In the "Quick Screen" title panel in Plate 10-4, I screened paint over the freezer-paper letters. When it was dry, I peeled the letters off. A similar process was used for "Dye Sticks," where the colors were scribbled on. The ironed-on freezer-paper letters could also be colored by brush painting, with crayons, or by stamping heavily around all edges.

This process always gives you negative letters: you color the background areas. To do the reverse, carefully cut letters from freezer paper, keeping the background paper intact. Keep the inside shapes from the e's and d's. Iron the background onto fabric, insert the inside shapes, and then add color to make positive letters.

## PRINTER

Your word processor and its printer offer a wonderful, versatile means of creating text of varying types, styles, and densities. The print-out can then be copied or copytransferred. Jody House's rhinoceros quilt in Plate 10-5 has a title taken from her computer print-out. It was photocopied onto a transparency for use with photo-emulsion screen printing.

Special heat-set ribbon is available for the printer (see Chapter 4); it allows you to iron the letters permanently onto fabric. The "Printer" title in Plate 10-4 shows an example of heat-set transfer in both reverse and right-reading. Lettering must be reversed on the print-out in order to read correctly when ironed on. The lettering in the chicken panel of Plate 4-11 is from heat-set printer ribbon.

Laura Lee Fritz used her ImageWriter for the text of her documentary newspaper quilt in Plates 10-6 and 10-7. Her fabric, stabilized with freezer paper, was run through the printer and then heat set. Additional examples can be seen in Chapter 4. Esther Cheal's garment in Plate 4-9 includes lettering from her laser printer.

## RUBBER STAMPS

Rubber stamps are a perfect method for adding words to fabric. Alphabets abound, so you have an array of size and style choices. It's fun (and undoubtedly therapeutic) to stamp those little blocks down. The first time I used words on a quilt, I was too chicken to stamp directly on the fabric blocks. Instead, I stamped words on small pieces of fabric, then appliquéd the words to the quilt. This is a safer method but less direct, and it leaves you with the appliqué to do. In "The Bread Quilt" (Color Plate 100), I used India ink and an old set of kids' stamps for the adjectives. A casual, irregular line was used in part because I like that look, but also because it's a lot easier (which may be why I like it).

Plate 10-5: Detail of "Preposterous Rhinosterous" by Jody House.
The words which encircle the captive rhinos were print-outs from the computer photocopied to a transparency and used in photo-emulsion screening.

Plate 10-6: "Extra Extra Extra" by Laura Lee Fritz, 36" x 60".
The entire front page of a newspaper was reproduced and hand-painted on muslin to create this newspaper quilt.

Plate 10-7: *Detail of "Extra Extra Extra" by Laura Lee Fritz.*

*Invisible nylon quilting thread was used for the seismographic pattern which covered the quilt. After the pieces were assembled, box outlines were hand-painted and headlines were sewn over the text areas.*

The words in "Sojourner Truth" (Color Plate 101) were done by a slightly different process. The quote was stamped on a paper cut to the size of the quilt's central area. Each letter was touched up as needed with a marking pen. Errors could be pasted over and re-stamped. The completed paper panel was then photocopied onto a transparency. As the quotation was too large to be copied all at once, I had to make several transparencies and re-assemble them with clear tape. The lettering was screen-printed in sections, as my largest screen wasn't big enough to print it all at once. The transparencies were exposed to sunlight on a photo-emulsion screen and printed onto cloth. Since preparation and set-up time were so great for just the one quilt, I printed enough lettering to make several different quilts. Each one used the same quote with varying photos, borders, and colors. Plate 10-8 shows another use of the same words. This time, each line was printed separately and the quote was strung out along the borders.

In Plate 10-9 stamped words are shown on paper (upper right) and on transparency. Discrepancies can be corrected on either the stamped original or on the transparency. The original can be inked, outlined, or embellished with dots and lines. Parts of the paper can be cut out to adjust spacing or make corrections, and can then be re-arranged and glued. When it is finalized, you can make the transparency. To correct a transparency, you can remove unwanted areas of ink with the point of an X-Acto knife; areas too light or missing can be filled with an opaque

marker. This allowance for change and correction is reassuring and helpful. The transparencies can be used with any of the light-sensitive methods (blueprint, brownprint, Inkodye) and with photo-emulsion screen printing.

Lettering for "The Van Dalsem Quilt" in Color Plate 51 is from a stamp set; it was also made into a transparency for photo-emulsion screen printing. After printing, inside areas of the letters were hand-colored with markers. In Plate 10-10 Lura Schwarz Smith's panel includes outline letters stamped directly onto the fabric, then colored by hand.

Alphabets are commonly available at office suppliers, stamp shops, or toy stores, and sometimes at printers' or craft and art supply stores. When you find a set, experiment on fabric scraps to get a feel for the amount of ink and pressure needed. Stamping is more successful on cotton, since some synthetic fibers let the dye or ink migrate or bleed. Read Chapter 9 for details of ink and permanence.

## THERMAL IMAGER

The stencils from a thermal imager are great for small letters, handwriting, and signatures. Prepare your original, make a plain b/w photocopy, enlarge it if necessary, and run it through a thermal imager, as described in Chapter 7. Dozens of prints can be made from one stencil. And it can be saved for re-use later. In Plate 10-4 the "Thermal Imager" title strip was done in this way: the outline letters were drawn on paper with an opaque marker and then photocopied; the copy was imaged and the letters were screen-printed in a single color; the insides of each letter were then hand-colored with markers.

## TRACING AND DRAWING

No need to panic if you think you can't print well. There are dozens of alphabets available, and lettering surrounds us. A magazine page or a newspaper ad may have a word or slogan you need. Change its size on the copier if necessary, then trace it in any of several ways. If you are using freezer paper or contact paper, you may be able to see through it well enough to make a pencil line. If not, put the original over a light table or a window. If print from the back of the page interferes, make a photocopy of the area you want to use, and trace that.

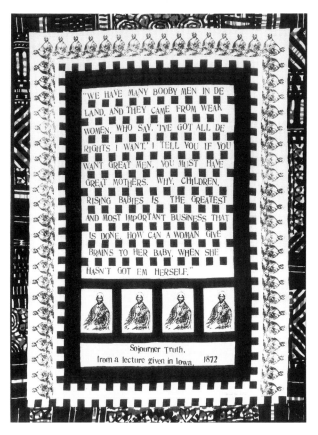

Plate 10-8: "Sojourner Truth" by Jean Ray Laury,
50" x 37½".

These letters and those in Color Plate 101 are printed from the
same screen but arranged in different ways.

Plate 10-10: Detail of "Northern Lights" by Lura Schwarz
Smith.

Lines of poetry are stamped from small alphabet letters into
flowing lines which echo the appliquéd shapes.

Plate 10-9:
Transparency sample by
Jean Ray Laury.

The stamped original, at
right, was copied onto a
transparency and used
for photo-emulsion
screen printing. The
cup, cut from paper, was
adhered to another
transparency.

In Laura Lee Fritz's singular work in Plate 10-7, she traced not only the letters but the photograph as well. Her process was a complex one in which she reproduced each part of the paper in accurate proportion to the rest. She first traced the paper itself, having obtained permission from the *San Francisco Chronicle* for this. The tracing was cut into sections which were projected with an opaque projector. With her calculator and yardstick in hand to keep proportions accurate, she then transferred the tracing to heavy white paper with pencil. This drawing was outlined with an extra-fine permanent-ink pen. Muslin was placed over the paper drawing and an outline of the images was made. Freezer paper was then ironed to the back of the muslin to stiffen it slightly. She painted in the black areas of letters and photo using a brush and Versatex, referring constantly to the original newspaper for shadows, lines, and textures. She next did wash areas for the gray, using a wet brush. The muslin did not absorb the dye evenly, as the warp threads drew the wet paint more than the weft threads, making the piece resemble ikat. The finished painting was heat set, and the pieces were then joined. The text involved the use of a printer.

## TYPEWRITER

When you have large amounts of writing to go onto fabric, some mechanical method will probably serve you best. If you can't run fabric through a copier or printer, use a typewriter. Chapter 4 describes ways of making this permanent; a wonderful example of typing on a quilt is shown in Plate 4-6.

Examples of lettering abound in this book. Robin Schwalb's "Gift of Tongues" in Plate 5-6 and "Projectionist Please Focus" in Plate 6-22 demonstrate her passion for printed words. Their visual and symbolic values are as great as their use and variability in communicating. Few processes will offer greater pleasure than those which allow you to add words and letters to your work. Embroidered letters are lovely; but, if you've got a lot to say, other methods are speedier and at least as interesting.

## TROUBLESHOOTING FOR LETTERING

Problem: You want bold, easy-to-read letters on a quilt but don't know which method to use.
Solution: The iron-on letters cut from freezer paper will be easiest. Color in any of the ways described.
Photo screen printing or any light-sensitive method lets you place large block letters in a contact frame.

Problem: When cutting letters freehand, your spacing gets way off.
Solution: Start with a strip as long as you want the finished word or words to be. Then estimate the space for each word, and cut these sections. It will then be easier to see how much space you have for each letter.

Problem: Your signature is tiny and detailed, but you'd like to reproduce it in script on fabric. How should you print it?
Solution: Write directly on the cloth with a permanent fine-line pen if you need only one signature. For multiples, make a stencil using the thermal imager and screen-print it, or copy your signature, make a transparency, and print with photo-emulsion screen.

# Additional Help

Processes mentioned in brackets following the entry word indicate where the definition applies. If no processes are listed, the definition is of general interest.

**ACETATE: See TRANSPARENCY**

**ACETONE: See SOLVENTS AND PROPELLANTS**

## ACRYLIC MEDIUM

This translucent, colorless, gel-like base, available in matte or gloss, is used as an extender with acrylic paints. It is sometimes used as a transfer medium.

## ACRYLICS

Acrylic paints are used for screening, stamping, painting, or stenciling. They can be cleaned up with water before they set, but they cure or harden to water-fastness. No heat setting is required. More opaque than textile paints, they also dry faster in the screen and add a slight stiffening to the fabric. When mixed with an acrylic medium or a transparent base, they can be used for screen painting, or they can be used from the tube in other processes.

## AIRBRUSH

Any standard airbrush can be used with textile airbrush inks, which are thin but intense in color. A simple, convenient home airbrush called the LetraJet Air Marker utilizes the LetraJet (made by Letraset), which connects a Pantone fine-tipped marker to canned propellant (Letraset's propellant or Badger's Propel). A fine spray is produced from a wide range of colors. As an alternative, Dye*namite by Carnival produces a textile dye in spray cans.

An atomizer or a small hand-held spray gun provides an inexpensive alternative. The spray is not as consistent, but with practice you will get a good airbrush effect. Use airbrush ink, or textile paint smoothed to a consistency which can be easily moved through the sprayer.

## AIRBRUSH INKS FOR TEXTILES

There are special inks made for use in airbrush equipment but which have other uses as well. They are thinner than textile paint, but not diluted in color. Because of their intensity, they are often used to paint color directly onto fabric through various transfer methods. The inks are thin enough to use on stamp pads. Some companies which make textile paints make airbrush inks in identical colors.

## ALTERING IMAGES [all transfers, photo silk-screen, direct copy prints]

Once you have reproduced a photograph or drawing on the copy machine, you're ready for the fun of introducing changes. Eliminate a crowded background or, with a quick snip, remove a political incompetent from the scene. You could introduce a friend into a photograph of the Beatles, or place your saintly sister-in-law at the table with the Apostles for the Last Supper.

You can alter images by using old photos as backgrounds (a little like the backdrops in photography stalls). They let your features shine through as Calamity Jane, Queen Elizabeth, or the Marlboro Man. Put yourself behind the wheel at the Daytona 500 or standing upright on a horse as it vaults over a water jump. Your cut-outs can stand atop the Himalayas, sit on the Eiffel Tower, or leap over the Golden Gate Bridge. None of this, of course, damages your original print.

Transparencies (either positive or negative) allow further play with the image. Create a double or simultaneous exposure, stacking transparencies to create collaged images. Your own portrait could be overlaid with the things filling your head on any given day — dreams, birds, bats, feathers, or heavy thoughts.

Both cut-outs and stacked transparencies are great fun. Doing straight photographs is intriguing at first, but adding what you know about the person gives depth and dimension to a portrait.

## BLOCK-OUTS [photo-screen printing, cyanotype, all light-sensitive printing]

Any opaque surface, whether flat or 3-dimensional, used to intercept sunlight and prevent exposure, may be referred to as a block-out. A cardboard star used in the contact frame in place of the negative or transparency is a block-out. A star drawn on a transparency makes a linear block-out. Your hand, placed on any sensitized fabric before exposure, becomes the block-out. Pick a leaf from your maple tree, place it on a fabric sensitized for blueprint, and expose it to the sun. The area protected by the leaf will not develop. After exposure, when the fabric is rinsed, the undeveloped sensitizers will wash out and a silhouetted imprint of the leaf will appear in the original fabric color (preferably white). The exposed area surrounding the leaf will develop into a color, in this case blue. If a caterpillar ate the middle of the leaf for lunch, that open area would also develop and appear in blue. In cyanotype, Van Dyke, Kwik-Print or Inko print, the developed image on fabric is the final print, but in photo-screen printing the developed fabric is the mesh on the screen, and another step is required to make the print. When paint is squeegeed through the screen mesh, the image will be a dark/light reverse of the light-sensitive fabric. The leaf block-out in a blueprint will produce a leaf in fabric color with a blue background; the leaf block-out in a photo screen will be the color of the paint, and the remaining area will the the fabric color.

Block-out designs can be applied to any transparent material for use in making an exposure. For example, if you wish to print an olive branch, the stem and all leaves (actual or paper cut-outs) can be glued to a sheet of acetate. This finished block-out (the design applied to a transparency) is used in the contact frame. This is easier than trying to arrange all the small leaf shapes directly onto the fabric in the darkroom.

Arrange stickers (the ones that third graders collect and put on their 3-ring binders) into block-out patterns on transparent film, or cut paper dolls or snowflakes and adhere them. Block-out sheets can be kept and re-used, an important factor in light-sensitive processes which produce single prints. Block-outs on transparency sheets can be flipped for mirror images.

Since block-out designs do not need to go through your copy machine, any transparent surface will do (glass, cellophane, lightweight tracing paper, etc.). Even plastic sandwich bags (heavier ones are better) provide an adequate backing for block-outs. The transparent area must let sunlight through.

### BRAYER [photo transfers, stamping]

This is a simple tool which consists of a free-turning hard rubber or plastic cylinder, 4" to 5" wide, with a handle. It is like a small paint roller and is used to exert even pressure over a flat area.

### CENTERING (aligning) prints on fabric

Centering is especially important on garments, or when your design must parallel the grain of the fabric. By folding and marking the center of your fabric (lengthwise and crosswise) and also marking the center of your design in the same way, you can assure accurate placement.

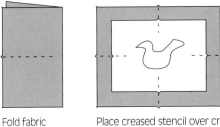

Fold fabric and crease

Place creased stencil over creased fabric. (Align creases of stencil and fabric.)

In quick-screening, make a fold on the grain of the fabric where the print is to be centered. Then make fold lines, also centered, on your freezer-paper cut-out. Align the folds before pressing the freezer paper in place on the fabric.

When screen printing a block or panel, fold your cloth on the grain and press it at the cut edges. Apply your design to the silk-screen frame so that it is approximately centered. Then measure to determine the exact center and extend that line to the top and bottom edges of the wood frame. Mark the frame with pencil, marker, or tape, then align those marks with the creases on the fabric. When these indicators line up, top and bottom, you will be centered side to side. Repeat at the sides to center it top to bottom.

To center a design on a T-shirt, fold the shirt down the center front as well as across. Center the design on the screen and align the folds to the marked screen, as described above.

For random designs, such as a pattern of screened stars, first prepare your frame for printing. Print several stars on paper, cut them out, and place them on your fabric until the arrangement satisfies you. Then place the screen over one of the paper stars, holding it just off the surface to align them. Tilt the screen, keeping one edge on the fabric, and slip the paper star out of place. Put the frame back down in the same place and print

### CLEAR WRAP

Transparent plastic kitchen wrap (Handiwrap or Saran Wrap) is used in the studio to protect surfaces from wet inks or paints. It offers see-through protection from moisture and retards drying time when used as a cover.

### COLORING OR TINTING PRINTS

All heat-set water-based textile paints or textile airbrush inks can be hand painted either thinned or thickened. Use a palette (a disposable plastic tray or plate), adding small dabs (¼ teaspoon or less) of color. Use a brush that has some stiffness (a flat-tipped oil-painting brush), but nothing as rigid as a stenciling brush. Pointed brushes will be needed for tiny details, but very soft-bristled brushes are difficult to control.

Thinned color: Textile paints or airbrush inks can easily be thinned and watercolored onto cloth. Dip the brush in color and add water on the plate until the color is dissolved. With the fabric print over an absorbent paper, brush color onto a small area and immediately blot with a paper towel. Blotting is essential to keep the color from bleeding or running. Paint until an area is complete. Dry and heat set (actually, you can go ahead and heat set small areas without waiting). This method gives you good control over the color but less control over the spreading. Constant blotting and heat setting will help. With a little practice you will learn to blend colors and avoid running. Color Plate 30 shows a pillow colored in this way. If the color is too pale, paint it again. Do not heat set over an embossed paper towel, as the raised pattern will show up in the print.

Thickened color: An extender is a translucent medium with a consistency similar to the paint, but without any pigment or dye. In silk-screening it is used to dilute a color's intensity without making it more liquid or runny. Mix a small amount of textile color with extender on a plate and paint an even, thin layer onto the fabric. It will not be necessary to blot or to heat set immediately, and there will be little or no problem of spreading or running colors. However, this thicker paint is more difficult to manipulate and slower to dry.

## CONTACT FRAME: See DIRECT CONTACT FRAME

## CONTACT PAPER [screen printing, stencil, improvised copy transfer]

This is self-adhesive paper made for household use; common brands are Con-tact, Magic Paper, and Grid-Grip. For most craft purposes, the clear (actually translucent) variety is preferred over the opaque colors. It consists of an adhesive plastic layer with a waxed-paper-like backing, and the sheets can be separated for use in silk-screen printing, stencils, etc. It can also be used as a copy transfer sheet.

## COPY TRANSFER

This is the process of transferring either a color or a b/w copy from a sheet of paper to fabric by any of a variety of means.

## CRAYONS [heat transfer]

Special crayons are made for designs on paper to be transferred by heat setting onto fabric. They contain disperse dyes and work best on synthetic fabrics. They are marketed by Binney and Smith Inc. as Crayola Craft Transfer Crayons.

## CRAYONS [fabric]

Special crayons are made for use directly on fabric. They must be heat set and are most permanent on synthetics. They are marketed by Binney and Smith Inc. as Crayola Craft Fabric Crayons.

## CUT-OUTS

Figures, letters, or images can be cut from paper (or any similar material) and translated to fabric in a variety of ways: 1) as block-outs in photo-screen printing or light-sensitive methods; 2) as stencils (also see contact paper) in screen printing; 3) as designs with dye transfer.

## CYANOTYPE (blueprinting)

In the blueprinting process, cloth is saturated with chemicals which make it light-sensitive. A block-out is then used to protect parts of the cloth. On exposure to light, the exposed areas develop the blue color characteristic of cyanotype.

## DARKROOM [photo-screen printing, light-sensitive methods]

Any room essentially free of outdoor light can be used for drawing or for working with light-sensitive materials. Photo-screen printing requires low lighting for preparation, and a darkroom is needed only to dry the screen. A closet will do: use a folded turkish towel to block light coming in under the door. When you must enter the room, shut the door quickly behind you. Or use a cupboard or drawer if you are drying only one or two screens.

For light-sensitive methods (cyanotype, Van Dyke, Kwik-Print, and Inko print) a laundry or small work area can be turned into a usable dark room by closing doors and blocking off all windows with black plastic (garbage-bag type) and masking tape. As a last resort, use a bathroom, but only if you have two. It is best not to mix this work with the living areas of your house.

For a work light, use a photo safe-light, a 75-watt yellow bulb, or a 25-watt incandescent bulb. Keep your bulb, black plastic, clothesline, and masking tape together in a box or drawer, so you can reconstruct your darkroom in minutes.

## DIRECT CONTACT FRAME

A frame can be set up to provide direct contact between sensitized material and a block-out before it is exposed to light. You can easily make an inexpensive contact frame to avoid purchasing one at a photo shop. It consists of a piece of wood (masonite, plywood, drawing board, an abandoned bread board, or any flat, rigid surface), ½" to 1" thick flexible foam pad, and a sheet of glass. All three layers should be cut to approximately the same size, a couple of inches larger than the largest negative or design you intend to use. A 10" x 12" frame is a good size with which to start.

If the weight of the glass is inadequate to produce a good contact, use small C-clamps or large clips (similar to those on clipboards) to keep the layers held tightly together.

## DISPERSE DYES

Disperse dyes bond permanently with synthetic fabrics at relatively low temperatures, making them convenient for home use. Also called sublimation dyes, the dyes sublime, or change, from a dry to a gaseous state with the application of heat and pressure. Thus, during heat setting, fibers expand or open and capture the fumes given off as the dyes sublime.

Available in liquid form (like Deka Iron-On), they can be painted to make dye sheets; in sheet form (Design Dye Sheets), they are already evenly painted onto a paper surface; in powder form (PROsperse or Aljo), they can be mixed and painted. The colors are fast to light and water on the appropriate fabrics. Care must be taken to avoid any breathing of the disperse dye powders.

## DISPOSAL [light-sensitive solutions]

Be environmentally responsible. Read all labels and dispose of materials only as directed. While information and directions are offered in this text, remember that regulations change from state to state, and even from county to county. For help, call your fire department, your local toxic waste disposal management, the health department, or the Department of Fish and Wildlife.

Plan and carefully estimate so that you mix only the amounts needed and you'll avoid any disposal problem. Small amounts of the solutions (the amounts used in this book are considered small) can be disposed of by diluting and flushing them down the drain with lots of water. Unless you plan to do production work or teach classes, the amounts used in single projects are regarded as minimal. For larger amounts, it will be important to check with your local agencies.

If you wish to neutralize any acid or alkaline solutions, first determine the level of acidity or alkalinity using a pH test kit (used for swimming pools). A pH 7 is neutral. If the solution tests alkaline, neutralize it with the addition of a mild acid, such as white vinegar; if it tests acid, neutralize it with a solution of soda ash or washing soda. The neutralized solution can then be diluted and safely washed down the drain with lots of additional water.

Remember: Always add acid to water, not the reverse.

Never dispose of one chemical immediately after another down a drain (even diluted), since this can cause a reaction, particularly with an acid and a base.

Never pour any chemicals into the ground.

To dispose of any leftover chemicals from light-sensitive processes, dilute them by putting a half cup of the solution into a gallon of water. Wash the mixture down the drain with ample water. Continue to run the water for several minutes.

If you cannot dispose of leftovers in these ways, place them in closed containers clearly labeled as to contents and delivered to a local toxic waste disposal.

## DYE STICKS [dye transfer, lettering]

Made by Pentel, these bright, easy-to-use colors are for direct use on cloth. They are permanent on cottons and the colors can be blended.

## DYE TRANSFER

The process of transferring dyes to fabric is an indirect method. Disperse dyes, for example, are painted on paper, then placed face down on synthetic fabric and transferred with heat. Dye transfer is also what happens in the laundry when your white blouse gets washed with something in non-permanent green.

## DYE TRANSFER PAPERS

Sheets of paper already coated with disperse dyes are available for use on fabric.

## FABRIC CRAYONS: See CRAYONS

## FABRIC FINISHES

Treatments are often applied to fabrics to make them wrinkle-free, crease-resistant, water-resistant, glazed, or polished, any of which may interfere with dye absorption. See PFP Fabrics.

## FABRIC FOR PRINTING : See PFP FABRICS

## FOAMBOARD [stamping, cyanotype]

This is a rigid white foam panel, available in various thicknesses, which is coated on both sides with white or colored paper. It is easily cut and lightweight. For most craft uses, the $\frac{3}{16}$" or $\frac{1}{4}$" thicknesses are adequate. Get foamboard from art-supply stores, picture-framing shops, or school suppliers. Large sheets are often used for displays or posters. The foil-covered sheets found at lumber yards or hardware stores are not suitable, since they are less easily cut, and it is difficult to make anything adhere to the metallic surface.

## FOAM CORE: See FOAMBOARD

## FREEZER PAPER [quick-screen, lettering, direct machine printing]

Reynolds, Magic Wrap, and Grid-Grip make plasticized papers, similar to that used for wrapping meats. They are inexpensive and available by the roll in some grocery or hardware stores. The plasticized side of the paper can be ironed onto fabric with a medium hot iron. The optimum temperature varies with brands, so test your paper. Adequate heat must be applied to secure the edges (as in quick screen), but overheating will make the paper difficult to peel off.

## GENERATION COPIES

A first photocopy of any material is referred to as the first-generation copy or print. A copy made from that copy is a second-generation print. As the copying proceeds through generations, some clarity and detail are lost. Therefore, first copies are always best for use in transfers.

## GLASS [all light-sensitive processes]

A picture-framing shop or glass company will cut glass to specific sizes, and many have pre-cut glass in standard sizes. Have them grind the edges of the glass, or fold fabric tape or masking tape over all the edges. Store the glass on edge on a shelf. Non-glare glass is not essential but is easier to work with in bright sunshine .

For light-sensitive methods, you need two sheets of glass, one to prepare your fabric and one to expose it. The glass must be larger (by an inch or two) than the largest negative or image you plan to use.

For silk-screen printing, the glass must fit the inside dimensions of the screen printing frame if you expose on the inside surface. To expose on the outside (or bottom) of the frame, the glass must be at least the size of the mesh area, and can be larger.

## HALF-TONE NEGATIVE: See NEGATIVE

## HAND PAINTING: See COLORING OR TINTING PRINTS

## HAZARDOUS MATERIALS

Several of the processes in this book use materials that may be hazardous.

The Federal Hazardous Substances Act requires labeling of all consumer art and craft materials which are potentially hazardous. The designations DANGER, WARNING, or CAUTION must be used, and the label must list what the hazardous ingredients are, what precautions to take, and the recommended first-aid treatment. None of the processes in this book uses any materials which are labeled DANGER, the most hazardous of the three.

If you intend to work extensively with any potentially hazardous product, request a Material Safety Data Sheet from the manufacturer. Some will include this when you buy their products, but others send them only when you request them. This sheet offers more detailed information, and you should read and keep these papers on hand.

Good references for fiber artists are the books listed by Michael McCann and by Shaw and Rossol. It is important to know and understand the materials you work with so that you can handle them intelligently and safely. A few good general rules for everyone are:

1. Don't use any hazardous substances in your kitchen.
2. Reserve measuring or mixing utensils for craft use only, and never mix them with kitchen ware.
3. Work with adequate ventilation, outdoors when recommended.
4. Allow no food, drink, children, or open flames near any potentially hazardous material.
5. Use masks, gloves, and safe-box when recommended.
6. Wash your hands and work surfaces thoroughly when you have finished.

When you have questions regarding products, there is help available through the Center for Occupational Hazards. The Center also publishes the Art Hazards Newsletter, important if you use the materials regularly (teaching) or extensively. You can often call on the chemistry department at a local high school or university. And, while fiber artists working at home actually have "minimal" amounts of materials, if there are questions of disposal consult a local waste disposal service, the Department of Fish and Game, or your Material Safety Data Sheet for disposal methods.

## HEAT SETTING

Follow the manufacturer's recommendations for heat setting printed fabrics. All recommend drying prints before ironing. Only artists too impatient to wait are familiar with the sizzling sound of hot iron on wet dye. If patience isn't one of your greater virtues, keep an iron for heat setting only: dyes burned onto the plate of an iron have a tendency to let go at inappropriate moments (usually on new or favorite light-colored shirts, and never on old ones you don't give two hoots about).

Once dry, fabrics can be heat set on the printed side for about 20 to 30 seconds. If you iron on the back side, or prefer to use a press cloth, increase the time to 3 minutes. Use as hot an iron as the fabric will allow. Fabrics which cannot tolerate 250° should not be used if you want permanence. Drying or curing prints in bright light before heat setting increases permanence. Allow several days before washing.

## INKODYE

This is a light-sensitive permanent vat dye in a leuco-base, which means the color is not evident until it is developed by exposure to sunlight or ironing (sunlight produces brighter colors). It is used for printing, stamping, dyeing, and screen printing . It will dye cotton, linen, and viscose rayon (free of finishes); its shelf life, if it is kept properly, is six months to a year.

Because it is light-sensitive, direct contact prints can be made on fabric treated with Inkodye in a process similar to blueprinting (called Inko prints). The dye must be stored and used in subdued light.

Inkodye must be carefully handled, with rubber gloves. It is best used outdoors (where you would do photograms or Inko prints anyway), as good ventilation is a must. Purchase dyes in liquid form to avoid handling and measuring powders. If you do use powders, a North respirator is recommended.

## IRON AND BOARD

Reserving an iron especially for heat setting paints and dyes is a good idea. Even with care, some paint will make contact with the iron and stick just until someone tries pressing a white shirt. Use an iron with a completely flat sole-plate, a non-steam version: steam vents leave small areas of undeveloped color during heat setting or dye transfer. You may have to haunt the thrift shops or garage sales to locate such an iron, but it can be found. A few craft suppliers (Cerulean Blue, Sax) sell new ones.

Keep a separate board for heat setting dyes. A piece of ½" plywood about 16" x 24", covered with padding and fabric, can be kept on your work table. Then you need not be concerned as colors or inks transfer to the cloth. Add another layer of fabric as needed.

## IRON-ON MENDING TAPE: See MENDING TAPE

## KODALITH [light-sensitive prints, photo silk-screen]

Also called a line film positive, it is an image on a transparent acetate. Contact prints made from Kodaliths or high-contrast positives are sharp and clear, since all areas are reduced to black or white, while grays are eliminated.

To determine if you need to have Kodaliths made, first select those photographs (b/w or color) which have strong dark and light contrast. Make a photocopy of each. If the image is clear it can be copied onto a transparency and used in a contact print. If the image is unclear and you wish to use it, have a Kodalith made at a photo lab.

## KWIK-PRINT

This is a printing method in which fabric is painted with a light-sensitive color, covered with a block-out, and exposed to sunlight. Color develops and is made permanent in the exposed areas, and it washes out in the protected areas. It is available in a variety of colors, in contrast to single-color blueprints or brownprints.

## LINE FILM POSITIVE: See KODALITH

## MENDING TAPE [copy transfer]

This fabric, coated on one side with adhesive, can be heat set to another piece of cloth. Made for mending or decorative purposes, it can also be used as a transfer medium, as described in Chapter 1.

## MINERAL SPIRITS: See SOLVENTS AND PROPELLANTS

## NATURAL FORMS

Any natural objects (such as leaves, branches, pebbles, or sticks) which are opaque can be used in printing processes. In light-sensitive methods, they would be used as block-outs. For dye transfer or stamping they can be used as the printing plates. Found objects or any man-made forms (raw spaghetti, strings, tools, wire mesh, screen) can be utilized in the same way.

## NEGATIVES [silk screen, light-sensitive prints]

Negatives are used in processes that involve photographic images. When they are used with light-sensitive methods, the dark areas inhibit the passage of sunlight and do not develop. They therefore wash out after exposure, making a reversal or a positive print. Black areas on the negative will be background color (usually white) on the print. Negatives are used in one-step contact prints, such as cyanotype, quick print, or Inko print. If the print from your negative is not distinct or clear, a half-tone negative can be made at a photo lab. It translates the gray areas to patterns of dots and will produce a clearer image.

## OPAQUER

An opaque liquid can be used to conceal something on a copy, print, or drawing. Special white opaquers made for use with the copier are referred to as white-out or correction fluid. In stencil or quick screen, opaque inks may be used to cover a background to keep its color from showing through, especially when you are covering a dark-colored fabric with a light-colored paint. In screen printing, an opaquer can be mixed with colors to make them less transparent. Some opaquers must be handled carefully, as they tend to be quick-drying.

## ORIGINALS

In the context of this book, an original is the finalized image which is going to be printed or transferred. Thus, the original may actually be a copy or a composite paste-up design from which the print is to be made. It is the starting point of the printing process. (In the discussion of copyright, I use the word in its usual sense.)

## PAINTS: See TEXTILE PAINTS

## PERMANENT MARKERS

These felt-tipped marking pens contain ink which is permanent and washable on fabric. Non-toxic fabric markers are available in a wide range of colors with wide or pointed tips. Among my favorites are Niji Fabric Colors, Marvy Fabric Markers, Fabricmate, El Marko, and Pigma Micron. For permanent black markers, try Sanford's Sharpie, Pilot's SC-UF, or the Finepoint System markers which come in various point sizes. All are permanent and require no heat setting (although it is recommended on the Fabricmate markers). I heat set everything on general principle. Use a dry iron, and press directly or cover the print with cloth or paper. Set the iron for cotton and press for 30 seconds, moving the iron. Marvy and Niji give brilliant color without streaks. Fabricmates are available in both brights and pastels, and the Pigma Microns make very fine lines. Marks-a-Lot are also very permanent wide-point markers. While markers are easy to use, it's difficult to blend marker colors or avoid stroke lines. Color Plate 29 shows an example of markers on fabric. Always test them on fabrics, as even permanent markers may bleed on some synthetic or treated fibers.

## PFP FABRICS

PFP fabrics are those which have been prepared for printing. Since finishes can interfere with the absorption of dyes, the best results are achieved on fabrics which have been scoured or degummed and/or bleached. Invisible lubricants, oil, dust, and impurities may all interfere with dye absorbency. Special untreated fabrics, made for dyers and printers, are available on order. You can wash and remove some finishes yourself. Because cottons are subject to wrinkling, they are subjected to the most surface treatments.

Starch, glaze, or sizing left in fabric will absorb dye or paint; then, when the fabric is laundered, the fillers wash out, taking some of the dye with them. Even if washability is not a concern to you, some fabric finishes inhibit dyes from penetrating the fibers. With a permanent marker, indicate on the fabric selvage the fiber content of materials you purchase, as it is important in many of the processes.

Treatments for wrinkle-resistance, water-repellance, permanent press, drip-dry, glazing, and soil resistance will not easily wash out. Some finishes cannot be budged. Use no additives such as water softeners, which may deposit a residue that interferes with dye absorption.

To remove finishes, one dyer recommends boiling fabric for 2 to 4 hours in the following solution:
- 1 gallon of water per ounce of fabric
- 1 teaspoon of detergent
- 2 teaspoons of soda

Another formula calls for the following for each washing-machine load:
- ¼ cup of Synthrapol (see Sources)
- ¼ cup of detergent
- ¼ to ½ cup of soda ash (similar to washing soda but without additives, it is available from pool suppliers or at dye companies)

The simplest recipe recommends:
- ¼ cup of Synthrapol
- Washer load of water

## PHOTOGRAMS [light-sensitive processes]

In light-sensitive processes, prints made by exposing objects rather than negatives are referred to as photograms.

## PHOTO TRANSFER

This term sometimes specifically refers to thermal transfer, but it more generally includes any method by which a photographic image is transferred to cloth. Solvent transfer of b/w copies is also referred to simply as photo transfer.

## POLYMER MEDIUM: See ACRYLIC MEDIUM

## POSITIVE [silk screen]

A positive, like a negative, consists of dark and light areas applied to a transparent or translucent sheet of acetate. It is used to block the ultraviolet light during exposure. A positive can be made by adding an image to acetate in any of several ways: 1) with brush or pen, using an opaque ink; 2) with transfer or pressure-sensitive letters, designs, or textures; 3) from cutouts of shapes, figures, or letters; 4) with natural forms (leaves or flowers); 5) by copying any drawing, signature, photograph, etc. onto a transparency. To apply a liquid to a smooth, clear surface, use a wet media paper. Tracing paper will work if it allows enough light to come through.

When a photograph is photocopied onto paper, the resultant positive copy can be solvent-transferred to fabric. When the photograph is photocopied onto a transparency, it will produce a positive for use in photo-screen printing, and the black areas will print in color. If the same positive transparency is used in a light-sensitive method, the dark lines will retain the fabric color and the background will develop.

The line film positive or Kodalith is a positive in which all grays have been eliminated and a photograph is turned into black areas on a clear base.

## PRE-WASH: See PFP FABRICS

## PRINT CLOTH

Fabric specially prepared for printing, usually pre-washed and without finishes, is sometimes sold as print cloth. It is a PFP fabric.

## PRINTING ON DARK FABRIC

Most water-based textile paints work best when a dark or bright color is printed onto light. Printing light on dark is more difficult. To make the light color more opaque and to prevent color bleeding, it is recommended that 1 part of the textile medium be added to 2 parts of paint. The medium tends to dry on the surface rather than to soak into the fibers. Deka's opaque white can be mixed with colors to make them less transparent. Other opaquers can be used directly on the fabric, followed by a final coating of the desired color. Sanford makes a base coat especially for use with fabric markers.

## REVERSAL

A reversal can be either of two changes that occur in printmaking. One reversal is the mirror image of an original; the other kind is between light and dark, or positive and negative.

Mirror-image reversals occur in some transfer methods and are an automatic result of the process. For example, solvent transfer of b/w copies and thermal transfer of color are both reversal methods. In each case, whatever appears on the copy will transfer backwards with images reversed. (Your hair will appear to be parted on the other side.)

In resist methods, we get a different kind of reversal. For example, in cyanotype a colored leaf placed on the sensitized white fabric will turn, upon exposure, into a white leaf on the colored fabric. This is essentially a reversal from positive to negative.

## SAFE-LIGHT

Photo-sensitive liquids can be handled under a low-level light without excessive exposure. Purchase a photo safe-light, a 75-watt yellow bulb, or a 25-watt incandescent bulb.

## SAFETY: See HAZARDOUS MATERIALS

## SCREEN-PRINTING FRAME [all screen printing]

A rigid wood frame over which a polyester mesh is stretched taut and stapled or corded into place holds both the stencil and the plate for screen printing. While silk was once commonly used, a polyester filament is now preferred, since it will withstand the chlorine bleach used to remove the photo emulsion. The fabric attached to the frame is referred to as a mesh or "the silk."

Available in all sizes, an 8" x 10" screen frame covered in a 12xx to 16xx monofilament polyester mesh would be a good starting size. A lower mesh size means a more open (or larger) weave, less detail in the print, slower drying, and greater ease in cleaning. A higher mesh size (over 16xx) is a tighter weave, gives finer detail, and clogs more readily. Anywhere within this range is good for fabric, on which very fine detail may be lost anyway.

A new screen must be degreased, or thoroughly cleaned. Use trisodium phosphate (TSP) or a powdered detergent in water. Rinse and dry.

Unless you have a resident woodworker, it will be less expensive to buy a ready-made frame than to make one (drive to the lumber yard, cut the wood, miter the corners, reinforce the frame, buy the special polyester, etc.). The frame must be rigid and free of any give. A small frame is not costly and, carefully treated, will last for years. The mesh can be replaced as needed.

## SECOND TRANSFERS [crayon transfer, dye transfer, heat-set printer ribbons]

Once an image has been transferred, a second transfer can sometimes be made, although it is never as brilliant as the first. Crayon transfer, computer heat-transfer ribbon, and dye papers can all be used to make multiple prints of diminishing clarity.

## SENSITIZERS [contact prints]

Certain chemicals utilized in printmaking processes are referred to as sensitizers because of their light-sensitive characteristics. They are used in the photo emulsion for screen printing, and in the sensitizing liquids for cyanotype, Van Dyke, Kwik-Print, or Inko prints. All sensitizers must be used with caution. Read all warnings and follow all directions carefully.

## SOLVENTS AND PROPELLANTS

These liquids are used to dissolve or dissipate other substances. In this book, most are used to dissolve copier ink or to transfer it. All solvents and propellants pose some health or safety hazard and must be used with adequate ventilation (outdoors or with a hooded vent) and away from open flame. Mineral spirits is combustible, turpentine is flammable, and acetone is highly flammable. Turpentine, a relatively common workshop solvent, is hazardous through skin contact, inhalation, and ingestion. If you have small children in your house, don't have turpentine. Mineral spirits and acetone are only slightly toxic. The specific uses of each are covered in Solvent Transfer, Chapter 1.

Solvents are present in some permanent marking pens, and they must be used with adequate ventilation. Look for non-toxic inks, read the labels on markers, and know what you are using.

Sprays often contain solvents and/or propellants, and the vapors must be avoided. Particles can stay in the air for hours after spraying, and the fine mist can be taken deep into the lungs. Use them only outdoors or with adequate venting. When another product will work, avoid aerosol sprays.

## SPRAY ADHESIVE

An aerosol adhesive is usually sprayed to each of two surfaces before joining them, often to mount photographs or art work. It makes a smoother bond than glue or glue sticks but must be used outdoors. Read labels carefully and avoid breathing the mist. Wear a mask.

## SQUEEGEE [all screen printing]

This flat, partially flexible tool is used to spread ink in a silk-screen frame for screen printing. For oil-based paints, squeegees have traditionally consisted of a rubber or plastic blade set into a wooden handle. For water-based paints, wood is unsatisfactory, as it often warps. Easier to handle and to clean are the thin, tapered, one-piece, all-plastic blades available from silk-screen companies. They come in 6" widths, but I cut some into 2" and 4" pieces as well. (They can be cut with a mat knife, though not easily.) The small squeegee is easy to handle. In lieu of a "real" squeegee, use a piece of cardboard (illustration board is a good weight) which will last for a number of prints. In a pinch, use a credit card, a spackling tool, or any similar flat, smooth object, but the squeegee has just the right degree of flexibility and rigidity. Unless you are printing yardage or using huge screens, small squeegees will be the most convenient.

## SQUEEGEE TECHNIQUE

The squeegee makes contact with the mesh, forcing paint through it. When the squeegee is held vertically, the least possible contact is made, and less paint is pressed through. As the squeegee leans more parallel to the mesh, the area of contact is greater and more paint is forced through.

A more absorbent fabric (cotton, velveteen) will need more paint, and thus a flatter squeegee. A thin, non-absorbent fabric, such as silk, will require the least possible paint. With practice, you will find it easier to determine the angle best suited for the piece underway.

## STENCIL

A stencil is any thin, flat surface material used to prevent paint from spreading to the protected area. In quick screen, freezer paper becomes the stencil. Thermal screens, contact paper, Mylar, photo emulsion, newsprint, acetate, stickers, or tape are all used as stencils.

## TEST SAMPLES

Keep records of your work. With each project, cut an extra piece of fabric on which to record a print or copy of the work. Write on it to indicate the processes used, fiber content, if it has been pre-washed, heat set, washed after printing, etc. Your test notebook should include unsuccessful trials as well, with exposure time, temperature, or other pertinent information. Kept in plastic packets in a 3-ring binder, they will be an invaluable reference source for later projects.

Test your methods and materials on the fabric you intend to use in any major project. Try the sample for sewing, quilting, cleaning, etc., as appropriate to your needs.

## TEXTILE PAINTS

Any paint identified as a water-based textile paint will work for most processes in this book. A few of the commonly used brands include Versatex, Cloud Cover, PROfab, Lumière, Deka, Neopaque, and Createx. Most colors can be easily mixed to produce tints, shades, and combinations. Deka makes an opaque white as well as metallic paints. Lumière Fabric Paints are available as opalescents or metallics which can be mixed with Neopaque Fabric Paints. Both are opaque on fabric, even on dark grounds. Lumière also makes an opaline which reveals two different colors in reflections. In addition to their textile ink colors, PROfab makes an opaque white #101 to which color concentrates can be added for opaque colors.

Water-based paints for fabric are usually heat set, though some will cure with air drying. All should be allowed several days of curing before being washed. Drying in direct sunlight before heat-setting increases permanence for some paints.

A medium, available with some brands of textile paints, can be added to the paint to delay drying time. A screen is less likely to clog with a medium added. Thickeners can be added to give the paint more body (making it more like sour cream and less like hand lotion). As colors vary in their viscosity, some thinner paints may benefit from this addition. Most textile paints, however, are made for printing and will work just as they are.

If dyes are used, such as Procion or Inko, a thickener will be needed to achieve the right consistency for screening. Dyes are sometimes preferred by designers because they do not change the hand of the fabric: it feels the same after printing as before, since dye is absorbed by the fibers and does not sit on the surface. Paints usually coat the fibers, adding a little stiffness to the cloth, while dyes penetrate the fibers.

Most textile paints change the texture or feel of the cloth very little. Acrylic paints (which are very opaque) have some desirable visual qualities, but they coat the cloth so that it is difficult to sew through. A pin or needle through the printed area will leave a hole. Opaquers tend to add density but also dry fast in photo-screen printing. Airbrush inks for textiles are intense in color, but thinner, and work well for direct painting or stamping.

## THERMAL IMAGER [direct machine printing]

In this machine, heat reacts with carbon to etch an image onto a special sheet made for this purpose. Fabric artists use it primarily to etch screens to be screen-printed. Either photographs or drawings can be etched onto screens.

## THERMAL SCREEN

This is the heat-sensitive sheet used in the thermal imager. The term also refers to the etched stencil produced and used for screen printing.

## TRANSPARENCY [photo silk-screen, light-sensitive prints]

A transparency is a clear sheet onto which an image can be transferred (in the b/w copier), or to which opaque papers or inks can be applied. The term also applies to the clear sheet with the image on it, ready for use. It is variously referred to as transparent film, a transparency, or an acetate, and in some copy shops you must specifically ask for a transparency for the overhead projector. They are sold as single sheets or by the box, and prices fluctuate greatly, so do some checking.

If your transparency is to be run through a photocopier, it is important to use one that is compatible with your copier. Buy those which are specifically recommended for your machine, as the degree of heat generated by machines varies, as does the heat tolerance of the transparencies. Using the incorrect transparency may cause it to overheat and warp, distorting the image. Or, even worse (heaven help you), it may melt in the machine. Whether or not it would actually burst into flame I do not know. Transparency boxes list the machines in which they can be used. Just think of your machine as a picky eater. Fed the right papers, all runs smoothly. But feed it something disagreeable, and there will be interior rumblings.

I have run transparencies of unknown pedigree through my own copier, though I always keep one hand free to unplug the machine at the first whiff of hot plastic. Nothing drastic has ever occurred. It is helpful to feed the transparency through the machine along with a sheet of white paper. The plain paper seems to absorb some of the heat. Some transparencies come with a thin sheet of paper separating them, and I always run those two through together.

Designs printed on the transparency must be opaque if they are to be used in a direct contact frame. If one appears to be pale gray instead of black, try setting the machine for a darker print. If it is already set at dark, you can make the lines more opaque by drawing over them with an opaque marker. This is easy with line drawings but difficult with photographs or sketches, and all you can do there is fill in pinholes or darken areas meant to be all black. Making two transparencies and stacking them may serve to help block sunlight. When they are perfectly aligned, tape them at the edges with clear tape and then use this double layer for exposure. You may have to try several machines to locate one which deposits more toner as it prints.

To prepare a drawing, diagram, or sketch for exposure, first enlarge or reduce it to the desired size on a copier. A small fern can be made the size of a full page, and a ladybug enlarged to grade B movie proportions. Make all corrections or alterations on the copies. Then make the final copy on a transparency which can be used for your contact print or photo-screen exposure. The transparency is also a way to store images for later use. If you intend to use wildflowers but don't get around to it until October, you'll be glad to have reserved the images.

The final copy should be as dark as possible without losing the background clarity. If your transparency does not seem opaque enough, make a second transparency, stack the two, and use clear tape to keep them perfectly aligned. This will usually produce a more opaque image. Some touching up is still possible at this point, and the sharp blade of a craft knife can be used to scrape away unwanted copier ink from the smooth surface. Fine-line permanent markers can be used to enhance the drawing.

## TRANSPARENT BASE

It is a gel-like extender, or base, used with paints or inks to alter their consistency for screen printing. The base is sometimes used as a transfer medium.

## UNTREATED CLOTH: See PFP FABRICS

## VAN DYKE PRINT

This is a light-sensitive print which is brown in color. It is also known as a brownprint.

## WHOOPEE

You have finished reading. Now the fun really begins. I know you will enjoy imagery on fabric as much as I do!

# SOURCES AND SUPPLIES

This list of suppliers is offered to help you locate the materials you need to get started, and at least one source is given for each item. While the list is extensive, you'll want to keep it current by adding new sources and revising phone numbers (which seem to change with alarming frequency). Always check local sources first, and check with manufacturers for the retailer nearest you.

## GENERAL SUPPLIES

Airbrush inks: 1, 3, 18, 21, 27, 31
Brayer: 1, 18, 21
Contact paper: 4, 6
Copy FX: 2, 9
Electric dry iron: 31
Freezer paper: 5, 6
Permanent marking pens: 1, 3, 15, 18, 20, 21, 30, 31
PFP fabric: 12, 15, 20, 27, 32, 33
Protective gloves and masks: 4, 6, 15, 20, 21, 27
Synthrapol: 20, 27
Transparency (acetate): 1, 2
Water-based textile paint: 1, 3, 19, 20, 27, 27, 30, 31, 35
X-Acto or craft knife: 1, 3

## CHAPTER 1

Acrylic mediums: 1, 18, 21
Bottled transfer: 3, 5
Caran d'Ache pencils and crayons: 1, 9, 18
Contact paper: 6
Mending tape: 3, 4, 5
PARO transfer: 2
Solvents: 1, 6
Specialty transfer companies: 2, 22, 23, 26
Thermal transfer sheets: 2, 28
Transfer medium: 3, 5
Transparent base: 1

## CHAPTER 2

Crayola Craft Fabric Crayons: 5, 9
Crayola Transfer Fabric Crayons: 1, 3
Fabricfun dye sticks: 1, 4, 31
PAROdraw: 1
Pastel dye sticks: 1, 3, 15, 31

## CHAPTER 3

Caran d'Ache pencils and crayons: 1, 9, 18
Deka IronOn Transfer Paint: 1, 3, 19, 20, 30
Design dye sheets: 1, 31
Disperse dye powders (Aljo and PROsperse): 11, 27
PAROdraw: 1, 2

## CHAPTER 4

Heat transfer ribbon for printer: 16, 17
Indelible typewriter ribbon: 16

## CHAPTER 5

Dye*namite: 1, 31
LetraJet Air Markers: 1, 2, 21
Lumière and Cloud Cover: 15
Mylar: 1, 3, 5
Silk-screen printing frame: 1, 3, 21, 31, 32
Squeegee: 1, 3, 21, 32

## CHAPTER 6

Kodalith and halftone negatives: 8
Photo emulsion (bichromate and diazo): 1, 21, 31, 32
Silk-screen printing frame: 1, 3, 21, 31, 32
Transparency: 1, 2

## CHAPTER 7

Plastic frames: 1, 31, 35
Thermal screen (stencils): 1, 9, 31, 35

## CHAPTER 8

Blueprint fabric, pre-treated: 12
Brownprinting chemicals: 24, 29
Cyanotype chemicals: 13, 29, 34
Inkodye: 1, 15, 32
Kwik-print chemicals: 24

## CHAPTER 9

Embossing powders: 3, 10
Erasers: 1, 3, 4, 9, 10, 21
Flexible printing plate: 1, 15, 31
Foamboard: 1, 3, 7, 21
Fun Foam: 3
Inks: 1, 10
Insoles: 4
Klay Gun: 1, 3, 21
Stamp pads (Color Cubes, Comotion, Fashion Stamp): 1, 2, 3, 10
Super Sculpey III and Fimo: 1, 3, 21

## CHAPTER 10

Opaque markers: 2, 21
Press-on alphabets: 1, 2, 9, 21

1. Art supply store
2. Copy shop
3. Craft and hobby store
4. Drug store
5. Fabric or quilt shop
6. Hardware store
7. Picture-framing shop
8. Photo shop
9. School supply store
10. Rubber stamp shop

11. Aljo Mfg. Co.
    81 Franklin Street
    New York, NY 10012
    (212) 226-3878

12. Blueprints - Printables
    1504 Industrial Way, #7
    Belmont, CA 94002-1201
    (414) 594-2995 and (800) 356-0445

13. Bryant Laboratory, Inc.
    1101 Fifth Street
    Berkeley, CA 94710
    (510) 526-3141

14. Cal Process Supply
    2836 — 10th Street
    Berkeley, CA 94710
    (510) 841-7477

15. Cerulean Blue, Ltd.
    P.O. Box 5126
    Seattle, WA 98105
    (800) 676-8602

16. Computer Friends, Inc.
    14520 N.W. Science Park Drive
    Portland, OR 97229
    (800) 547-3303

17. Connections
    3065 Research Drive
    Richmond, CA 94806
    (800) 643-0800

18. Daniel Smith
    4130 First Avenue South
    Seattle, WA 98134-2302
    (800) 426-6740

19. Decart Inc.
    Lamoille Industrial Park, Box 309
    Morrisville, VT 05661
    (802) 888-4217

20. Dharma Trading Co.
    P.O. Box 816
    San Rafael, CA 94915
    (800) 542-5227

21. Dick Blick
    P.O. Box 12676
    Galesburg, IL 61401
    (800) 634-7001

22. Gramma's Graphics, Inc.
    20 Birling Gap, NFSB-P9
    Fairport, NY 14450
    (716) 223-4309

23. Imagination Station
    7571 Crater Lake Highway, #103
    White City, OR 97503
    (800) 338-3857

24. Light Impressions
    439 Monroe Avenue
    Rochester, NY 14607-3717
    (716) 271-8960 or (800) 828-6216

25. Photographers Formulary
    P.O. Box 950
    Condon, MT 59826
    (800) 922-5255

26. Photo Textiles
    P.O. Box 3036
    Bloomington, IN 47402-3063
    (800) 388-3961

27. PRO Chemical & Dye Inc.
    P.O. Box 14
    Somerset, MA 04726
    (508) 676-3838 or (800) 2-BUY-DYE

28. Quick-Way Color Copies
    100 East Ohio
    Chicago, IL 60611
    (312) 943-3662

29. Rockland Colloid Corp.
    302 Piermont Avenue
    Piermont, NY 10968
    (914) 359-5559

30. Rupert Gibbon & Spider Inc.
    P.O. Box 425
    Healdsburg, CA 95448
    (707) 433-9577 or (800) 442-0455

31. Sax Arts and Crafts
    2405 South Calhoun Drive
    New Berlin, WI 53151
    (800) 558-6696

32. Screen Process Supplies Mfg. Co.
    530 MacDonald Avenue
    Richmond, CA 94801
    (510) 235-8330

33. Testfabrics, Inc.
    P.O. Drawer O
    Middlesex, NJ 08846
    (201) 469-6446

34. VWR Scientific
    600 S. Spokane Street
    Seattle, WA 98134
    (206) 575-1500

35. Welsh Products, Inc.
    P.O. Box 845
    Benicia, CA 94510
    (707) 745-3252 or (800) 745-3255

Advance DM-888 Photo Emulsion is a brand name of J.R. Advance Process.

Air Marker is a trademark of LetraSet U.S.A.

Aleene's Fabric Stiffener is a trademark of Artis, Inc.

Aljo dye is a brand name of Aljo Manufacturing Co.

Badger's Propel is a brand name of Badger Air Brush Company.

Ball Mason jar is a brand name of Ball, Inc.

Bondex is a registered trademark of Wrights Home Sewing Co.

Caran d'Ache Neo Color is a registered trademark of Caran d'Ache.

Cloud Cover paints is a trademark of Cerulean Blue, Ltd.

Color Box is a trademark of Co-motion Rubber Stamps, Inc.

Con-tact is a registered trademark of Rubbermaid, Inc.

Copy Trans Heat Transfer is a brand name of Quick Way Color Copies, Inc.

Crayola Craft Fabric Crayons is a trademark of Binney & Smith, Inc.

Crayola Transfer Fabric Crayons is a trademark of Binney & Smith, Inc.

Crayola's Color Works is a trademark of Binney & Smith, Inc.

Createx paint is a trademark of Color Craft, Ltd.

Decal-It is a registered trademark of Plaid Enterprises, Inc.

Deka IronOn Transfer Paint  and Fabric Dye are registered trademarks of Decart Inc.

Delta Fabric Paints is a registered trademark of Delta/Shiva.

Design Dye is a registered trademark of Design Dye.

Dr. Scholl's Air-Pillo is a registered trademark of Schering-Plough HealthCare Products, Inc.

Dye*namite is a trademark of Carnival.

El Marko pens is a registered trademark of Flair.

Fashion Stamp Ink Pads is a trademark of Tulip Productions.

Fimo is a registered trademark of Eber-Casteel.

Flexi-Cut is a brand name of Dick Blick.

Foiling Around is a trademark of ESP Crafts.

Formatt is a trademark of Graphic Productions Corp.

Fun Foam is a registered trademark of Westrim Crafts.

Geotype is a brand name of Geographics Inc.

Gocco is a brand name of Welsh Products.

Grid-Grip is a trademark of the KVP/Service Products Division of James River Corp.

Handiwrap is a registered trademark of Dow Chemical Company.

Holden's Diazo is a trademark of Standard Screen Supply.

Hunt Speedball is a registered trademark of Hunt Manufacturing Co.

Hyplar is a registered trademark of Grumbacher.

ImageWriter II is a registered trademark of Hewlett Packard.

IMPRINTZ is a trademark of Stewart-Superior Marking Equipment Company.

Inkodye is a trademark of the Screen Process division of Golden Value Inc.

Itoya Finepoint is a brand name of Itoya.

Klay Gun is a brand name of Kemper Manufacturing, Inc.

Kodalith is a registered trademark of Kodalith.

Krylon Workable Fixative is a registered trademark of Borden, Inc.

Kwik-print is a brand name of Direct Reproduction Corporation.

LaserJet III is a registered trademark of Hewlett Packard.

LetraJet is a trademark of Letraset U.S.A.

Letraset's Copy FX is a trademark of Letraset U.S.A.

Letratone is a registered trademark of Letraset U.S.A.

Lipton's Tea is a brand name of Thomas J. Lipton, Inc.

Liquitex is a registered trademark of Binney & Smith, Inc.

Lumière is a trademark of Cerulean Blue, Ltd.

Magic Cover is a registered trademark of Kittrich Corp.

Magic Transfer Paper is a brand name of Dharma Trading Co.

Magic Rub is a brand name of Faber Castell.

Marks-a-Lot is a registered trademark of Dennison Manufacturing Co.

Marvy is a trademark of Marvy Company.

Mylar is a registered trademark of E. I. duPont de Nemours & Co.

Naz-Dar is a brand name of Naz-Dar Co.

Neopaque is a trademark of Cerulean Blue, Ltd.

Niji is a brand name of Yasutomo & Co.

Panasonic KX-P 124 is a brand name of Matsushita Electric Industrial Co. Ltd.

PARO is a trademark of Graffoto, Inc.

Pantone is a registered trademark of Letraset U.S.A.

Pelikan ink is a brand name of Günther Wagner.

Pellon is a registered trademark of Freudenberg Nonwovens.

Pentel's Fabricfun Pastel Dye Sticks is a trademark of Pentel Co., Ltd.

Picture This is a trademark of Plaid Enterprises, Inc.

Pigma Micron is a registered trademark of Sakura Color Products Corp. of America.

Pilot SC-UF is a registered trademark of Pilot Pen Corporation of America.

Pink Pearl is a trademark of Faber Castell.

Plexiglas is a registered trademark of Rohm & Haas.

Poly Print is a registered trademark of Hunt Manufacturing Co.

Procion is a registered trademark of Imperial Chemical Industries, Ltd.

PROfab, PRO Thick F, and PROsperse are brand names of PRO Chemical & Dye Company.

Reynolds is a brand name of Reynolds Metals Company.

Rubkleen is a registered trademark of Faber Castell.

Sanford Glad Rags is a trademark of Sanford.

Sanford Sharpie is a registered trademark of Sanford.

Saran Wrap is a trademark of Dow Chemical Company.

Sculpey and Super Sculpey III are registered trademarks of Polyform Products.

Spra-Ment is a registered trademark of 3M Adhesives Systems.

Staedtler Mars Plastic Grand is a brand name of Nürnberg.

Stitchless Fabric Glue is a brand name of Slomons.

Sure-Stamp is a trademark of Cerulean Blue, Ltd.

Synthrapol is a trademark of Imperial Chemical Industry, Ltd.

Thermo-Fax is a registered trademark of 3M Adhesives Systems.

Transfer-It is a trademark of Aleene's division of Artis, Inc.

Velcro is a registered trademark of Velcro USA Inc.

Versatex is a brand name of Versatex Co.

X-Acto is a registered trademark of Hunt Manufacturing.

# Photo Credits

Stan Bitters: Color Plate 100.

Bill Ferguson: Plates 8-1, 8-2, 8-8. Color Plates 85, 86.

Joni Goss: Color Plate 13.

Mike Hopiak: Plate 9-20.

Schecter Lee: Color Plate 49.

Leonard Migliore: Plates 4-7, 4-8. Color Plates 35, 36.

Carol Olson: Plate 6-13.

Sharon Risedorph: Color Plates 48, 71.

E. Z. Smith: Plates 1-2, 1-8, 1-9, 1-11, 1-12, 1-16 to 19; 2-1 to 5, 2-7; 3-1 to 5; 4-1 to 5, 4-9 to 12; 5-1 to 4; 6-1 to 5, 6-8 to 12, 6-14, 6-17, 6-19; 7-1 to 4; 8-5 to 7, 8-9; 9-1 to 19, 9-21 to 24, 9-26, 9-27; 10-2 to 5, 10-8 to 10. Color Plates 11, 12, 14, 17, 20 to 25, 27, 29 to 34, 37, 40, 41, 51, 53 to 57, 61 to 65, 72, 74 to 76, 96, 97, 101.

Ken Wagner: Color Plates 42, 46, 47.

The portrait in Plate 8-7 is by Chris Kausch.

The newspaper in Plates 10-6 and 10-7 is reproduced by permission of the *San Francisco Chronicle*.

Plates 1-1 and 2-6, and Color Plate 1, are courtesy of The Women's History Project, Santa Rosa, California.

All other photography is provided courtesy of the artists.

Jean Ray Laury's many books and magazine articles are well-known to readers of fabric and craft publications. While all her writings focus on folk arts and crafts, the styles range from cartoons about quilters to documentation of women's history, from children's stories to practical advice for disorganized quiltmakers, from instruction for quilted clothing to patterns for children's quilts.

She has been honored by a wide range of women's and arts organizations for her accomplishments, her quilts have been widely exhibited in museums and corporate collections, and she has been inducted into the Quilters Hall of Fame.

With a B.A. in art and English from Northern Iowa University and an M.A. in design from Stanford University, Jean has also been a free-lance fabric designer, and she has written and designed for many magazines. Although she has taught academically from junior high through the college level, she prefers teaching adult groups of highly motivated quilters and designers.

Jean has taught quiltmaking on four continents, lectured extensively, and is a popular presenter for her knowledge as well as for her humor and charm. Students are always amazed at her ability to clarify and simplify every technique she teaches. Her work has always been known also for its originality: in this book she now teaches many of her technical innovations for creating imagery on fabric.

# Fine Quilting Books From C & T Publishing

An Amish Adventure, Roberta Horton

Appliqué 12 Easy Ways!, Elly Sienkiewicz

The Art of Silk Ribbon Embroidery, Judith Montano

Baltimore Album Quilts, Historic Notes and Antique Patterns,
Elly Sienkiewicz

Baltimore Beauties and Beyond (2 Volumes), Elly Sienkiewicz

Boston Commons Quilt, Blanche Young and
Helen Young Frost

Calico and Beyond, Roberta Horton

A Celebration of Hearts, Jean Wells and Marina Anderson

Christmas Traditions From the Heart, Margaret Peters

Crazy Quilt Handbook, Judith Montano

Crazy Quilt Odyssey, Judith Montano

Crosspatch, Pepper Cory

Design a Baltimore Album Quilt!, Elly Sienkiewicz

Fans, Jean Wells

Fine Feathers, Marianne Fons

Flying Geese Quilt, Blanche Young and Helen Young Frost

Friendship's Offering, Susan McKelvey

Happy Trails, Pepper Cory

Heirloom Machine Quilting, Harriet Hargrave

Irish Chain Quilt, Blanche Young and Helen Young Frost

Isometric Perspective, Katie Pasquini-Masopust

Landscapes & Illusions, Joen Wolfrom

Let's Make Waves, Marianne Fons and Liz Porter

Light and Shadows, Susan McKelvey

The Magical Effects of Color, Joen Wolfrom

Mariner's Compass, Judy Mathieson

Mastering Machine Appliqué, Harriet Hargrave

Memorabilia Quilting, Jean Wells

New Lone Star Handbook, Blanche Young and
Helen Young Frost

Perfect Pineapples, Jane Hall and Dixie Haywood

Picture This, Jean Wells and Marina Anderson

Plaids and Stripes, Roberta Horton

PQME Series: Milky Way Quilt, Jean Wells

PQME Series: Nine-Patch Quilt, Jean Wells

PQME Series: Pinwheel Quilt, Jean Wells

PQME Series: Stars & Hearts Quilt, Jean Wells

Quilting Designs from Antique Quilts, Pepper Cory

Quilting Designs from the Amish, Pepper Cory

Story Quilts, Mary Mashuta

Trip Around the World Quilts, Blanche Young and
Helen Young Frost

Visions: The Art of the Quilt, Quilt San Diego

Visions: Quilts of a New Decade, Quilt San Diego

Working in Miniature, Becky Schaefer

Wearable Art for Real People, Mary Mashuta

3 Dimensional Design, Katie Pasquini

For more information write for a free catalog from

C & T Publishing
P.O. Box 1456
Lafayette, CA 94549
(1-800-284-1114)